With appreciation and best wishes
from the graduates of th[...]on.

William M[...]

Claremont, California

March 23, 1991

Handbook for
Basic Types of
PASTORAL CARE AND COUNSELING

Handbook for Basic Types of PASTORAL CARE AND COUNSELING

HOWARD W. STONE
WILLIAM M. CLEMENTS

EDITORS

Abingdon Press
Nashville

HANDBOOK FOR BASIC TYPES OF PASTORAL CARE AND COUNSELING

Copyright © 1991 by Abingdon Press

This book is printed on acid-free paper.

Library of Congress Cataloging-in-Publication Data

Handbook for Basic types of pastoral care and counseling / Howard W.
  Stone, William M. Clements, editors.
      p. cm.
    Supplement to: Basic types of pastoral care & counseling / Howard
  Clinebell.
    Includes bibliographical references and index.
    ISBN 0-687-16540-7 (alk. paper)
    1. Pastoral counseling—Handbooks, manuals, etc. I. Stone, Howard
  W. II. Clements, William M., 1943– . III. Clinebell, Howard,
  1922– Basic types of pastoral care & Counseling.
  BV4012.2.C528   1990 Suppl.
  253—dc20   90-39832
                                                                  CIP

MANUFACTURED IN THE UNITED STATES OF AMERICA

In Honor of Howard Clinebell
Who defined basic types of pastoral care and counseling

Completely Revised and Enlarged

BASIC TYPES OF PASTORAL CARE & COUNSELING

RESOURCES FOR THE MINISTRY OF HEALING & GROWTH

HOWARD CLINEBELL

This book helps ministers and seminarians develop maximum skills in the basic caring and counseling methods by

- giving an overview of the theological foundations, historical heritage, uniqueness, and mission of pastoral care and counseling,

- highlighting those types of caring and counseling that are normative in a person-centered, non-specialist ministry,

- reviewing the procedures that are fundamental to all caring and counseling that nurture healing and growth,

- encouraging the use of the reality-practice method in learning pastoral care and counseling.

ISBN 0-687-02492-7   Abingdon Press

CONTENTS

Marriage and Family

Appendix

PART ONE:

FOUNDATIONS OF PASTORAL CARE AND COUNSELING

INTRODUCTION

William M. Clements

The *Handbook for Basic Types of Pastoral Care and Counseling* is designed to stimulate your thinking about the ministry of pastoral care and counseling. Through these pages, each author invites you to enter into a process of dialogue. We hope that the exchange between you and each author will prove to be a stimulating procedure. The authors are keenly aware that innovative expressions of ministry often flow from new conceptions. We anticipate that after you read and digest these ideas, you will do some things differently in your ministry—adding here, consulting there, even bridge building across previously experienced chasms—resulting in additional professional and personal satisfaction. Perhaps you will discover yourself using new reflective skills, sparked by your experience of a rich dialogue, as you think through again the basics of your ministry of care and counseling—this time with different perspectives suggested by your reading of the *Handbook.*

Every author has been closely associated with Howard Clinebell and the "revised model" that was first elaborated in his *Basic Types of Pastoral Counseling* (1966) and greatly enlarged and revised in his *Basic Types of Pastoral Care and Counseling* (1984). The contributors to the *Handbook* are colleagues of Howard Clinebell who have chosen this means to wish him well in his continued ministry of lecturing, writing, and consulting. The authors bring creativity and energy to their topics and encourage you to enter into productive dialogue about your ministry. They contribute to a significant extension of the revised model that envisions our movement into the twenty-first century.

This *Handbook for Basic Types of Pastoral Care and Counseling* is an eminently practical book. You will find concrete approaches and models for pastoral care and counseling, designed by experts who have devoted years of professional ministry to the subject areas from which their chapters flow.[1] Each chapter has been contributed by a noted authority who is aware of the time, energy, and conceptual demands that can either energize or deplete other aspects of the general ministry of the church, such as worship, preaching, group leadership, teaching, and visitation. Taken in its entirety, the *Handbook* facilitates movement toward wholeness and liberation centered in the Spirit, themes that are nurtured and empowered by Howard Clinebell and by each kindred spirit who has contributed to the *Handbook*.

Each chapter serves as either a natural extension of or a valuable supplement to Clinebell's *Basic Types of Pastoral Care and Counseling*. While the *Handbook* can and will stand alone on its own merits, perhaps its greatest use will be found as a supplement to *Basic Types* in introductory seminary courses, or possibly as a text for advanced courses in pastoral care and counseling that build on the revised model developed by Clinebell. Students who read the *Handbook* as a supplement to Clinebell's *Basic Types* might want to relate chapters from the *Handbook* to those from *Basic Types*. Asking the question "How might a dialogue between an author in the *Handbook* and Clinebell develop?" could be an innovative way to stimulate the imagination.

Helpful techniques for learning might include staging an imaginary conversation using the method of role playing. One person would be "Clinebell," while another person might play the role of an author from the *Handbook*. How are the themes and emphases in each comparative chapter complementary or harmonious? What are the discontinuities? How might you harmonize the ideas or techniques in your ministry if you were combining the best of each chapter? For example, John Cobb's chapter "Pastoral Counseling and Theology" (chap. 1 in the *Handbook*) might be used in a dialogue with "Clinebell" about his chapter on the "Mission, Biblical Bases, and Uniqueness of Pastoral Care and Counseling" (chap. 3 in *Basic Types*), as might Hunter Beaumont's chapter on "Encountering Sin in Pastoral Counseling" (chap. 2 in the *Handbook*.) How might a conversation develop among Clinebell, Cobb, and Beaumont? I would like to be present for that interchange! Even more challenging, in my imagination, might be the conversation between Masamba ma Mpolo, based on "Cultural Collisions: A Perspective from Africa" (chap. 6 in the *Handbook*), and Clinebell, based on his interest in transcultural counseling as found in the chapter on the "Foundations of All Types of Care and Counseling" (chap. 4 of *Basic Types*).

In a real sense, however, the potential dialogue between the internalized authors from the *Handbook* and the internalized Clinebell has equal possibilities for creativity, if you are reading the *Handbook* on your own. Do not hesitate to try each chapter from the *Handbook* in more than one dialogue with chapters from *Basic Types*. Allow yourself to be creative and to experience the excitement of a new journey.

If, on the other hand, you are a pastor in active ministry who is already familiar with Clinebell's revised model, you will find the *Handbook* a rich resource for ministry. Solid theory is combined with innovative practice—two qualities that are always valuable in ministry. Your understanding of the revised model can serve as a bridge to the *Handbook*, allowing you to digest and to apply the many new ideas directly to your pastoral situation.

The essential plan of the *Handbook* is simple and direct.

There are two parts, each of which is further subdivided. Part one concerns some of the foundations of pastoral care and counseling and is subdivided into two components: Theology and Ethics, and Social Dimensions. Part two deals with the practice of pastoral care and counseling and is subdivided into three components: Imagination and Prayer; Grief and Depression; and Marriage and Family.

Foundations of Pastoral Care and Counseling

Part one presents some of the essential elements of pastoral care and counseling. Theology, ethics, and social awareness are foundational components of pastoral care and counseling that undergird this *Handbook*. Important information is distilled by leading scholars from the United States and from abroad. You will be stimulated and challenged to rethink some of the basic assumptions you have brought to the *Handbook* from your previous experience and study. You may well find yourself employing some new categories or applying tried and true concepts in a novel fashion to help evaluate and strengthen your ministry.

Foundation chapters probe outwardly in two directions. First, within our own rich theological heritage, sustaining theological and ethical roots are explicated and applied to the situations we find ourselves in day by day. Only the most relevant issues and concepts have been chosen for discussion. The interplay between theory and practice should prove fascinating and stimulating as you extend the discussion in your own mind. Second, some of the important, though often neglected, social dimensions of pastoral care and counseling are explored. We are reminded that pastoral care never involves only two people—the social milieu is always powerfully present, whether it is explicitly acknowledged or not.

Theology and Ethics

In his chapter "Pastoral Counseling and Theology," John B. Cobb, Jr., explicates the continual interplay between the great polarities of the human condition. The dynamic interchange between legalism and antinomianism is highlighted for us in the human situation—whether it is experienced in a counseling session or through historical theology. Likewise, the dialectic of whether human nature is essentially good or evil is clearly set forth on both theoretical and practical levels. Grace versus works, and determinism versus freedom, two classic themes, are presented as helpful polarities that illuminate the inner dialogue of personal growth and change. The subtle allure of the dualism encompassing body and spirit is shown to obscure more of reality than it illuminates, through the continual preoccupation with "substances" in each case. Cobb proposes the reality of "events" and "moments of experience" as an alternative means of transcending these dualistic dichotomies and elevating our awareness of the "embodied character of the human person." Cobb's concluding discussion of the concept of *salvation* recaptures the richness of the ancient term while confronting the poverty of the concept in modern language.

In his chapter on the encounter with sin in pastoral care, Hunter Beaumont discusses sin and virtue, by using concepts from gestalt therapy and the theory of the fragile self process. Beaumont illuminates narcissism in the light of the traditional seven deadly sins and then posits the seven virtues as an effective antidote to narcissistic behavior. The role of love in the healing process is shown to be crucial in breaking the paradox of narcissism. Both the theoretical and the operational levels of pastoral care and counseling ministries benefit from Beaumont's thought-provoking proposal.

How does the pastoral specialist integrate ethical considerations on the applied level, in the actual give-and-take interplay that characterizes pastoral care and counseling in the real world of confusing human problems and discontinuities? James Poling allows us to participate with him as he grapples with some of the profound ethical issues involving normative principles and theological vision. The pastoral counseling he provides for a case involving child sexual abuse illustrates the proposed ethical method.

Social Dimensions of Pastoral Care

The second section introduces the social dimensions of pastoral care with Bridget Clare McKeever's moving and challenging chapter "Social Systems in Pastoral Care." She takes us with her as she makes a pastoral call in the home of a family who is just experiencing the devastating and tragic loss of a young child. As she discusses the case and the principles that might have applied, she challenges us with her call for personal and collective conversion in sacramental dialogue with people, formed by values that are different from the secular values that have been adopted unconsciously and uncritically from the culture of the majority. The poor and the oppressed are shown to be our teachers as we move toward "a finite shape of God's saving grace."

Paul Schurman catalogs grim examples of cultural and racial ethnocentrism from the pages of American history in his chapter on cross-cultural pastoral care and counseling. Deep mistrust, anger, guilt, and despair need not be the only results of confrontations between cultures, however. Schurman gives us hope for the future as he describes an educational process in cross-cultural perspectives aimed at fostering a better understanding of differences—and similarities. We are left with a much deeper appreciation for the reality that all ministry is cross-cultural in some sense when we consider the contexts within which we live and minister—"male-female, gay-straight, hearing-deaf, and so on." The cultural collisions described by Schurman prove merely preparatory, however, for the even more powerful cross-cultural confrontation in Africa, presented in the next chapter.

Masamba ma Mpolo raises searching questions in the context of pastoral care from Africa. How best to care for people who are themselves cross-cultural, who are, in a sense, innocents caught in the midst of a powerful collision between cultures, is the fundamental question posed in this final chapter in part one. Basic assumptions about monogamy and polygamy are carefully examined as examples of cultural assumptions that have been either rejected or accepted as being primary to the pattern of life. Acquiescence to a particular view is the mediator of acceptance or rejection within the church or the culture. But what is, in fact, fundamental for faith about either position? Does the grace of God hinge on this question? Does each position contain uncritical assumptions, merely adapted by the respective culture at a pivotal moment in its historical development, one being African and the other Western? Must all cultural assumptions be accepted only in one way or the other? What would your position be in such a context? What is your position on similar questions in your context today, where the same metaissues exist, but clothed in other cross-cultural garments?

CHAPTER ONE

Pastoral Counseling and Theology

John B. Cobb, Jr.

The pastoral counseling movement is most intimately informed by developments in the general counseling movement. These, in turn, are intimately related to certain schools of psychology. As a result, the theory and practice of pastoral counseling are more influenced by psychologists than by theologians. This separation of an important aspect of pastoral practice from systematic theology has frequently been criticized. Too often, the criticism has implied that fault lies with writers on pastoral counseling, who should base their directions for practice on theology. If blame is appropriate at all, however, it falls at least equally on theologians, who address themselves to the problems posed by the discipline of theology more than to those that arise out of the real needs of churches and their members.

Whatever the lack of explicit connection of pastoral counseling with systematic theology, there can be no counseling or theory of counseling that does not have a view of the human situation. Indeed, the multiple schools of counseling reflect diverse views of this situation. The differences among them often parallel differences that have appeared in the history of Christian thought. In this sense, all theories of counseling have theological assumptions and

18

convictions; alternately, we could say that all theological positions have psychological assumptions and convictions.

In this chapter, I propose to identify schematically a range of issues, which may be called either *theological* or *psychological* (or *philosophical*, for that matter), that are important for pastoral counseling and that have also been important in the history of Christian thought. I am not proposing that pastoral counselors should first determine the "orthodox" view on each topic and then adjust their theory and practice accordingly. On the contrary, the church's teaching needs to be informed by pastoral experience just as much as pastoral practice needs to be informed by traditional doctrine. Nevertheless, I urge pastoral counselors to continue to become more aware of the relationship of what they are doing to the cumulative wisdom of the church, and that the barriers that still separate the discipline of pastoral counseling from the discipline of theology will continue to crumble.

My list of topics relevant to both theology and pastoral counseling should be recognizable across a wide spectrum of positions. In my presentation of the issues, I am not aiming at neutrality, however. Instead, I am commending positions that seem to me to make sense for both theology and pastoral counseling.

Legalism and Antinomianism

The pastoral counseling movement has involved from the beginning reaction against pastoral legalism in dealing with personal problems. For many generations, pastors were viewed, and usually viewed themselves, as watchdogs over the moral behavior of their congregations. The dominant perception of the church and its leadership appeared in terms of its role in raising the moral standards of the community, especially in areas of sexual behavior, personal honesty, kindness, and social responsibility. Church leaders felt that this required the disciplining of an unruly human nature, a discipline that could be internalized in each person only as the community and its leaders encouraged this by precept and by example. There might be personal sympathy for the strains and stresses imposed on individuals by collective pressure toward "high" moral standards, but pastoral instruction and demand remained firmly on the side of urging individuals to conform at any cost.

This cost has been enormous. It has entailed all sorts of repression, with all sorts of deleterious consequences. It has led to social ostracism of those who refused to conform to the prescribed patterns of righteousness. It has generated hardness and rigidity on the part of those who did conform, including the pastors who were responsible for enforcing the rules. It has led to neuroses and psychoses. The pastoral counseling movement has been keenly sensitive to these destructive effects of ecclesiastical legalism and has provided a context in which the real feelings and real needs of people can be expressed and discussed without moral judgment.

Theologians generally have supported this opposition to legalism, but gradually both theologians and pastoral counselors have come to recognize that freedom from legalism is not enough. The problems of people who do not internalize the norms of the community are no less serious than the problems of those who do. Meaninglessness supersedes repression as the besetting enemy of health in many instances.

This recent shift in dominant social pathology from repression to meaninglessness is a recurrence of an age-old problem for Christians in the swing from legalism to antinomianism—that is, to a rejection of all moral concerns. Paul himself knew that his attack on legalism was sometimes misunderstood in an antinomian way. He strove to clarify the distinction between Christian freedom and antinomianism. He was sure that those who know Christ or are filled with the Spirit need no rules. In their freedom they go far beyond what the law requires.

Actually, this simple point can be stated in a quite secular way. Those whose lives are ordered to encompassing ends act so as to attain those ends. They do not need moral rules to guide them. If the end to which they are committed is quite inclusive, such as the good of the nation, their actions will generally correspond to what the laws designed to ensure socially constructive behavior will require. Thus they fulfill the law, or at least the basic intention of the law, without needing to be committed to the law or bound by it. The issue is that of idolatry—whether the end is encompassing enough. If it is not, then what functions in this liberating way for one group leads that group into conflict with others. If the end is beyond all possibility of such conflict, then it is the true God. Augustine could say: "Love God and do as you please." The problems of legalism and antinomianism are left far behind.

Pastoral counseling, however, is not geared to eliciting ultimate commitment. Where commitment is present, counselors may be able to free parishioners from the confusions of legalism and antinomianism, but the evocation of commitment and the critique of inadequate commitment belong more to the preaching and teaching functions of the church. Pastoral counseling that is cut off from these functions has limited potential.

The Badness or Goodness of Human Nature

The legalistic habit of mind is typically associated with the view that human nature cannot be trusted, that it is essentially sinful. Because, in this view, people's natural tendencies are to act selfishly, and because selfish behavior is antisocial, human nature must be controlled. The reaction against this view has been that human nature should be allowed to express itself, that much of its apparent evil results from its repression, that when it is not distorted by adverse social controls, its expression will be both personally fulfilling and socially enriching. In short, human nature is essentially good. This positive judgment of human nature has tended to dominate pastoral counseling. It is associated with a view that the goal of life is self-realization, or self-actualization. The self that is to be actualized is usually understood to be unique to each individual. It consists in the particular potentialities of that person. Hence, the actualization of native potentialities tends to become the overarching goal of counseling.

Most pastoral counselors, like most theologians, realize that these anthropological views are too simple. Human nature is neither the enemy to be overcome nor the ideal to be realized. The hypothesis that perfect child-rearing methods would lead to adults without antisocial tendencies has not been tested and cannot be tested in a world composed of adults like ourselves. Actually and concretely, we must deal with the way human beings are shaped in a very imperfect world. In this world, the effort to discover a purely good potential may well be therapeutically valid in many cases, but it can also encourage an exaggerated individualism and even narcissism. The task of counselors, like the task of theologians, is to understand the relationship of constructive and destructive forces or tendencies within people and to find ways to support the constructive ones.

The Christian myth of origins proves itself again and again a fruitful source of reflection on human nature. Read in a quasi-historical manner, it suggests that our ancestors in the gathering societies (hunting was not, in fact, very important to primitive economies in most cases and is not included in the biblical myth) were free from the conflict of personal and social good that is so central to the moral conflict. They were not free, however, from the appetite for knowledge, and this appetite led to sexual self-consciousness and the shift from the gathering society to the agricultural and pastoral ones. With this shift there arose backbreaking labor and jealousy. In this new world, human evil has been a pervasive and persistent problem both personally and socially. There is no way back to the earlier innocence. Our hope is that through and despite our sinfulness there will come into being a new order in which, without loss of knowledge, we can regain the ability to live together in harmony with one another and with all creation.

Like most readings of the myth, this one assures us that the deepest level of our being is not evil. We are created good. It also warns us that we cannot solve our present problems by recovering that original condition. That is irrevocably lost. We must deal with the evil that is genuinely part of ourselves as well as with the given reality of our world. For such health and growth as is possible to us in the world in which we live, it is as important that we acknowledge the evil within us as it is that we affirm our inherent worth and capacity for good.

Grace and Works

Legalism calls for the exercise of will to control the evil tendencies of one's nature. It is, therefore, inherently a religion of works. The pastoral counseling movement has reacted against a works-righteousness. The church, however, has learned over the centuries how difficult it is to replace legalism with anything other than another legalism. In the case of pastoral counseling, the tendency of the new legalism is often the opposite of the old. Instead of ruling against the expression of negative feelings, it has often encouraged such expression. Instead of demanding self-abasing service to the neighbor, it has often required that the parishioner affirm her or his own rights.

The goal, of course, is to avoid arousing feelings of guilt and unworthiness based on a new set of moral demands. Indeed, one of the requirements is to cease feeling guilt and unworthiness. The problem is that recognizing that one should not feel guilt can end up compounding the feelings of guilt rather than doing away with them. Equally, the goal is not to belittle the importance of morality in human life and interpersonal relations.

The alternative to legalism and antinomianism is a life ordered by the love of God, but such a love can also appear as a demand that one is guilty for not obeying. Indeed, the commandment of love, rather than freeing those who genuinely hear it from the burden of law, can become the most burdensome of all laws because the inability to obey is so profound. Augustine responded to his awareness of this problem with another oft-quoted expression: "Command what Thou wilt, and give what Thou commandest." Genuine salvation can come to us only as a gift. Furthermore, we can live with our failure to measure up to the standards we have internalized only if we also believe that we are accepted and loved without regard to these failures. This is the double meaning of grace that is so central to an authentic Christian theology.

Pastoral counseling has succeeded better than any other aspect of the pastoral role in this regard. Unconditional acceptance has been deeply a part of the counselor's role. Sometimes this has been wrongly interpreted to mean that the counselor should avoid showing, or even feeling, any moral judgments. Unconditional acceptance of that sort can be dangerous in encouraging antinomianism. True unconditional acceptance is acceptance of persons despite their acknowledged sinfulness. Only in this way can it model God's love.

A special difficulty arises in the clarification of the grace that is, or can be, present in human relations and the grace of God. Does the counselor's grace function as the grace that is finally needed, so that reference to God's grace is not required? Does it model God's grace so as to enable the parishioner to understand and to apprehend that grace? Or does it mediate that grace, so that in experiencing the counselor's acceptance one is in fact experiencing God's grace? The answer, I think, is all of the above. True graciousness in human relations is, in itself, and without reference to God, redemptive. The graciousness of another human being enables the recipient to identify elsewhere the working of grace, specifically God's grace. God's grace is both immediate and mediated, and in its mediated form, it does come to the recipient through the counselor.

Determinism and Freedom

Legalism tends to accent freedom in the sense of assuming the ability of people to obey or to disobey the law. Reactions against legalism often seek causal explanations of behavior and personality traits, thus removing them from the sphere of choice. Indeed, deep-seated tendencies of thought, strengthened by modern science, indicate that everything that happens has, in principle, a causal explanation. The implication is that whatever happens had to happen. In short, the conclusion of this line of reflection is metaphysical determinism. The existential implication is that we are not responsible for what we are or do.

Some forms of counseling share in the determinist world view, assuming that present feelings and behavior are the result of past events. Acceptance of this view can be a source of great relief to a client. The burden of guilt associated with the view that one is responsible for what one is and does can be removed in this way. One can then hope that the agency of the counselor will introduce new factors that will lead to feelings and behavior that are more satisfactory. The client can be largely an observer of the changes occurring. The limitations of this attitude are apparent to most counselors. In fact, a number of counseling theories have reacted strongly against the result of this deterministic mind set. They emphasize the immediate responsibility of the client, not for the past, but for the present. They encourage clients to understand themselves as choosing to respond in the present as they do. The danger here is that clients come to take responsibility for features of the situation, including their own feelings and behavior, that are in fact beyond their control.

This swing of the pendulum between total determinism and total freedom has been found not only in counseling theory but also in the wider history of thought. Within philosophy, advocates of determinism are numerous, whereas the affirmation of genuine freedom is rare. When freedom is affirmed, the position can be extreme. Jean-Paul Sartre is the most thoroughgoing supporter of the view of total freedom on the part of human beings. Christian theology has always resisted unqualified determinism, although some of the writings of Martin Luther come very close to accepting it. As a minimum, theology has been committed to holding people responsible for their sin. It has held this view in uneasy tension, at times, with the apparent implications of divine omnipotence.

Pastoral counseling has expressed the tensions of both the Christian tradition and the counseling theorists. Some have leaned toward the therapeutic power of causal explanation of what is now occurring. Others have leaned toward the therapeutic power of emphasis on present choice and responsibility. Most have tried to balance these two elements, whether or not they could articulate a theory of how they are related. I suggest that practical experience indicates truth in both points. A theory that displays the truth of both can be helpful both theologically and practically. Most of the feelings and behavior that characterize a human being at any moment are determined by the past. They are not subject to current choice. On the other hand, it is never the case that present feelings and behavior are exactly and totally determined by the past. In some measure they are being decided as they happen. Choice is a real factor. Furthermore, however tiny the effects of choice may be in any moment, cumulatively they can be quite large. The choice at the moment may be nothing more than to continue the conversation with the counselor, but that choice may make another choice possible a little later— namely, to acknowledge for the first time a feeling of anger toward one's children. That choice may open the way to other choices about how to talk with the children more openly, and so forth. Identifying accurately where the areas of current choice really are, while also acknowledging the givens within one's own feelings and behavior as well as the wider situation, is far better than sweeping suggestions of total determination or total responsibility.

Within such a differentiated analysis, it is also possible to identify the working of grace. One can identify the role of the counselor in establishing a context in which certain choices become possible that would not otherwise be possible. At a still deeper level, it becomes possible to identify God as the giver of all freedom and the One who calls us to the right exercise of that freedom.

Embodied and Transcending

Much of Christian tradition has downgraded the body. Despite official theological rejection of a dualistic separation of soul and body, much of Christianity has held to the salvation of the immortal soul as the goal, and has often viewed the body, especially its sexuality, as the major enemy. Much of Christian spirituality, at least until very recently, has denigrated attachment to the body, often using ascetic means of accenting the primacy of the soul over the body.

Modern Western philosophy, on the whole, has furthered this dualism. What was a religious tendency in Christianity became metaphysical in the philosophy of Descartes. For Descartes, the body is merely a machine. Adopting the perspective of the experiencing subject as ultimate, empiricism and idealism alike go beyond dualism in their relegation of the body to the realm of appearance, or phenomena.

Materialists reacted against this, arguing that only the material world, including the body, is truly real, so that the soul or mind is merely epiphenomenal.

Psychology, like modern thought generally, has been confused and inconsistent on these issues. Its actual preoccupation has been with the soul, or psyche. Some of the psychological tradition arose out of the natural sciences and treated subjective events as by-products of physiological ones. Some of it arose out of the empiricist tradition and viewed behavior as part of the phenomenal world given to the observer. Some of it arose out of the idealist tradition and described the subjective content of experience and how it shapes the perception of the external world. Psychotherapy has been influenced in theory and practice by all of these. Counseling, on the other hand, has been influenced chiefly by empiricism and idealism, and pastoral counseling by idealism. Thus pastoral counseling has drawn on traditions that give primary status to the soul, or psyche. It may theoretically acknowledge that bodily events have causal efficacy on psychic ones, and it does find its access to the soul through bodily events, but it seeks above all to effect change in the psyche. Yet, its own practice indicates that the sharp separation of body and soul is erroneous, and much pastoral counseling aims to deny and to oppose this separation. In this effort, it shares a concern with contemporary theology. Few theologians today explicitly affirm dualism either of the religious variety or of the metaphysical sort. The recognition of the importance of the body and that the Bible opposes its sharp separation from the soul is now almost universal. The problem is how to understand this union of body and soul theoretically and how to implement its implications practically.

At the theoretical level, I propose that we stop thinking of bodies and souls as substances, and shift to thinking in terms of events. An actual human experience is an event, and the flow of experience that constitutes the soul is a succession of such experiences in which each event is deeply informed by its predecessors. What happens in the brain and in other parts of the body also consists of events.

This shift from substances to events will not get us far if we then proceed to classify events into two types: physical events and mental events. Events do not lend themselves to such classification. A moment of human experience certainly has mental elements or aspects, but it also has bodily or physical ones. Similarly, if we focus on cellular events in the body, and especially in the brain, there is no reason to say that these events are merely physical. The reality seems to be not that there are two types of events, disconnected from each other, but that there are many types of events, all of which take account of one another and influence one another. They differ greatly, but that does not place them in discrete metaphysical categories.

This means that careful analysis of human experience is appropriate. Among its causal determinants, some lie in past moments of experience. Others lie in the bodily events that inform the experience. These, in turn, are of many sorts. The major current influences may be from bodily organs or glands, from visual or auditory stimuli, from posture, or from blood chemistry. These bodily events should also be understood as being partly autonomous from psychic events but also partly affected by them. Human feelings and attitudes are affected by chemical, organic, and glandular events, as well as by posture and bodily movements. At the same time, changes in feelings and attitudes that are not the by-products of changes at these levels can also influence bodily events. The reality is so richly interconnected that the effort to deal with the body without attention to the soul, or with the soul without attention to the body, is based on a false dualism and has negative effects. Pastoral counselors can take the lead in sensitizing the whole church and its theologians to the concrete meaning of the denial of dualism and the embodied character of the human person.

Faith

The church has always placed a heavy emphasis on right belief. The demand for right belief often becomes legalistic. The rightness of a particular belief is asserted on authority, with the warning that refusal to accept it carries penalties both here and hereafter. This is a profound corruption that has done inestimable harm. It has, among other things, brought the whole of church teaching into disrepute.

Nevertheless, the church has been correct in asserting that what one believes is important. The argument that has arisen in reaction to inauthentic and authoritarian teaching, that not belief but practice is important, is misleading. Of course, practice is important, but the question remains as to what practice is desirable. That cannot be answered apart from what one believes about human beings and the wider world in which they take part. In this chapter, I have noted a set of beliefs that have informed counseling in various ways. Each school of counseling is based on a system of belief, that affects the way counseling is practiced. One cannot judge the several types of practice by a single neutral norm of success, for the understanding of what constitutes success is itself a function of the system of beliefs.

Sometimes an effort is made to avoid this relativization of criteria of successful counseling by arguing that the issue is whether the client has been satisfied, but the appeal to a criterion of that sort is just as dependent on a belief system as is any other. In this case, the belief system in question is a purely individualistic one, with respect to which many questions can be raised from the perspective of other belief systems. If this is true, then pastoral counseling has particular reasons to clarify the belief system that determines its goals as well as its methods. The goal should be to advance parishioners in a direction indicated by an understanding of Christian existence that arises from the interaction of tradition with present experience. Of course, this goal does not preclude offering counseling to others, just as it does not preclude feeding the hungry and giving water to the thirsty, but it does preclude assisting others to realize goals that are personally or socially destructive when considered from a Christian point of view.

When pastoral counseling is done within a congregation, there need be no objection to working together with the parishioner quite explicitly toward the goal of a fuller Christian existence, accompanied by appropriate supporting beliefs. Working with persons who have no Christian commitment who come for help is a more delicate situation, since acceptance of Christ should certainly not be made a precondition for this sort of help any more than for any other form of help. However, a counselor who is convinced that certain beliefs support human health and growth should not conceal this fact from the counselee. I have suggested, for example, that sorting out the features of experience that are determined by the past, by the body, by the counselor, by God, and by the counselee can be healing and conducive to growth.

Although the distinction between *belief* and *faith* can be exaggerated, it is real. *Belief* points to the way we understand our reality; *faith* points to a trust in some feature of that reality, justified by that system of belief. For Christians, it is appropriate to put relative trust in many things, but unconditional trust should be directed only to God. Can this belief about faith play a role in pastoral counseling?

Anyone in a healing profession must have confidence in something. With physicians this can work in two general ways. They may think of the body as something material, and hence passive, an object that can be manipulated into new and better forms by physical or chemical interventions. In this case, what is trusted is the power of the interventions. Or they may think of the body itself as an active agent in the production of health and growth, which is being blocked by particular impediments from realizing its goal. Physicians then remove obstacles to the effectiveness of a life process that is itself the primary agency of health and growth. Trust in that process guides their work.

Counselors can also view matters in either of these ways. They can view the clients' souls as primarily passive objects that can be improved by altering the stimuli that impinge upon them. Or they can see their role as removing obstacles to a process of self-healing and growth that is native to the soul itself. In that case, trust in that process guides their work.

From a theological point of view, the attitude that one is removing obstacles is superior. Life itself is the primary agency of healing and growth. Human interventions are not the cause of life. Human interventions can, however, remove obstacles to the effective and normative working of the life that is the presence of God in the world, so that trusting in the power of life, as it works in body and soul alike, is trusting in God.

To trust in God calls for attention to what God is doing, to making oneself sensitive to what God requires, to aligning one's will with God's aims and call. It requires a shift from an attitude of control and manipulation to one of openness and receptivity. Discernment and discrimination become more important than trying to shape events to meet the projected goals. Of course, the God who speaks to us in the life processes of our bodies and souls addresses us also through other people, through tradition, and especially through those saints and spiritual giants who have lived from and for God with peculiar fullness. We can test our discernment against theirs and in community with others who seek to understand God's call today. Yet, all of these complexities count for nothing, compared to the basic attitude of trust in the life that flows through us. Pastoral counselors can work in the context of such a faith and can encourage their counselees to live with such a faith.

Individual and Social

Everything I have written thus far would be compatible with a strong form of individualism—that is, with the view that the individual psyche is self-contained. This view has been widely influential both in Christian theology and in counseling theories. Philosophically, this is the doctrine that the individual psyche's relationship to other psyches is external. Excluded is the idea that the relationships among psyches are constitutive of each of the psyches that is thus related, meaning that the character of a soul is affected by its relations to others, which depends on a doctrine of internal relations. The point can be stated more clearly if we think of events instead of things. Let us assume that the soul is the flow of human experience and that this flow can be analyzed into the successive experiences that make it up. Now, consider one of these experiences. The doctrine of internal relationships asserts that this experience is largely constituted by the way past experiences and bodily and environmental events enter into it. It is, to a large extent, its appropriation of these other events, but in addition, there is its own creative response.

If this is the correct way of viewing the human soul, then a major element in determining what a person is at any moment is that person's environment. As that environment changes, the person changes. In some environments the person may be loquacious; in others, taciturn. In some environments the person may be affectionate; in others, defensive. In some environments the person may be self-assertive; in others, submissive. There are, indeed, few character traits that are wholly independent of the environment.

Of course, changes that take place in one environment will have some effect in another. Internal relationships are those to one's own past experiences as well as to the current environment, so that new experiences have an effect on later experiences, regardless of the difference of environments. Yet, the extent of these changes can easily be exaggerated. Christians over the years have learned that a conversion experience is unlikely to change very much about a person's character unless the experience is continuously reenforced. Unless the conversion is followed by altering the dominant environment—for example, breaking with former associates and finding one's new context within the church—the conversion is likely to be followed by a lapse into former patterns.

Counselors have had a similar experience. Changes that take place in the clinical context do not readily carry over into patterns of relating within the family. The person as a family member is not greatly changed by changing the person as a client. This reality has led from individual counseling to group counseling, and especially to family counseling. If the individual's problems arise from patterns of relating within the family, then the individual can be helped only as those patterns are changed. Rarely can the individual effect those changes healthily. Hence, the involvement of the counselor with the entire family is more promising than working with the individual.

Obviously, this principle does not apply only to families. The problems of individuals can be generated in the workplace and in educational institutions as well. Often these problems cannot be resolved in the very different context of the counselor's office. They require changes in the patterns of relating within the context in which they arise.

Theologically, this expresses insights that were especially vivid in the writings of Paul. He depicted the church as the body of Christ, in which all members were integrally related to one another. This is in part a relationship that is envisioned as existing through Christ, but Paul also saw that we are members one of another.

Adjustment and Social Transformation

In both theology and counseling, the deeply entrenched individualistic habit of mind has been associated with the view that the structures of society are given and that the need is for individuals to adjust to these "givens." The church through the centuries has counseled such adjustment in all kinds of ways, from Paul's argument that those who rule do so with God's authority to the idea that we should accept whatever happens as an expression of God's will. Counseling has generally dealt with disturbed people who have found it difficult to adjust to the situations in which they have found themselves, and it has undertaken to help them make that adjustment.

In the history of the churches in the United States, other motifs have also been prominent. Many religious groups came here from Europe because they refused to adjust their corporate life to the requirements of governments there. They sought to order society in accordance with their own convictions, and the New World gave them an opportunity to do so. In the late nineteenth century, the suffering of workers during the Industrial Revolution evoked a new movement within the churches, the Social Gospel. Here again, the goal was to reconstitute society rather than to adjust to it. This social activist theme has been part of the life of the American church ever since.

For some time, this social activism seemed to be at the opposite pole from pastoral counseling in the life of the church. Pastoral counseling dealt with individuals, helping them to adjust to society and to realize themselves or to actualize their potentials in whatever context they found themselves. Social activism tried to change the context. These two functions could be seen either as complementary or in actual opposition.

The situation is changing, however. Pastoral counselors have come to realize the ambiguity of helping people to adjust to given situations when those situations are profoundly unjust or destructive. Feminists, above all, have driven this point home. So much of therapy and counseling over the years has been done by men helping women to adjust to a patriarchal society. For many counselors, the continuation of that pattern is not acceptable. Counseling needs to strengthen people to resist and to change the situation rather than to adjust to it. Also, the counseling situation itself must be examined to determine whether it can contribute to such strengthening, especially when it consists in a male counselor and a female counselee.

The implications of these questions are very radical. They challenge the isolation of counseling from the whole life of the church or community. Only as the goals of the whole community are clear can there be an adequate context for dealing with the personal problems of individuals, which still constitute the main focus of pastoral counseling. How this will change pastoral counseling cannot yet be clearly envisaged, but it may have a healing effect on pastors who can see their roles as preachers, administrators, teachers, and counselors in a more integrated way.

Certainly the importance of counseling will not diminish. To engage in efforts at social transformation and to participate personally in the deep social changes that are involved are inevitably taxing and disorienting. Our need as individuals to find help in dealing with these new situations is keen and urgent. The services of pastors able to offer such help will be in great demand. The magnitude of the need is such that churches must find ways to make use of the capabilities of all their members to help one another. The line between mutual support of friends and formal pastoral counseling may well erode. Just as what has been learned through the analysis of society and the church's responsibility to work transformatively within it and upon it needs to inform counseling, so what has been learned in the practice of counseling needs to inform all reflection about how to work for social change. Perhaps we can find ways so to support one another and understand one another in the midst of our efforts to overcome injustice that such efforts can become occasions for personal growth and renewal rather than of exhaustion and burnout.

Salvation

Pastoral counseling is not accustomed to using the word *salvation*, because in the setting of the church, the meaning of that word has become constricted. To most people it suggests an otherworldly outcome of what happens in this life. Even when its use does refer to present existence, its connotations are often narrowly religious. This narrowness and other-worldliness are not characteristic of the use of the term *salvation* in the Bible. There, salvation can be from a variety of dangers and evils to a variety of outcomes. This broad use is current in ordinary language today. People are saved from drowning. Institutions are saved from bankruptcy. Nations are saved from conquest. In this ordinary and biblical language, there is no difficulty in saying that people go to counselors seeking to be *saved* from some acute problem or misery.

Our thinking would be better informed also in theology to start again with the general use of the term *salvation*. We can then ask from what Christ saves us and to what are we saved. The answer need not narrow down to one single point, such as "from sin" or "from death" or "from the devil." Perhaps the salvation we most need today is from nuclear holocaust, from ecological degradation and famine, from massive injustices, from plagues, from meaninglessness, from our collective self-destructive tendencies. These forms of salvation are intimately related to those from sin, death, and the devil, but the forms of salvation should be stated explicitly. It is equally important to speak of being saved from drug abuse, from uncontrollable rage, from depression, and from a host of other personal problems.

If the church is to have the importance today that it once had in people's lives, it must make credible the claim that Christ is the Savior in this whole range of ways. An otherworldly salvation that is not intimately involved with these worldly needs segregates the church, as its bearer, from the world God loved and loves, the world for which Jesus lived and died. This separation is wholly unacceptable. With respect to one range of human misery from which people seek salvation, pastoral counselors are those best qualified to help.

The breadth of this understanding of salvation does not mean that it has no definition. The idea of salvation implies some notion of what is evil and what is good. Those who believe in the patriarchal family as the basic unit of any healthy society will not want to be saved from it; whereas those who see patriarchy as the root of all evil long for such salvation. Those who see capitalism as the best form of economy, making possible both wealth and personal freedom, will certainly not want to be saved from that; whereas others, who view capitalism as a system of exploiting the poor for the sake of the rich, will regard nothing as more important than salvation from it. For some, salvation involves liberating the body from all repression; for others, it is gaining control over the desires of the body and subordinating it to higher values. For some, salvation means freedom from the shackles of responsibility to others and the oppressiveness of life in community; for others, it means freedom from individual isolation, participation in the life of a community.

To share responsibly in the process of salvation, any Christian needs an understanding of the nature of *Christian* salvation. For the pastoral counselor who is directly involved in facilitating the saving process, this need is doubly urgent. Pastoral counselors may prefer to speak of *health* or *wholeness* because salvation is too easily misunderstood as belonging to a segregated religious sphere. The word is not of primary importance. What is of primary importance is that pastoral counselors are clear as to what constitutes *genuine* health or wholeness or salvation and that in becoming clear about this, they relate their vision to the cumulative wisdom of the biblical and Christian traditions.

Clear thinking about salvation should help to overcome another duality that is emerging in the roles of pastors. The role of pastor as counselor arose out of the tradition of the care of souls. Yet, it has developed in such a way that today when Christians want to deepen their inner lives or consider their discipleship more seriously, they ask the pastor to function in a quite different role. The role of spiritual director appears quite separate from the role of pastoral counselor. This, surely, is unhealthy. The care of souls must include both elements indissolubly.

For pastoral counseling to carry forward genuinely the ancient tradition of the care of souls, it must separate itself further from secular therapy. Therapy can too easily be based on a model of restoring people to the capacity to function satisfactorily in society as it now exists. That can be a proper moment in pastoral counseling, certainly, but it cannot provide the basic model. The goal of pastoral counseling needs to be something like growth in grace, the strengthening of Christian existence, enabling Christians to be more effective disciples, or salvation. Such a goal will enable pastoral counseling to be spiritual direction as much as it is therapy.

Conclusion

The general thesis of this chapter is that any form of counseling entails judgments about many of the same issues as those that have been discussed in the tradition of Christian theology. I have identified some of the more obvious issues. If

I am correct that these issues are important to counseling, then it behooves counselors in general to be clear as to where they stand on them. Many counselors are committed to theoretical positions that do express such commitments clearly. Pastoral counselors have the specific responsibility to think about how the positions they adopt relate to the discussion that has occurred within the church as theologians have reflected on the same issues.

I have tried to make clear that this does not mean that theologians are the authorities and that pastoral counselors are obligated to accept their views. On the contrary, generations of counseling have given rise to a body of understanding of human beings that provides the church with new opportunities for theological reflection. It is as important that theologians be informed by what is learned in counseling as that counselors be informed by theological traditions, and both need to be informed by what is learned from others, including, as noted above, the contemporary feminist movement.

The seminary has a particular responsibility to overcome the compartmentalization it has adopted from the university. As long as theology and pastoral counseling strive to be academic disciplines, neither will be appropriately open to the other or to insights from other sources. The need to understand today's world and how we can act appropriately within it is too important to be treated in fragmented and fragmenting ways. We may rejoice that among the leaders of the pastoral counseling movement there are those who have pointed the way to wholeness here, too. Of these, no one has done more for the pastoral counseling movement, or for the healing of the church as a whole, than Howard Clinebell.

CHAPTER TWO

Encountering Sin in Pastoral Counseling

Hunter Beaumont

In this chapter, it will be suggested that narcissism may be considered a form of sin that has as its cure the development of virtue. The argument may seem capricious, a quixotic juxtaposition of theological and psychological systems of thought and language. Or perhaps it seems as if the argument stigmatizes persons living in a narcissistic pattern, labeling them psychological sinners. This is not my intention. It is my earnest hope that the reader will find this perspective of value in working with the narcissistic issues of parishioners and clients—and with his or her own narcissistic patterns.

In recent times, many people have shied away from the concepts of sin and virtue because childhood's painful preoccupation with the fear of sin and the quest for virtue produced only a paralyzing form of guilt and depression, instead of the promised well-being and joy. Such an approach to sin and virtue will not be of help here. Similarly, clients have reported feeling dismissed by some counselors, "You are just narcissistic," as if their struggle and suffering were inauthentic. In the following discussion, the concepts of sin and virtue and narcissism are changed as they are brought into dialogue with one another. Their meanings are altered, with sin and virtue becoming once again life-affirming resources and narcissism becoming something more than an ugly stigma. As in much of pastoral counseling theory, our task here is to allow the traditions of religion and psychotherapy to interact with each other—informing, correcting, and driving toward synthetic formulations that are more complete than either alone.

Gestalt Therapy and Narcissism

The German word *gestalt* is a complex and fascinating word that has no exact English equivalent, although in its most common translation it means "pattern" or "form." A melody is a gestalt, remaining recognizable even when played on different instruments or when sung in different keys. In this sense, a gestalt is an idea that the human mind recognizes in many different situations. *Gestalt* has other meanings as well. It has a meaning very similar to the concept of *system* in family systems theory or of *role* as in "social role." The family system is a pattern of behavior created by the individual family members interacting with one another, but it also influences and shapes the behavior of the individual family members. *Gestalt* in this sense means both the system that is formed and the pattern of roles and expectations that organizes the family.

In German, *gestalt* can also be a verb. "To gestalt," in this sense, means to organize, to arrange, or to produce something in a certain way. To gestalt is active. For example, one might gestalt a relationship, which means that the partners of the relationship are active in creating the relationship. From this perspective, people do not just have relationships; they make them. They do not just have experiences; they make them.

In the gestalt therapy way of looking at things, awareness is a creative process of gestalting one's experience through relating to the world and to others. How does this work?

Counselors, for instance, listening to their clients and parishioners speaking about problems, create experiences synthesized from many different elements. They do not pay attention to everything the clients do, but rather choose some of the elements of behavior to notice and ignore others. They see the clients' lips moving and the way they sit and move; they hear the sound of the words, the rhythms and modulations of speech. They recognize the meanings of words and the flow of thoughts. They consider possible interventions and remember other similar clients. Perhaps they think about shopping for a child's birthday present, or finishing a lecture or a sermon. Each of these components of experience—selecting, seeing, hearing, remembering, and so on—occurs simultaneously in different locations of the brain, and the mind creates a seamless, unified experience.[1] In this way counselors gestalt their experience of their clients and do not even notice their own creative actions. Their gestalted experience of the client is sometimes different from the clients' experiences of themselves. Thus gestalting becomes an active creating of experience.

As people gestalt their experience of others, so too are they involved in gestalting themselves. In every situation they create themselves a little differently. In a gestalt therapy context, self is best understood as being a process of gestalting one's own being in relation to others.

Narcissism

There are three major definitions of the psychotherapeutic term *narcissism,* and there are myriad minor ones. Although Freud was not the first to use the term *narcissism,* it was he who brought the term into popular usage.[2] Freud saw in the narcissist's self-absorbtion, egocentrism, and difficulty in relationships signs of a self-love gone out of control.

The second major view of narcissism sees it as being a deficit in the structure of the personality, the result of an unfulfilled developmental task.[3] The growing child may not have had the opportunity to learn how to live independent of external affirmation and validation. The adult narcissist who puts on a display to be the center of attention has a common motivation with the two-year-old child who dances for admiring adults: to get an affirmation of self-worth reflected in the mirrors of admiring faces.[4] In the child, the behavior is appropriate; it serves the purpose of helping the child to know that he or she is a valued person, that he or she is wanted and loved. The same behavior by the adult can be inappropriate, a sign that the adult has not learned to be independent of external affirmation to maintain a feeling of self-worth.

From a gestalt therapy perspective, the narcissistic pattern describes persons who tend to look into the world to get validation for their own being. Their self-gestalting is fragile,[5] and they need other people's affirmation to stabilize it. They are dependent on, or are *addicted* to, the affirmation of others to maintain a sense of their own inner well-being. When the hoped-for validation comes, they feel good; when it does not come, they may experience an inner collapse, temporarily becoming less competent than usual, exploding into rage, shame, or depression. The subjective experience of inner collapse can be dramatic, like a kind of psychological paralysis—the person may temporarily be unable to think clearly, may have trouble looking others in the eye, may wish to disappear.[6] Thus the narcissistic pattern describes persons who are constantly threatened by the collapse of the self-gestalt when external affirmation is not forthcoming.[7]

It is common to hear such statements as "Everyone needs a little praise now and again." While this statement may well be true, such sentiments ignore the degree to which the narcissistic addiction to praise supports dependency on other persons' good opinions and undermines personal freedom. If a person only feels good when praised, if praise and criticism are not equally valued, then there is a temptation to act in a way that pleases others, to act in order to get praise and not for the intrinsic value of the action. In this pattern, appearances may become more important than reality.

One minister with unusual candor came into counseling complaining of stress and anxiety. He soon revealed his longing for closeness and affirmation, which resulted in his having an affair with a woman with whom he felt very much understood and appreciated. In spite of having compromised his relationship to his parishioners, he felt he could not live without her.

From this perspective, narcissism is neither self-love nor a deficit, but rather an addiction to affirmation from others, a dependence on the opinions of others for feelings of self-worth. Relationships take on an instrumental quality;[8] maintaining good appearances can become more important than true interest in others.

Narcissism and the Seven Deadly Sins

The pattern of behavior that is so carefully described in the psychotherapy literature under the term *narcissism* has been described much earlier in the theological/religious language of sin and virtue. The "seven deadly sins" are not moral condemnations, but rather accurate phenomenological descriptions of the patterns of narcissistic behavior.

To the modern ear, the seven deadly sins—lust, pride, covetousness, envy, sloth, anger, and gluttony—do not always seem as sinful. A little lust, for example, has its place in contemporary marriage, as does a little gluttony on Thanksgiving Day and Christmas. In excess, however, they can take on an addictive quality that impinges on free choice. It is just this addictive quality that distinguishes a healthy enjoyment of life from sin as a destructive force.

Pride and Covetousness

Pride and covetousness may be considered methods of guarding the self by identifying the self with admirable things or with an admirable self-image or "false self." Persons living in the narcissistic pattern identify themselves with their possessions (covetousness) and with their image of themselves, their status and abilities (pride). Criticism of either may be felt as an attack on themselves. Such a person's inner sense of well-being is dependent upon his or her self-image and upon the valuation of her or his possessions by others. All relationships take on an instrumental character; other people are instruments to get affirmation.

Here is an example that I like because it is typical of the little things of which our daily lives are made. It is not dramatic, but it is representative of the thousands of little prides we all have. A man came into a counseling session mildly upset about an incident that had occurred during his winter vacation. It had snowed heavily, and in clearing the snow away from his own car, he noticed that the snow had blocked another hotel guest's car. Thinking to do this unknown person a favor, he carefully leaned his broom against the guest's expensive car and began to shovel the snow away, congratulating himself in his mind about what a considerate person he was. The owner of the car, who had been watching from the hotel window, hurried downstairs and angrily told the man to get his broom away from the car. Instead of the expected thanks and affirmation for his courtesy, the shoveler got angry criticism for his inconsiderate leaning of the broom.

It is easy to recognize that the owner of the car felt personally violated, almost as if the broom had been lain against his own person. What was done to his car was done to him. At the same time, however, the snow shoveler's upset was connected to his own investment in his self-image as a charitable person. He had tried to manipulate the owner of the car into giving him some affirmation. Two proud men spoiled a beautiful winter day, one proud of his car and the other of his self-image.

Covetousness, then, is not just coveting other persons' things. It is the general attachment to material things to bolster feelings of self-worth. Pride is not just the feeling of being proud; it is the attachment or addiction to an image of oneself and to getting affirmation for it from other persons. There is a simple test for pride: If criticism hurts, then you have an attachment to self-importance.

Pastoral counselors and clergy commonly confront two other forms of pride. One is the pride that every minister and every counselor must combat. It feels good to be able to help people in need. What a subtle seduction! How many of us could really do without the feeling of being the helper, without the feeling that we are good at what we do? The insidiousness of pride was demonstrated recently as a group of ministers was working to become more aware of their own narcissistic behavior. They discovered and confessed their pride in the growth of their congregations and Sunday attendance, their pride at counseling successes. Some mentioned their love of preaching, of being before an admiring audience. Others mentioned subtle competition with one another for rank and prestige in the community. Then one of them suddenly discovered that they were at the moment engaging in a subtle competition to see who could notice and reveal the most narcissistic behavior.

The other form of pride is the pride of the believer who lives in a feeling of righteousness, like the Pharisee praying loudly at the front of the Temple. This self-image seduces us into a false belief that we are right and that others are not. The picture of ourselves as being good persons becomes an armor, a psychological corset holding a fragile self together; take it away and the self collapses into shame. Certain media evangelists come to mind, who preach righteousness and collapse into teary self-pity when their own transgressions come to light. When they chastised their parishioners the week before the revelations of their own sins, they acted as if their own transgressions didn't exist, thereby maintaining their good image, but doing some damage to truth.

Sloth

We usually think of sloth as being laziness. As I have described them, persons living in the narcissistic pattern are dependent upon others for self-validation. When the praise and appreciation comes, they feel good; when it does not come, they feel bad. In this way they are dependent upon the actions of others, and they expect other people to do something for them that they are not able to do for themselves—to give them a feeling of inner stability and worth. They enter relationships with the need to get. In this way, they "instrumentalize" their partners, assigning to a partner the function of filling the emptiness of their own beings. They often hold others responsible for their own unhappiness, seeming not even to notice what they may have contributed to the problem.

A young divorcee in counseling told the tale of one disastrous relationship after another, of being badly used by the men in her life and nevertheless of falling in love over and over again with inappropriate partners. As we unraveled her experiences, she began to recognize a pattern in which she fell in love with an idea, with a hope, instead of with a person. She began to live a dream each time in which "Mr. Right" would love her so perfectly that she would feel whole inside, healed and openly loving. The beauty and power of this dream she lived was so overwhelming that she forgot to notice that the men she chose weren't "Mr. Right" at all, until it was too late. Because of her motivation in the counseling, she soon was able to recognize that she was trying to use the men to fix her own inner self and that they were singularly inappropriate for this task. Her capacity to feel openly and intensively made it very easy for her to believe that love and being in love are the same.

Behavior becomes slothful when we expect others to do something that we can, but don't, do for ourselves. This woman's behavior was slothful in the sense that she wanted healing from her partners, and because of this she wasn't ready to love them with no strings attached. Her love had a goal, and because of this she was disappointed again and again. In the course of the counseling, she did make progress in the direction of affirming her own inner worth, independent of men's admiration, and she became better able to choose wisely.

Lust and Gluttony

Lust is the pleasure principle of life, the criterion for behavior that we do what feels good, not necessarily what is good for us. Gluttony describes the addictive quality of so many behaviors. Freud has made clear to us that one dimension of human behavior is biological/genetic programming. That is not all there is to humans, but it certainly is one important factor. In its sexual guise, lust can bring spice and excitement into a healthy relationship. In its excessive forms, it denigrates persons, reducing them to lust-satisfying instruments. Persons who are dependent upon external validations are especially vulnerable to these excesses. They may do things to please others, sometimes losing a feel for what is psychologically healthy for themselves.

We must eat to live, and eating gives pleasure. It is well known that some habits of eating support health, while others are harmful to health. Decisions of how much to eat and what to eat may be made according to what is healthy, but far more often are made according to the principles of lust and gluttony. Hunger and appetite often are divorced from each other. The urge to eat may have nothing to do with the body's need for nourishment. People may feel hunger even when there is no need for food; they may eat too much, or to sate hungers that cannot be satisfied with food. We know, in fact, that many people are eating themselves to an early death because they do not distinguish between the various hungers, and they do not recognize the difference between eating for health and eating to sate addictive excess.

There are, of course, hungers for things beyond food—desires for possessions (covetousness), for power and admiration (pride), for sex (lust). Gluttony is thus choiceless consuming to satisfy unknown hungers without regard to the natural needs of the body. Above all, in persons living in the narcissistic pattern, there is often a deep inner sense of emptiness and a yearning to be whole. Clinical experience shows that people often interpret these sensations as sexual hunger, food hunger, or hunger for closeness and intimacy. Such persons may seek to fulfill these longings through a long series of relationships, as did the woman we discussed above. They may consume materially, accumulating a wonderful home and fancy cars. They may seek fame and fortune. Many arriving at middle age are faced with the realization that this "eating" yields no lasting satisfaction. One great tragedy of narcissism is that people are convinced that they must get something to still their hunger, must consume something or possess some commodity in order to feel inner peace. They then pursue activities that not only do not fulfill their longings, but that may actually prevent them from finding their longed-for inner peace.

Envy and Anger

Envy is more than a feeling; it is a primitive act of spoiling another person's joy. In its simplest form, envy can be observed in children playing together when one of them has a special toy or when one gets special attention. One child may spoil the other's satisfaction by damaging the toy or by interrupting the attention, even to the extent of provoking an "accident." It is astonishing how often and how subtly envy occurs in adult interactions. Counseling groups are one good example. While one person works on some theme, enjoying the group's attention, another person may become angry or bored or sad, turning the group's attention away from the first person. Even in the workings of church committees, one person may spoil another's joy, pointing out obstacles. Such behavior can, of course, be constructive, motivated by positive forces, but sometimes it is not.

Similarly, anger has healthy forms that contribute to cleansing, to building communication in relationships, and to the protection of the self, but it also has forms that are excessive. Persons living in the narcissistic pattern are vulnerable to sudden shifts of mood, to sudden violent angers. It is essential for them to learn to distinguish between healthy anger, which protects and cleanses, and the exaggerated anger of narcissistic rage. This anger does not build relationships, nor does it cleanse. It is destructive and manipulative. It punishes those who have failed to grant the validation and affirmation necessary to maintain a stable self. Counselors working with battered women, for example, will recognize the pattern in which a husband, addicted to affirmation from his wife in the form of sex or service, becomes enraged and violent when she does not flatter him as he wishes.

Virtue and Healing the Narcissistic Process

To many laypersons, the phrases *narcissistic process* and *the seven deadly sins* may sound foreign. As we have seen, however, when viewed phenomenologically, both concepts become tools that help us to understand the suffering of the people seeking us out for help.

Narcissism is not merely pathological, the consequence of

developmental misfortune. Far beyond that, it is also an expression of the human condition. Human life begins with a separation and ends with a return. In between, there is freedom to seek the source of life and the realization of the human potential. Narcissism has the paradoxical advantage that it engenders psychological suffering, which motivates people to continue their own birth.

From the phenomenological point of view, sin is human action that creates useless suffering and detracts from love and fulfillment of the human promise. In this final section, it is our task to place virtue within this same perspective.

Virtue and the Treatment of Narcissism

Kohut has told us that the self must be restored in a process something like reparenting and that it will never be fully healed. Jung suggested that we may set out on the path of individuation, like a medieval quest to seek self (he clearly saw a connection between self in this sense and the experience of God). For Kohut, the self has been damaged and must be restored; for Jung, it must be developed. They agree that the character must be transformed even when they do not agree just what this means. Gestalt therapists see the task as being to improve the connectedness of persons to their environment and to other people. From the religious perspective, it is to "Repent; go and sin no more."

Most psychotherapists and many pastoral counselors would have trouble giving that directive to their clients. It sounds brutally insensitive, hollow, superficial, and even threatening in some way. Psychotherapy through the years certainly has accumulated impressive evidence for the futility of trying to cure sin/narcissism by means of inducing more neurotic fear and guilt, by giving more injunctions that the client does not carry out. Anyone who has had counseling experience with the narcissistic process (or with his or her own narcissistic issues) knows the helplessness with which good intentions to "sin no more" meet the addictive forces. Insofar as sin has been understood as a desperate attempt to bolster a fragile self-process, one cannot simply abstain from sin until the structure of the self is strengthened. Yet, the task of strengthening the self remains. Just how are we to go about it?

Virtues as Resources for Growth

In a creative study, Beg has pointed out that virtues may be seen as being skills or resources, not just as moral qualities.[9] Thus courage, honesty, patience, humility, charity, prudence, and love are all skills to be developed and not primarily moral qualities that people have. Rather, they are things people *do*. This switch of perspective is essential to our argument: Virtues are resources, not qualities. Thus, from a gestalt therapy perspective, the treatment of narcissism is not just the restoration of a damaged self and not just the fulfillment of the individuation of the self-archetype, although both of these models are useful. Rather, it is the enhancement of the self through increasing connectedness to others. The virtues are the skills of contact, the skills that make it possible to connect to another person, not just instrumentally in order to stabilize the fragile self, but in a truly loving "I-Thou" moment.

But how do we learn virtue? Let us look first at how we do not learn it. The teaching of virtue has traditionally been based on two false assumptions: on the fear of God's punishment and on the idea that the child's will should be able to enforce itself on the entire personality. According to this teaching, children (and adults) were frightened with visions of punishment in the world to come. From our phenomenological perspective, the suffering that results from living in the narcissistic style is God's punishment. There is no other. The addiction to praise and the lack of true freedom are the death that is the wages of sin. The life of the person caught in a narcissistic pattern is hell enough. What is important is to teach God's promise of redemption, not God's vengeance. All attempts to teach true love and freedom through fear are doomed to failure.

In the same way, the will of a child or of a person in the narcissistic pattern is underdeveloped and is not in a position to rule the whole personality. When one function of the personality attempts to force its will upon another function, the self fragments, one function working against the others. Regardless of which function wins the struggle, the self is divided. The method of teaching virtue with "shoulds" can only be counterproductive. What people learn are hypocritical pretensions, to act as though they were not narcissistic. They learn to lie and to conceal and to deny, and all of these make the healing task of characterological transformation more difficult.

Narcissism as sin is turning away from God, for the narcissist seeks love from another person as if love had not already been freely given by God. "Repent; go and sin no more" means that people living in the narcissistic pattern *can* learn to feel inner worth, to gestalt an integrating self capable of loving without making itself dependent upon external affirmation. *To repent* means to recognize that the narcissistic efforts to stabilize the self cannot succeed. It means to learn to relinquish the attempts to gain love by performing for others' admiration. *To sin no more* must not be understood as meaning repression of the narcissistic behavior, for that, too, is pride, an investment in a false self. It means to begin the long and difficult task of truly learning virtue, admitting each narcissistic sin, relinquishing it with gentle firmness, and then turning to face God once more.

The great paradox of narcissism is that sin blocks the love narcissists so eagerly seek. Persons living in the narcissistic pattern believe they must be loved in order to be healed, but this is a distortion of the situation. *To feel loved* is not the solution to the narcissistic pattern. The solution is *to learn to love.* All the efforts to gain love, the pride in accomplishments, covetousness of possessions, consuming to fill nameless hunger, the endless quest for the perfect partner who will love enough, the spoiling of others' joy, the anger, the shame—not only do these not help, but also they prevent one from gaining the goal. From this perspective, the narcissistic pattern is not the deficit of love the child received (although it is true that many of these persons *did* experience a deficit), but rather it is the person's failure to develop his or her capacity to love.

Virtues are the skills that make this development possible. Honesty is the skill that makes it possible to track the subtle variations of the addictions and the self-deceptions. Humility makes it possible to surrender pride and the attachment to self-image, to accept failure and criticism. Courage makes it possible to face shame, to peer into the dark and lonely places within us. Faith of the heart is not belief; it is knowledge. It is the experienced truth that when one faces fear, that fear loses its power and shrinks in size. Charity makes it possible to act with gentle kindness when one feels hurt and angry, to remain contactful in the face of fears of abandonment and the loss of love. Prudence makes it possible to discriminate between "needs" that feed the self-image and "foods" that nourish the soul. Patience makes it possible to accept the difficulty of the task and to endure discouragement, to release failure and useless criticism. All of these are skills that can be learned, and when mastered they are resources of enormous value. But, of course, all of these are not enough. Human effort is not enough. All of this is possible only through God's grace and love. To accept that we are loved makes it possible for us to affirm the connectedness of God's kingdom and the love of others and of ourselves. The virtues are resources made available by God. Their correct development and implementation is the human contribution. To love is both the goal and the solution.

CHAPTER THREE

Ethics in Pastoral Care and Counseling

James Poling

All interventions by pastors and pastoral counselors involve ethical decisions.[1] We perceive and respond according to our norms about the family, about marriage, about parenting, about just relationships between male and female, and about the social context from which persons receive the choices they have to make. But most pastors are not trained to think ethically about their counseling. We don't know the difference between norms and rules, between decisions based on principles and decisions based on goals, between moral and nonmoral goods. The language of theological ethics is a strange one for pastoral counselors. Howard Clinebell instructed his students to attend to the ethical issues involved in our pastoral counseling.

> Counseling on ethical, value, and meaning issues is not just one special type of pastoral counseling. These issues are present, at some level, in all human dilemmas and problems, often in subtle or implicit form.

As Don Browning makes clear, the church is called to be a community of moral inquiry, guidance, and formation. The minister's role is to facilitate this process in the congregation and to help "create, maintain and revise the normative value symbols of his society."[2]

This chapter is designed to respond to Clinebell's challenge.

To be more effective with our ethical responsibility, we must know something about ethics, but we must adapt the ethical discussion to fit our pastoral context.

The Debate Within Ethics

One of the first questions clients often ask their pastor is "What should we do?" They seek help because they have gotten themselves into a fix and don't know what to do. They come to their pastor for ethical guidance, and the responses of the pastor are based on ethical assumptions. Theological ethics is a discipline that tries to sort out the nature of responsible, ethical decision-making.

Great controversy swirls about the nature of ethics. Ethicists have long been divided between those who believe that ethical decisions must be based on universal principles and those who believe that ethical decisions must be based on consequences. This is the traditional debate between the deontologists and the teleologists.[3] Deontologists believe that there are eternal or universal laws that can be known by reason or by religious insight. Human life is moral when it conforms to these principles. Teleologists believe that a moral state can be said to exist only when what is good is increased and what is evil is decreased. In this view, adhering to a rationalized moral law in the midst of destructive consequences is patently immoral.

If a pastor introduces any ethical dilemma into a group discussion, it is predictable that the group will divide into two camps, illustrating these ethical methods. Some will appeal to some form of natural or God-given law, and some will appeal to the situation and its context. For example, is child abuse wrong because human life is sacred, or is it wrong because abused children frequently become abusive parents? These two forms of ethical thinking are usually understood in any lay group.

There have been two recent critiques of traditional ethics.

One critique is represented by Stanley Hauerwas, who argues that both deontology and teleology are wrong. Both types are crisis-oriented ethical methods. They both assume that ethical decisions arise only when there is a dilemma that cannot be easily resolved. In contrast, Hauerwas argues that the true focus of ethics should be the formation of community life. In *Community of Character*, he says that every particular community has a narrative about its identity that defines its values and gives clues about the kinds of persons needed in that community.[4] When there is an ethical crisis, the main question is not one of principles or consequences, but rather, "What kind of community are we? What values do we intend to promote? What kind of character do we want?" In order to answer a question about behavior, one must first ask about the particular community in which that question arose. Even the definition of the ethical question will be shaped by the community context. Essentially, Hauerwas's position questions the usual definitions of authority. Traditional ethics assumes some "universal experience" that can be asserted, which has the effect of establishing as normative the perspective of the one acting. Hauerwas posits a radical pluralism in the world, characterized by lack of consensus about values and virtues, which has the possibility of granting power to those whose voices are not usually heard in the ethical debates. Particular communities present their ethical visions by the way they live their loyalties and commitments. This view is consistent with James Fowler's definition of faith as the way one lives one's commitments and loyalties.[5]

The second critique of traditional ethics, liberation theology, defines ethics in terms of social justice and liberation. That is, traditional ethics is criticized because it implicitly accepts the present structures of power and dominance. Who decides what principles are relevant to a particular situation? Who decides what consequences are tolerable? Those with privilege and power are comfortable making such judgments on behalf of others, but in a situation of oppression there is not equal power to consider choices and then make rational decisions. For example, in the African-American experience, the meaning of behavior must be understood within the context of racism. The black family historically has struggled to define its identity and values within a context of racial oppression. The ideology of the nuclear family has been especially destructive in the African-American community. Therefore, ethics must take that witness into account.[6]

Similarly, feminist theologians see women's experience as the normative context for ethics. They criticize traditional ethics for having a male bias that does not understand the inequality and injustice women face. The economic inequality that women face in the United States has an especially destructive effect on marriage and family, and it often leads to forms of physical and sexual abuse that men do not have to deal with.[7]

Liberation theology redefines ethics in relation to social criticism. Ethical questions and ethical methods will be very different when seen from communities that are oppressed than when seen from the ideology of the dominant culture. The relationship between suffering and power is the key to ethics.

A Case of Child Abuse

One way to illustrate these various types of ethics is to examine an ethical dilemma in ministry. I have picked the issue of child abuse because of the increasing numbers of adults who were abused as children and who are turning to their pastors for ethical guidance and counseling.

For several years, I have been working as a psychotherapist with parents who are abusive to children. In one case I worked for two years with a divorced father, Tom, who had engaged in anal intercourse with his nine-year-old son during weekend visits. Many ethical issues were raised for me by this case, in addition to the difficult psychodynamic issues. I had an ethical responsibility to provide quality psychotherapy for Tom, who lived in terrible intrapsychic pain and loneliness. But what was my ethical responsibility toward the son? Toward the son's family, his mother, and her boyfriend? Toward the system of child protective services and the court? How could I work toward building trust with Tom if he was afraid I would report any impulses or misbehavior to his ex-wife or to the police? What was the scope of my responsibility to the whole network of people involved in this case? Suddenly, my usual ethical commitment to the client's growth alone fell into question. I was faced with issues about my basic beliefs about the nature of the family, about the use of power in therapy, and about the limits of confidentiality.

The Nature of Ethical Reflection

How does a pastor do responsible ethical analysis on such an issue as child abuse? Usually we have a strong emotional reaction that something is terribly wrong in such families. But on what basis are any of these things wrong? Four types of ethical arguments are possible.

1. *Violation of God's law* (deontological ethic or "ethic of intuition"). The Ten Commandments and their restatement by Jesus are accepted as universal ethical standards. Several laws are involved in cases of child abuse: Honor your father and mother; you shall not kill; you shall not covet; love God and love neighbor as self. This type of ethics argues that certain standards are given in the nature of things, the violation of which results in the destruction of the moral fabric of human community. Based on these principles, a family may be a part of the natural order that must be protected against harm by the society—that is, children should honor their parents. But children are human beings who should be protected from

harm by adults, even if the harm comes from the parents. Parents should not kill or covet their children's innocence and liveliness to deal with their own depression or childhood trauma. The ethical issue is how to balance the various rights of individuals and groups to obtain the best approximation of the way God intends life to be. Abusive families raise questions about the way various traditional principles are applied to daily life.

2. *Destructive consequences* (teleological ethic or "ethic of purpose"). In a case of child abuse, a destructive sequence of events is set in motion, which increases evil and decreases the possibility of good, sometimes over many generations. Abused children sometimes become abusive parents. While the rights of the family and the rights of children are both good, the evaluation of what action will create the most good for the most people is always a contextual one. Pastors must not be so concerned about maintaining consistent principles that they miss the nuances of particular situations. It may be possible that respecting the rights of the parents is best in one situation, while protecting the child against the parents is best in another situation. The criteria must be based on a realistic evaluation of each situation.

3. *Violation of community character and narrative* ("community ethic"). In situations of child abuse, the community or society needs to reformulate its character in relation to families and children. In the United States today there is conflict about the meaning of personhood and its place in the family. In order to understand the public concern about child abuse today, we must explore the narratives that inform the relationship of children and families. Recently I showed a videotape, produced by a public television station in Seattle, Washington, to my class.[8] In the program was an interview with a disgruntled parent who was denied the right to adopt a ten-year-old girl. While the family was waiting for the adoption process to be completed, someone anonymously

reported the parents for child abuse. The county's child protective services investigated that report and eventually took the child from the home. The parents sued the department and had the decision overturned. The adoption went through, but the father was so angry that he formed an organization to promote the rights of parents who have been harassed by overly zealous state agencies. One result of such activities was pressure in the state legislature toward ensuring that state law supports the rights of parents and preserves the integrity of the family against government intervention.

This interview was part of a documentary program on the death of a child near Seattle. Because of fear of pressure from parents' rights groups, Child Protective Services apparently mishandled this case. Warning signs that the parents were a danger to their three-year-old child were ignored. Family unity was preserved, and the child was beaten to death by his father. The ensuing controversy grew and the state eventually changed its bias toward protecting parents' rights and mandated child protective departments to be concerned foremost with the protection of children.

Who is right? Is society's first responsibility toward the child or toward the family unit? According to a community ethic, such cases illustrate a society that is struggling to define its character—in this case the nature of family life and the individual rights of children. What is right is not reducible to either the family or the children, but some definition of the appropriate relationship between families and children that will enlarge the character of all citizens. Such a story becomes a parable that focuses the ethical debate about community identity and values.

4. *Social injustice* ("liberation ethic"). A liberation ethic raises questions about the violation of power. Traditional ethical discussions tend to ignore issues of power and oppression. One of the characteristics of children is that they are powerless to influence their fate. Attending to the real

suffering of children would be a challenge to the dominant ideology about "good" parents and would require a reexamination of how all children are parented in our society. Likewise, child abuse tends to blur the inequality between men and women. One of the reasons why child abuse is not dealt with more effectively is that men who are so-called heads of the family would have to be challenged, and the relative powerlessness of many women to protect their children would have to be explored. Such a study would begin to uncover the depths of patriarchal oppression of all women and children.

Race and class issues are other important aspects of liberation ethics. Often in notorious child abuse cases, the family that is vilified in the press serves as an example to the public that mistreatment of children is primarily an issue of the poor or ethnic minorities. (In the case of Tom, my client, poverty was an issue. His inability to support himself economically was a part of the oppression he had to bear in addition to his personal pathology.)

An Ethical Method

In order to develop a fully realized ethical method of pastoral praxis, we need a workable method for moving from ideas to decisions. Identifying four types of ethical thinking is not enough. How do we move from an abstract metaphor, such as "God is love," to concrete answers to the question "What are Christian forms of adequate parenting?" A dialectical movement from concrete decisions to abstract generalizations and back to concrete decisions is required. Such movement involves three levels: (a) the level of story and metaphor; (b) the level of middle axioms, or rules based on values that provide concrete guidelines for behavior; and (c) the level of decisions or actual choices in concrete situations.

If we combine the four types of ethical questions with the move from ideas to decisions through middle axioms, we develop a more complete ethical method. Moving from the most concrete to the most abstract, we have the following components:

1. Decisions
2. Rules (middle axioms)
3. Norms (intuition and purpose)
4. Social analysis of oppression and power
5. Community story and vision (theology)

This method can be conceived as a hierarchy of levels, with movement up and down in a rhythm between practice and reflection.[9]

Ethical Reflection on the Case of Child Abuse

How does this method work in terms of cases of child abuse? When I work with abusive families, I am suddenly faced with decisions that may affect many persons—the parents, the children, the extended family, and the social services and criminal justice systems. How do I act so that I provide maximum protection for children while also providing a context in which the parents can deal with some of their needs? How can I help these persons to become better parents while they are trying to recover from their own childhood experiences of being abused? These decisions involve both ethical and psychodynamic issues, but the ethical questions can only be resolved by some form of disciplined ethical reflection.

Certain rules emerge from my initial reflections. I must provide a climate of trust in which the parents can talk about the intrapsychic deficiencies and social oppression that contribute to their abuse. I must provide maximum protection for the children. I must cooperate with the authorities who have legal responsibility for child protection. But one of the problems with such rules is that they seem contradictory, at least on the surface. How can I cooperate with authorities and also develop trust with the parents? How can I encourage the parents to discuss their intrapsychic pain while trying to monitor their interaction with their children? How can I avoid being manipulated by parents who are so narcissistic that they feel their right to control their children is more important than their children's right to avoid abuse?

These contradictions drive me to the level of norms. What principles can help me to sort out my inner conflicts? How do I evaluate the consequences of the various purposes that are important to me? One of my principles is that people should do no injury to one another, and another is that just relationships are based on mutual respect. I must do everything in my power to encourage these parents to treat their children better. This will be based partly on my ability to treat the parents with respect in spite of their deficiencies, but it may also be based on my willingness to set clear limits with them concerning their treatment of their children. If I ignore their abuse of their children, then I am showing disrespect for them and for their children. I must find a way to set limits on their behaviors. But I am still in a dilemma from a teleological point of view. If my purpose is to help this family to change so that the parents' treatment of their children is better, I cannot expect a miraculous change overnight. I must be able to tolerate some ambiguity in exchange for the possibility that they will remain in therapy long enough to change. If I am rigid in my expectations of their behavior, they may not stay in treatment long enough to get any benefit. The long-term consequences of reducing the violence while keeping the family intact may necessitate some tolerance on my part of behaviors that I don't like or that are repulsive. But how do I judge when the consequences are more good than evil, and when am I colluding with the pathology of these parents, rather than facing the painful possibility of my ineffectiveness as a therapist?

The conflict at the level of norms raises issues about the social context that defines our interaction. Because I am middle-class, white, male, educated, married, and have healthy children, I have a certain view of the family. I am involved in a situation in which I function as an agent of social control based on certain ideas and values that are normative in the society.

My client Tom is a single parent who has been convicted of child sexual abuse. He is barely holding on to a factory job, and if anything goes wrong, he could be unemployed, poor, homeless, without health insurance, and perhaps without friends. He is one step away from being excluded from the protection of the social system. Given his fragile situation, his relationship with me is highly symbolic. On the one hand, I am a symbol to him of social respectability. I have the education, the economic support, and the normative family situation that make it likely that society will reward me for promoting its values. On the other hand, I represent the social class that is the source of his oppression.

It is in contrast to men like me that he is judged to be inadequate and expendable in our society. It may well be that his abuse of his son was one of the few outlets for his rage at mistreatment by society. When I decide to make a moral issue out of his child abuse, I am being very selective about the range of ethical issues that impinge on his life. Perhaps his situation would be better addressed if I were to help him find a better job, better housing, better economic support, and a community of love and caring.

What is my ethical basis for choosing psychotherapy as the option that best serves his needs? This social analysis does not necessarily rule out psychotherapy, but it might mean that the effectiveness of psychotherapy with this client will be nullified unless I can address the issues of classism in our relationship. The more I work with clients caught in the criminal justice system, the more latent discontent I hear about issues of class, race, and gender.

Finally, the social analysis raises basic questions about human nature, community, and God. By facing the ethical dilemmas of this case of child abuse, and by uncovering my own ambiguous social location as a part of the problem, I have raised profound questions of theological vision and story. What configuration of individual and social evil is disclosed in this case of child abuse? From a distance, I am horrified to hear that a father has engaged in anal intercourse with his nine-year-old son, but the closer I get to the actual father, the more I discover my own complicity. My horror at his sin is the reaction of one who lives in the protection of social respectability. My indignation toward him is a direct expression of the sin of a society that needs an oppressed minority to justify its values. It is in contrast to this father that I understand myself as "good" in a moral sense. And it is my silence about his social situation and its consequences for him and his son that provides the very context in which such abuse occurs. Of course, there is something pathological in this father that contributes to the horror of his action, but I share in responsibility for the social situation that activates his pathology. I am among the silent respectable leaders who ignore children when they are abused by their parents. The suffering of these children and these parents labels me as "righteous" only because I don't have to face this particular sin. I have never been arrested for child abuse, and so I don't have to feel the harshness of society toward those who are outside its protection.

If I share moral complicity, then my moral response requires personal involvement. While my client is the one who sexually abused his son and lives with the intrapsychic and social consequences of his action, I share the same theological condition of sin. My rage can find other outlets than child abuse. I can express my rage through my prejudices toward those in poverty, those who are marginalized because of gender, sexual preference, social class, or ethnic heritage.

Society gives me socially acceptable outlets for my needs for power and control, so I do not need to abuse my children in the way Tom does. Tom's "otherness" confirms my righteousness. Only when I can identify in myself the same propensity toward sin that I find in Tom can I reintegrate the projections that protect my fragile defenses. I am horrified in his presence because I am secretly horrified at my own sin.

I am also morally implicated because Tom would not be accepted in my church community. Not only has the church been silent on issues of child abuse, but the church has also engaged in the same scapegoating of child molesters as the rest of society. The rhetoric about forgiveness in the church does not extend to those who are so damaged by life and society that they abuse their own children. Rather, the church defines its morality in contrast to such men as Tom. In spite of the church's profession of the love of God for all humankind, the practice of love does not extend to Tom. Part of the reason why he is not present in church is that "his kind" are not included among those for whom the church has an evangelistic mission. His very existence is an indictment of the church's hypocrisy.

Where is God in this situation? To the extent that God is expressed through the body we know as the church, God is absent for Tom. But insofar as God is known in the world in the incarnation through Jesus Christ, there is no sin beyond the power of God. While church and society may sharply distinguish between my respectability and Tom's depravity, the gospel says that Jesus came for sinners. Through my work with Tom, I learned something about God's love. There is hardly a more difficult sin to face in oneself than the sin of molesting an innocent child. Tom's courage in facing his own sin became a source of revelation to me about the nature of God. Where there is suffering, God is active, providing resources for new life. Even though Tom's life was circumscribed so brutally by childhood pain, adult pathology, and social marginality, God was present, giving him courage to live day by day and strength to respond to my bungling attempts to be in communion with him. Through my work with Tom, I received new faith in God's redemptive power.

Conclusion

I believe that pastors and pastoral counselors need to become more skilled in theological ethics. Every situation of personal and corporate life includes conflicts of normative principles and theological vision. I have tried to illustrate a method by which ethical reflection on situations of pastoral counseling can lead to constructive propositions about God. I have suggested a way in which the conflicting forms of ethical reflection can be integrated into a method for pastoral care. I think Howard Clinebell is pleased to see his vision for pastoral care extended by his students. It is to his work that this essay is dedicated.

CHAPTER FOUR

Social Systems in Pastoral Care

Bridget Clare McKeever, SSL

An article in the October 27, 1988, edition of *The Los Angeles Times* caught my attention. It began: "Dayna Lorae Broussard was buried in Whittier on Wednesday—nearly two weeks after she was allegedly beaten to death in an Oregon farmhouse by members of the group her father founded to help inner-city children. She would have celebrated her ninth birthday Monday." The article went on to state that authorities were conducting a child-abuse investigation of the Watts-based Athletic Association. It also quoted excerpts from the eulogy delivered by the pastor of the church where the funeral service was conducted:

> Little Dayna has had difficulties. She was cut off at an early age. But you know this was the plan of God. Little Dayna is through the suffering of this world. She won't have to face what you and I face. She's free. . . . Now [Dayna] while you're pure, while you're trusting, before you have reached the age of accountability. . . . Now your life will be an example for all to follow.

The eulogy made no mention of the horrible circumstances of the little girl's death.

The article reminded me of a tendency, which many of us in

pastoral ministry share, to evade the hard questions, to embalm consciences with soothing platitudes when we ought to rock the foundations of complaisance. It brought to mind an event that occurred in 1982, one in which I, too, took refuge in superficial answers to ultimate questions, when I ought to have first sought the less comforting proximate answers to the question of why a child had died.

It was a few days before Christmas, and the parish was humming with that excited busyness that precedes great feasts. The manger was in place in the sanctuary, awaiting the "bambino." Parishioners were dropping by with donations of poinsettias. As I was about to leave my office to join the decorating party, my phone rang. I lifted the receiver, hoping that this would be a simple inquiry about the times of the services and that I could continue on my way. The woman on the other end sounded Hispanic. She was sobbing. She wanted me to come to her home right away because the three-year-old son of her neighbor had just been killed by a truck.

In my eighteen months in this three-thousand-family parish, I had never visited the neighborhood she described. In fact, I did not even know that anyone lived down that alley between a Goodwill store and a cheap motel on a busy highway. When I arrived at the location she described, I found that indeed there was a little colony there, housed in a row of wooden, two-room shacks. I had no difficulty finding the house of mourning. A few people were standing around the stoop, the women sobbing, the men silent and blank-faced. I felt really out of place—a white woman, well fed and well clothed, not knowing a word of Spanish, invading the sacred space of their grief.

Inside, in the tiny living room-kitchen were three children, a boy of about ten and two younger girls. They were making iced tea. I told them who I was, and immediately a respectful shyness descended. I asked the boy, who spoke English, where his parents were. He said that his mother had collapsed after the accident and had been taken to a hospital emergency room. His father was in the bedroom; did I want to speak to him? I did. The children crowded me into the only other room, which contained a double bed and little else. A short man in beige pants and a brown windbreaker sat on the bed, staring at the wall. I put my hand on his shoulder and said, "I'm sorry." I hoped he would understand the tone, if not the words. He patted the bed beside him, indicating that I should sit down. He understood that I was the nun from the church, and that gave me access to the world of his pain. We sat in silence. Sobs shook loose from his chest. My tears dripped onto the coverlet around a wadded tissue. Where do the children sleep? I wondered. Probably on the floor and on the couch in the living room. There was nowhere else. After a while, the father, still sobbing, reached under the bed and pulled out a cardboard box. He searched in the contents until he found a photo of a little boy of about two years old—black curly hair, smiling shyly, sitting on a truck tire. You could see the folds of baby flesh around his belly button where the little shirt had slipped out of his pants. We held the picture between us, looking and sobbing.

Later that day, I heard the story of the accident from the woman who had phoned me. The family had come from Mexico about two years previously. The mother cleaned houses. The father collected newspapers and empty cans from the trash left out to be picked up by the city disposal service and sold them to recycling centers. He and his wife would take turns minding the youngest child, Manuel. December 22 had been the father's turn. He had taken the child along as he pushed his handcart from trash bin to trash bin. He did not notice a person jump into a large truck parked alongside the curb; neither did he notice that Manuel no longer held on to the handcart shaft as he had told him to do. Someone was yelling. The truck was starting up. The father turned in time to see the back wheel pass over his son.

There is nothing like the tragic death of a child three days before Christmas for bringing out the compassion of a parish. Food poured into the little home. The local supermarket sent boxes of dry goods. Parishioners donated wrapped Christmas gifts for the children—more than they had ever seen in their lives. The local mortuary donated the casket and provided a free funeral service. The church was packed for the funeral mass.

I visited the family off and on during the following weeks. We mixed some English and some Spanish, talking about the loss and the pain. Gradually my visits became fewer; by June I had moved on to another assignment. Externally, nothing had changed for the family. Maria, the mother, was still cleaning houses, and Raphael, the father, was still collecting papers and cans. They no longer took turns minding a little three-year-old son.

That was 1982. Yet, that experience still haunts me with a sense of futility and guilt. It was a great human interest story for the local newspaper. It brought the Anglo, Asian, African American, and Hispanic communities, the poor and the deprived, and the adequate and the rich together for a few days—at most, a week. Then their lives went on their parallel ways.

When I read newspaper accounts like the one cited at the beginning of this article, I am reminded that I still have unfinished business with that event in 1982. When I scrutinize my guilt, I believe that it arises from my failure to examine and address the causes of the tragedy. The futility comes from the feeling that my intervention changed nothing. It gave the impression that people cared, but I and the community only cared to the point where we could respond without changing. We did not want to change, and we left the family as we had found them—powerless in an overwhelming and oppressive system.

It seems to me that some of the frustration I feel with traditional pastoral care and counseling is similar to that felt by the pioneers in systems therapy. Even when we seem to effect some healing and to engender new life, the fragile plant transplanted back into the stony ground of the old system soon withers. We owe it to the honesty and dedication of such pioneers in systems therapy as Murray Bowen, Thomas Akerman, and Don Jackson that the shortcomings of individual therapy were laid bare and the foundations of an alternative approach were laid. More and more, systems theory is becoming to family therapy what psychoanalytic theory is to individual therapy. However, we in the pastoral domain have yet to devise or to find a comparable theoretical foundation with which to address the complex multiple systems in which those families with and to whom we minister are entwined. Systems therapy is meeting its limits (just as individual therapy did before it) when the relatively healed and renewed family system leaves the office, hospital, or clinic and attempts to maintain its growth in a web of other systems that do not favor such growth.

In the case of the family described above, even the best of systems grief counseling is liable to fail, or to have minimal restorative effect, so long as the role of the wider systems—political, social, economic, and so on—in the death of their child is left unaddressed. In 1982, I saw this family as a grieving one, the victims of a tragic accident, the recipients of the compassion and charity of the parish and civic community. Now, I see this family as the victims of a socioeconomic system in which the parents could not find, or were debarred from finding, the kind of work that would have provided decent food, shelter, and safety for their children. I see the tragedy as one calling not merely for compassion and charity, but also for indignation and justice.

But, it might be argued, we pastoral counselors are not by profession social workers, much less social activists. It is not, therefore, the purpose of this chapter to suggest that we depart radically from the ground of our discipline. The purpose is, rather, to consider how a theology of liberation may help us to refocus ultimate meanings of what we do and to reflect on ways in which we might begin to apply systems theory beyond the family to the wider systemic web.

Theological Basis of Paradigm Shift

In *The Community Called Church*, Juan Luis Segundo, speaking of the ecclesial community, draws from Paul in describing Christian revelation as knowledge of the *mystery*. For Paul, Segundo states, "mystery signifies a divine plan, hidden but universal in its operation, that runs through history." This plan, according to Segundo, operates on two planes. First, the Incarnation and Redemption operate from the beginning of the human race until its demise. Second, the knowledge of God's plan of redemption operating as mystery is present in the church only from the coming of Christ.[1] As I read Segundo's explication of Ephesians 1:1-10 and 3:1-21, I see that a fundamental aspect of our call as church is to discern how God is acting redemptively in the world at a given point in history. Liberation theology insists that theology must emerge from praxis done in a specific historical context. The question of how God is acting in a person's life can no longer be asked. Rather, we must ask how God is acting in a person's life and in the multiple systems in which his or her life is entwined. And this question can be validly discerned only by those persons who are aware of being an active part of, but are not embedded in, these systems. Knowledge of the mystery must be sought in the ways it is incarnated, not only in human persons, but also in human systems. Leonardo Boff puts it this way:

> Theological reflection does not just start off from itself and elaborate its thinking on the basis of its own sources in the Bible, tradition, and ecclesial magisterium, and past theology. It is also rooted in the cultural reality in which it is immersed, and it reads and interprets reality from that context.[2]

Boff offers a theological construct with which the praxis theologian may discern the systemic scene: the dual construct of *grace/dis-grace*. The focus of theological reflection becomes a process of discerning the possible fruitful ground of grace and the stony soil of dis-grace within a given system.

Social Analysis and Theological Reflection

Social analysis is to systems what psychoanalysis is to individuals. It is a method of uncovering the roots and causes of life-blocking processes. As such, it is a necessary tool in discerning the sources of incarnated grace and disgrace. At this point in history, when human existence depends on viable interpersonalism, it is imperative that as church and as stewards of the mystery, pastoral-care ministers allow the homeostasis of middle-class paradigms of pastoral counseling to be challenged by the signs of the times.

Just as personality theory models are maps and not replications of persons, however, so too, any given social analysis is a map, a more or less helpful tool for understanding and action. It is important that theological reflection not be conceived and practiced as the collusive colleague of any particular schema for understanding social reality. It must be an enlightened collaborator with and critic of any and all models. As Boff states, "It examines such readings [of social reality] and then accepts the interpretations that seem to dovetail best with reality and faith."[3]

Dermot Lane, another liberation theologian, points out that "the mystery hidden from eternity and now revealed in Jesus Christ: the mystery of the Father's love for his people, the call of all to unity in Christ and the gift of the salvation in the Spirit . . . is available only in and through the realities of community, history, people and politics."[4] The mystery is not, however, coincidental with these finite incarnations; it transcends them and calls them to account.

Grace and Social Systems

In the Vatican II document *Gaudium et Spes*, the Roman Catholic Church called its members to interpret the signs of the times in light of the gospel.[5] The words addressed to the just and the unjust, "I was hungry and you gave me to eat, thirsty and you gave me to drink" (Matt. 25:35 RSV), provide us with a gospel norm with which to interpret the signs of the present times. We live in a world that presents both a dis-graced visage and a graced countenance. On the one hand, as Dermot Lane says, it is a world "that is divided into the haves and have nots, the rich and the poor . . . a first world of extravagant waste and a third world of extreme want."[6] Moreover, it is a system of mutual dependency, in which the existence of the poor is necessary for the extravagant maintainence of the rich. It is a world that radically challenges the conscience of the Christian.

On the other hand, never before in history has there been more possibility for the improvement of the quality of life for all humankind. "The advances of modern science and technology have made it possible to reduce the gross inequalities that exist in the world. . . . Now for the first time nature and history are more and more under the control of humanity."[7] Both the means to solidify human oppression and the power to inaugurate a future full of hope are in our hands. Up to this point, however, it is apparent that in most parts of the world the level of homeostasis in the socioeconomic systems has solidified around a privileged minority and a marginalized and impoverished majority. In such a situation, the only sign of the effective entrance of the Word of Salvation can be the destabilizing of such a system.

Systemic Sin

A major theological issue for the pastoral counselor is that of sin. Traditionally, sin has been perceived basically as the rebellion and disobedience of the individual against God. This understanding of sin has served to keep the consciousness of the Christian focused on the oppressed individual. Who are more liable to rebel and disobey than those bowed down under the rod of the powerful? Thus religion could be used to control the underling by branding any movement toward liberation as sinful disobedience. Rarely is it seen that *hubris* is both the luxury and the sin of the powerful, or that sin has a systemic side. Speaking of Latin America, Leonardo Boff says:

> One of the great defects of Christian reflection has been its failure to consider the structural side of problems. Theological tradition has engaged in minute analysis of the individual person and his or her conscious life in rejecting God or undergoing conversion. But it has done little to spell out the institutional and structural forms of grace and dis-grace. . . . The nicest and most well-intentioned people may still be living within a structure that produces oppression. They may be personally opposed to any and every sort of privilege, but still their class status may place them among the favored members of discriminatory society. Unwittingly, perhaps even against their will, they may be part of a structure that fosters structural injustice. This fact shows us once again that human beings in their present condition are both oppressors and oppressed, both just and sinful.[8]

What Boff says of Latin America is equally applicable to other socio-cultural situations, such as that in North America, where women and ethnic minorities are embedded in oppressive systems.

The Pastoral Counselor and Socioeconomic Systems

The pastoral counselor is, by profession, often present and witness to destabilizing moments in systems. These moments are enfleshed in the tragic episodes that force individuals and families to reach out for help—death, domestic and gang violence, alcohol and drug addiction, and all the other afflictions that haunt the culture of poverty. Too often, however, we ministers perceive the locus of grace and dis-grace only within the individual psyche or, at best, within the family system. Consequently, we prescribe for the symptom rather than seek the roots of the disorder in the extended systems.

Pastoral Counseling: A Diagnosis

Though there are probably exceptions, it seems to me that the present office-counseling system is poorly equipped to address the phenomenon of systemic disgrace and to facilitate systemic grace. The ethnic groups who constitute the poor and marginalized are not accustomed to seeking counsel in the formal setting of a center, much less paying for it. For them the healing intervention of the church is expected and experienced (when it happens) within the praying, worshiping faith community of the prayer group, the Bible study group, the church-related society, and the base community. More recently, it is experienced in the church-sponsored social action groups that aim to empower the marginalized.

Specialization has led to the situation in which the pastoral counselor is just a counselor and no longer a pastor who leads worship, preaches, and administers sacraments. As a result, the counselor no longer has access to the means of healing and reconciling through social praxis within and beyond the faith community. In some ways, the pastoral counseling system itself, constrained by financial and legal exigencies, finds itself enmeshed in the very systems it would seek to challenge.

Roman Catholic Social Ethics

Each morning, as I drive to my job teaching pastoral care and counseling in a small graduate program, I am assaulted by the evidence of systemic disorder and oppression. My car radio announces the night's death-and-injury toll in the current gang warfare: infants in arms sprayed by bullets from cruising automobiles, grandmothers wounded as they sat on their front stoops, youths stabbed or shot. As I leave the freeway and join the work traffic along the inner-city streets, I drive past the homeless, covered with rags and newspaper, still sleeping in doorways. It seems as though my pastoral efforts do not make a ripple in the great sea of misery. Yet, I belong to a church that has for centuries given a clear mandate to its members to become actively concerned in matters of social justice, the right to work, and the promotion of national and international peace.

In the past ten years, the Roman Catholic bishops of the United States have produced two documents that have challenged and encouraged, and also disturbed, many both within and outside the fold: *The Challenge of Peace and Our Response* and *Economic Justice for All.*[9] The reason these two documents have not met with the same benign neglect as have historical papal social documents is that they bring the Catholic Church's social teachings onto our own turf and make their implications explicit in terms of our own systems. The bishops, to quote a familar cliché, have stopped preaching and have begun to meddle. These documents have disturbed us because of a shift in our ecclesiology. No longer is the church merely those authoritative "others." *We* are the church, and as such we stand both judged and challenged in the light of our social ethical beliefs.

The Challenge of Peace and Our Response is a complex document that seeks to balance a fundamentally pacifist stance with a realism that forces its authors to admit that sometimes war may be an unfortunate necessity in order to defend human dignity and rights. For me as a pastoral counselor, however, the main issue is contained in this statement:

> The issue of war and peace confronts everyone with a basic question: what contributes to, and what impedes, the

construction of a more genuinely human world? If we are to evaluate war with an entirely new attitude, we must be serious about approaching the human person with an entirely new attitude. The obligation for all of humanity to work toward universal respect for human rights and human dignity is a fundamental imperative of the social, economic and political order.[10]

As a pastoral counselor, I need to have a perception (albeit a heuristic one) of what constitutes a genuinely human person and a genuinely human world. This perception of person must go far beyond the traditional anthropology that informed intrapsychic therapy and is well described in Robert Bellah's *Habits of the Heart*:

> She [an interviewed therapist] understands that human relationships require give-and-take, that you must work hard for the satisfactions you expect in life, and that you are ultimately responsible for your own life. But this clear-sighted vision of each individual's ultimate self-reliance turns out to leave very little place for interdependence and to correspond to a very grim view of the individual's place in the social world.[11]

The Challenge of Peace and Our Response suggests that interdependence is basic to both human personhood and a humanized world. Today, a principle of unity that implies interdependence is clearly made imperative in the necessity of economic and political interdependence. However, such interdependence must be undergirded by a moral interdependence that leads individuals and groups to cooperate with one another in building a world that fosters human life in the image of God. As the pastoral document states, "We are living in a global age with problems and conflicts on a global scale, either we shall learn to resolve these problems together, or we shall destroy one another."[12]

The second document, *Economic Justice for All*, enunciates six basic principles that might form a substructure for the pastoral counselor's perception of a genuinely human world:

1. Human dignity can be realized and protected only in community.
2. Every economic decision and institution must be judged in light of whether it protects or undermines the dignity of the human person.
3. All people have a right to participate in the economic life of society.
4. All members of society have a special obligation to the poor and the vulnerable.
5. Human rights are the minimum conditions for life in community.
6. Society as a whole, acting through public and private institutions, has the moral responsibility to enhance human dignity and protect human rights.[13]

Clearly, as *Economic Justice for All* indicates, the key dynamic in a humanized world is the actualization of productive interdependence. A symptom of the failure to effect creative interdependence is the fact of material poverty, a major obstacle to the human development of more than thirty-three million Americans.

The norms of human dignity and the preferential option for the poor compel us to confront this issue with a sense of urgency. Dealing with poverty is not a luxury to which our nation [or the pastoral counselor] can attend when it finds the time and resources. Rather it is a moral imperative of the highest priority.[14]

Poverty is not confined to the anonymous people on the skid rows of our cities. It is something that is liable to happen to anyone at any time. Some may be newly laid off from work. Some may be unable to work because of illness or other disabilities. Some, particularly women, may be divorced and depending on an unreliable child-support check and a low-paying or underpaid job to support a family. A large number of persons are poor solely because they belong to racial minorities. While one out of every nine white Americans is poor, one out of three black and Native Americans and one out of four Hispanics suffer from poverty.[15] From the ranks of these come for counseling—if they can afford the fee—persons with the symptoms of marital and family discord, alcoholism and drug dependency, depression and anxiety, and the various other ills that we diagnose and treat as though they had no socioeconomic relevance.

The NCCB document on the economy suggests two principles that should underlie action against poverty. The first is the principle of *social solidarity*. All members of society are responsible for alleviating the plight of the poor, and the effort to do so must call all people together into one concerned and compassionate community. The second is the principle of *participation*. The solution in keeping with human dignity is one that enables people to take control of their lives. Poverty is not just lack of material resources; it is the marginalization of peoples, which debars them from participation in the social, political, and economic life of the nation. It means being not only deprived but also powerless.[16]

In his most recent social encyclical, *On Social Concern*, Pope John Paul II elaborates on the principle of *interdependence*, translating it into a fundamental Christian virtue. He describes interdependence as a relationship-determining system that translates theologically into the virtue of solidarity. Solidarity is not a sentimental empathy, nor is it a vague feeling of distress at the misfortunes of others. It is *committed action* in the service of others because "we are all responsible for all."[17]

A Tragedy Revisited

In the light of what has been said about the deformative effects of social systems on individuals and groups, and the necessity of a systemic paradigm in assessing the nature of human problems and in taking steps to remedy human ills, let us look again at the bereaved family described at the beginning of this chapter. What follows is a suggested plan of pastoral care and counseling that is expanded beyond traditional grief counseling.

I. Immediate crisis care and family counseling that would involve:
   A. Helping them through their initial shock, allowing them to express feelings of hurt, anger, guilt, etc.
   B. Helping to provide for immediate practical needs.
   C. Assisting with funeral arrangements.
   D. Helping the family to plan the funeral service.
II. Follow-up grief counseling that would involve:
   A. Encouraging the family to explore the systemic roots of the tragedy.
   B. Helping them to network with social organizations, such as UNO, EVO, SCOC, and VOICE,[18] in order to work toward a betterment of their economic situation.
   C. Helping the family to continue to articulate their grief in terms of its individual, familial, and social dimensions.
   D. Helping the family to plan and to celebrate ritually their grief at the time of the first month's memory and the first anniversary of the child's death.

The follow-up would also involve the parish community in the following ways:

A. In the funeral sermon, some mention would be made of the social conditions that contributed to the tragedy, care being taken to avoid "guilt-tripping" the community.
B. At an appropriate time after the funeral, a more extensive consciousness-raising sermon would be preached.

C. Members of the faith community who are interested in exploring the issue of social justice would be invited to form a theological reflection group, shaped after the base community model.
D. This group would be encouraged to become a leaven for change in the larger faith community.

The process described above would have as an aim the participation of the wider community in the mystery of death and resurrection. This death and resurrection would involve a dying to old perceptions of reality, to old clichés and stereotypes, and a rising to a new and fuller life of perception and action. As Leonardo Boff says, persons who have undergone such a conversion "realize that if they are to be graced personally, they must also fight to change the societal structure and open it up to God's grace. . . . They will feel a need for pardon every day and they will not be able to rest content with a pharisaical reliance on a wholly inner Christian life."[19]

Christian Wholeness in Systemic Terms

In the social encyclical letter *On Social Concern,* Pope John Paul II describes Christian holiness in a new, yet old, way. He indicates that it involves a clear commitment to solidarity with the oppressed,[20] in other words, to living the injunction implied in Mark 10:42-45:

And Jesus called them to him and said to them, "You know that those who are supposed to rule over the Gentiles lord it over them, and their great men exercise authority over them. But it shall not be so among you; but whoever would be great among you must be your servant, and whoever would be first among you must be slave of all. For the Son of man also came not to be served but to serve, and to give his life as a ransom for many." (RSV)

This concept of wholeness and holiness envisions an *imago Dei* who is not just an individual person but also a *we*, a person whose existence cannot be experienced apart from the rest of humankind.

Healing the Diseases of Affluence

It is not only in ministry to and with the oppressed that the pastoral counselor must be rooted in a systemic model. The human ills of the culture of affluence have the same source as those of the culture of poverty. The oppressor is also marginalized in the sense that she or he is cut off from the fundamental human family. Lacking a sense of human solidarity, and experiencing a meaning vacuum, such persons strive vainly to fill their lives with the palliatives of material things and political power, and, when the pain of emptiness becomes too great, alcohol and drugs. In the long run, healing for the wounds of the oppressor must involve solidarity with the oppressed. For them, salvation comes through the poor and oppressed. They need the water of life from the fingertips of the Lazaruses of this world (see Luke 16:19-31). For them the journey toward wholeness must involve, as Pope John Paul II states in *On Social Concern*,

> a moral value which men and women of faith recognize as a demand of God's will. . . . [An awareness] of the urgent need to change the spiritual attitudes which define each individual's relationship with self, with neighbor, with even the remotest human communities, and with nature itself; and all of this in view of higher values such as the common good. [21]

Pastoral Identity and the Systemic Paradigm

The paradigm shift that the awareness of systemic sin and systemic grace involves has implications for the identity of the pastoral counselor. First, it means that we ministers must recognize and own the extent to which we are fused into oppressive systems, not excluding the churches to which we belong. This means that to a great extent we live, more or less unconsciously, secular majority values rather than gospel values. Our identity as persons and as ministers has been contaminated by such values, including the values of our patriarchial religious systems. Such a situation calls for personal and collective conversion, and such a conversion can take place only in dialogue with those who have been formed with different values—the poor, the oppressed, women. Such dialogue will involve hard work, suffering, and, one hopes, some joy. If it is to lead to conversion, it will, above all, need to be a *sacramental* dialogue, a finite shape of God's saving grace. Wholeness and holiness, for all of us, means tending toward that state for which Jesus prayed on our behalf: "That they may all be one; even as thou, Father [Mother], art in me, and I in thee, that they also may be one in us, so that the world may believe that thou hast sent me" (John 17:21-22 RSV).

CHAPTER FIVE

Pastoral Care
Across Cultures

Paul G. Schurman

José is a senior in a suburban high school in a Midwestern city. His family has recently moved from the Southwest. José is a second-generation Mexican American. His father is a hard-working sales manager who has recently been promoted to a more responsible position in his company. José is an excellent student and is in line for an academic scholarship for college. However, the family went to their pastor to discuss what has developed as a serious school and family conflict.

José had submitted for his American history class an essay that was critical of the point of view presented in the class's textbook and defended by the teacher. José wrote a well-documented paper dealing with the development of the Southwest from a Mexican-American perspective. The teacher gave him an "F" on the project, but offered him the opportunity to rewrite his paper. José's family tried to persuade him to comply, arguing that the college scholarship was more important than the project. But José refused. If you were their pastor, what would you do to assist this family with its crisis?

A young pastor of an Asian Pacific immigrant group has recently graduated from seminary and is seeking ordination in a mainstream Protestant denomination. You are sitting on the denomination's board of ministry, participating in a discussion of this person's pastoral-counseling exam. He has written a study of a typical pastoral care situation in his immigrant parish wherein he receives a telephone call for help from a woman parishioner who has been physically abused by her husband during a family argument. The pastor decides not to intervene directly in what he felt was "a family matter." Most board members are ready to flunk the pastor on his exam. How about you?

Incidents such as these are coming to my attention with increasing frequency. Perhaps this is due to my location in the Los Angeles area, referred to in *Time* magazine as "the new Ellis Island." In a single recent year, nearly 100,000 immigrants settled here.

Immigrants have made their way to California before, of course. "We find ourselves suddenly threatened," the last Mexican governor of California reportedly said in 1846, "by hordes of Yankee immigrants whose progress we cannot arrest."[1]

In 1940, only one-eighth of Californians were foreign-born. Today everyone in Los Angeles is a member of a minority group; the 1980 census showed an Anglo population of 48 percent. This is not only an inner-city phenomenon, but is true of Los Angeles County as well. And what is true of Southern California is becoming the case in every major urban area in the United States, indeed throughout the world. Our cities are increasingly becoming mirror images of the global village.

Effective ministry, including the ministry of care and counseling, will require us to take giant steps in our understanding and appreciation of this new reality. The literature in the mental health field documents that we have come a long way from our very limited and highly prejudiced views of just a few decades ago. I will offer a very brief overview of this historical perspective so that we can appreciate the roots of the problem, and then I will suggest some directions for continued progress.

Historical Overview

A century ago, G. Stanley Hall, founder of the *American Journal of Psychology* and first president of the American Psychological Association, described Africans, Indians, and Chinese as members of "adolescent races" in a stage of incomplete growth.[2]

Less than seventy years ago, in July of 1921, W. M. Bevis, of St. Elizabeths Hospital in Washington, D.C., wrote an article in *The American Journal of Psychiatry* titled "Psychological Traits of the Southern Negro with Observations as to Some of His Psychoses." The article contains such racist ideas as "All Negroes have a fear of darkness . . . are careless, credulous, childlike, easily amused."

Carl Jung also wrote about the "childishness of the Negro": "What is more contagious than to live side by side with a rather primitive people?" he asked in the context of a discussion of American behavior.[3] At the Second Psychoanalytic Congress in 1910, Jung explained the cause of American sexual repression as "living together with lower races, especially with Negroes. Living together with barbaric races exerts a suggestive effect on the laboriously tamed instinct of the white race and tends to pull it down." This was Jung's explanation for the "strongly developed defensive measures" in American culture.[4]

Sociologists were equally prone to racist formulations. Dr. W. I. Thomas, at the University of Chicago, provided scientific justification for discrimination in his theory of "consciousness of kind." He claimed that race prejudice was an instinct "originating in the tribal stage of society." This instinct supposedly provoked a "reflex of repulsion" at the mere sight of physical features different from those of the beholder.[5]

For decades census figures and other statistical formulations were fabricated to prove that freedom was pathogenic for blacks since it violated their need for submissiveness to authority. When blacks ceased being treated as property, they were viewed by many as defective. From theories of genetic inferiority to later, more subtle, theories of cultural deprivation, we can trace the painful history of white racism.[6]

In the article "The Role of the Behavioral Scientist in the Civil Rights Movement," in *American Psychologist* in 1968, Martin Luther King, Jr., pointed out that social scientists have played little or no role in disclosing the truth about the plight of minorities. He claimed that "it was the Negro who educated the nation to the brutal facts of segregation by dramatizing the evils through nonviolent protest."

If white Americans have mistreated any other group as disgracefully as they have the African Americans, it would have to be the Native Americans. Their appalling plight is well-documented.[7] One out of three Native Americans will be jailed sometime during his or her lifetime, and one out of every two families will have a relative die in jail. From 25 to 35 percent of all Indian children are separated from their families and placed in foster homes, adoptive homes, or institutions. Average income per year is approximately $1,500. Unemployment of tribal members ranges from 40 to 80 percent.

Anthropological evidence indicates that the paleo-Indians of North America arrived here some 40,000 years ago. Their history has been all downhill since the arrival of the Euro-Americans. The conquering settlers viewed the Native American as an inferior being. "Cultural lag" theories were invoked to justify demeaning behavior and to repress any feelings of sympathy or understanding for the Native Americans. Hundreds of thousands of men, women, and children were forced from their homes to walk "trails of tears" to be relocated on useless land. Those who were uncooperative were massacred. Some fifty-five treaties, during President Andrew Jackson's two terms in office, were masterpieces of intimidation, bribery, threats, misrepresentation, and fraud.

Though other minority groups have fared somewhat better than the African Americans and the Native Americans, the record of discrimination and lack of understanding includes them all. The original immigrants from Spain, native Indians from Mexico, and their *mestizo* progeny founded permanent settlements in what is today northern New Mexico, subsequently spreading throughout the Southwest. The 1970 census reported nine million Hispanics, the majority claiming Mexico as their country of origin. These figures are swelling rapidly as immigrants from South and Central America, as well as Mexico, come into the United States, both legally and illegally. The common assumption is that Hispanic culture is homogeneous, whereas it is actually an aggregate of many distinct subcultures. These people have been exploited as cheap labor in the farming industry and the clothing "sweatshops" of Los Angeles, as domestic help, and as day laborers in the housing industry. They have contributed enormously to the economy of this country; yet, the income for Hispanic males is considerably lower than that of Anglos. In 1973, 22 percent of the Hispanic population was described as "low income," compared with 11 percent of the general population.[8] The "macho" label has been denigrated by the Anglos to denote aggression, sexual promiscuity, dominance over women, and excessive use of alcohol. In Hispanic culture, the concept involves dignity in personal conduct, respect for others, love for family, and affection for children.

Asian Pacific peoples represent another cluster of cultures that have been indiscriminately lumped together. Our ethnocentric tendency is to view the United States as the center of the world (look at most maps of the world printed in the United States), and thus we refer to the Asian countries as the "Far" East. "Far from what?" my Asian students often ask.

The 1970 census reported over a million and a half Asian Americans residing in the United States, but the current estimates are over two million, representing the cultures of

Japan, China, Korea, the Philippine Islands, Vietnam, and various Pacific Island groups. There are some myths about certain Asian groups' being "model minorities," but Asian Americans, too, have a history of inhumane treatment by Anglos. Beginning in the 1840s, Chinese immigration was encouraged as a source of cheap labor for building railroads and working in the gold fields of California. With the completion of the joining of the Union Pacific and the Central Pacific Railroads in 1869, competition for jobs became fierce, and white laborers saw the Chinese as a threat. Though originally based on economics, the anti-Chinese sentiment was fed by feelings of white supremacy. The Chinese were denied rights of citizenship and were viewed by many as "heathen" and "subhuman." The Chinese Exclusion Act of 1882, a racist immigration law, was not repealed until 1943. The cliché "not a Chinaman's chance" reflects these conditions.[9] There were massacres of Chinese in Los Angeles in 1851 and in Wyoming in 1885.[10]

The Japanese began to immigrate to the United States in large numbers in the 1890s. They found employment in the canneries, the mines, and on the railroads. Many of them were attracted by their backgrounds to farming and gardening, where they were very successful. The Japanese received some of the same treatment as the Chinese and together they represented a threat that the white establishment referred to as "the Yellow Peril." California enacted the Alien Land Law in 1913, forbidding immigrants to own land. Most Americans are by now aware of the discrimination and criminal acts committed against the Japanese Americans during World War II, when over 100,000 were held in concentration camps.

With the restrictive immigration laws directed at the Chinese and Japanese, business owners were forced to find another source of cheap labor. The new labor source was discovered in Puerto Rico and the Philippines. The hostility from white labor groups toward these cheap sources of labor was misdirected, since it was the owners, not the laborers, who created the situation.

Derald Sue, a pioneer in cross-cultural studies, explains that on close analysis, the status of most Asian Americans does not support the success story.[11] Even though the median income of Asian Americans is higher than that of most minority groups, the figures do not take into account that there is a higher percentage of more than one wage earner in Asian families than in white families. Asian seminary students, working in immigrant congregations in Los Angeles, report that both spouses working long hours takes a real toll on family life, creating problems especially among the teenage population. Asian family life often breaks down under the pressure of surviving. Most Asians are overqualified for the types of jobs available to them in the United States. Financial success is one means open to them for maintaining self-esteem, and so they often work several jobs to avoid shame. The results are often disastrous for the family.

Asian Americans view the stereotypical "model minority" myth as having functional value for those in power. The stereotype asserts the erroneous view that any minority group can succeed in a democratic society if they work hard enough. The myth is seen as a divisive concept used by the dominant establishment to pit one minority group against another, and it has the result of shortchanging many Asian groups from receiving necessary resources.

Though this historical overview has been extremely brief, it provides an important background for viewing the problems associated with a ministry of care and counseling across cultural lines. These descriptions of suffering suggest causes for suspicion and mistrust, at best, and for outright rage and defiance, at worst. And even though the most terrible examples of blatant and open racism are behind us, we hope, there is yet a massive task of identifying and addressing all the intricate and subtle institutional forms and expressions of discrimination.

Hope for the Future

Certainly, the research and emerging literature dealing with cross-cultural issues are sources of hope. Within the mental-health field, there is a new level of sensitivity as well. Members of the American Psychological Association at the Vail Conference in 1973 recommended that

> the provision of professional services to persons of culturally diverse backgrounds not competent in understanding and providing professional services to such groups shall be considered unethical. It shall be equally unethical to deny such persons professional services because the present staff is inadequately prepared. It shall, therefore, be the obligation of all service agencies to employ competent persons or to provide continuing education for the present staff to meet the service needs of the culturally diverse population it serves.[12]

The mental-health disciplines have been white middle-class in their formulation of philosophy as well as in their patterns of service delivery. The culture-boundness of these disciplines is, at least, in our consciousness now. Practitioners are increasingly aware of the extent to which their professions have served the dominant culture primarily, and how they have imposed on persons of diverse cultural backgrounds a narrow picture of mental health. Indeed, the hallowed notions of individual development, growth, and self-actualization must be considered culturally biased when imposed on Asian Americans and Native Americans, who are more family- or group-centered. The culturally encapsulated professional may function unwittingly as a tool of his or her own political, social, economic, or theological value system.

Professional education in all fields—law, medicine, theology, as well as the social sciences—has lacked an effective cross-cultural perspective. Curricula in the future should include components dealing with consciousness raising, affective issues, knowledge base, and professional skills. Such study would focus not only on nonwhite ethnicity, but also on white ethnicity. Most Euro-American immigrant groups did not begin to refer to themselves as "white" until they arrived in the United States. They were Germans, Swedes, Norwegians, Italians, Poles, and so on. What some writers are referring to as the "new ethnicity" or "new pluralism" has promise for helping us to abandon the white/nonwhite dichotomy.

I have observed this transition in my own students in a course on cross-cultural perspectives in pastoral counseling, which I have been teaching for about a decade. Several years ago, most white students elected to do research on a nonwhite ethnic group. This year every white student in the class focused on his or her own ethnic roots. This was very useful to the nonwhite students as well, giving them a clearer understanding of white ethnic diversity in the United States.

Pastors and pastoral counselors, along with other professional groups working with families, are playing active roles in influencing the structure of family relationships. These negotiations involve much more than simple personal arrangements among family members. Family structure grows out of the family's cultural tradition. Various therapeutic strategies and/or religious rituals also reflect cultural values. Indeed, every aspect of a ministry of care and counseling is filtered through our personal cultural perspectives as well as the inherent value assumptions of our respective psycho-therapeutic and/or religious traditions.

"Ethnicity remains a vital force in this country, and a major determinant of our family patterns and belief systems," write McGoldrick, Pearce, and Giordano.[13] Our forebears fostered the metaphor of the "melting pot" for this new nation, based on the premise of equality. We are not, in fact, all equal yet in this society, and we apparently have no intention of "melting." A more appropriate metaphor is that of a "salad bowl." Even among white ethnic groups, there is substantial evidence that ethnic values and identification are retained for generations after immigration.[14]

An increasing number of mental health practitioners have seen the value in moving from the myopic vision of an intrapsychic view to a focus on the family system. The narrow medical model led to placing labels of mental disorder on behavior we did not understand, whereas when the same behavior was viewed in the context of the family, it made perfect functional sense. Likewise, we now need to widen our angle of vision to see the family in its social and cultural contexts. Patterns that have until now been labeled as dysfunctional or defective may be seen as creative adaptations to an oppressive milieu. Problems can be neither diagnosed nor treated adequately without understanding the frame of reference of those seeking help as well as that of the helping person.

Spiegel was one of the first to set up a program for ethnicity training (in Boston), followed by Sluzki and Schnitman (in the Family Practice Residency at the University of California). Others are developing such opportunities. I am not aware of training at this depth in other professions, including theological schools, though efforts are being made to globalize the perspectives of curricula in many schools.

David Augsberger's ground-breaking volume *Pastoral Counseling Across Cultures* is an indication that serious consideration is being given to this area in theological education. Augsberger states:

> Anyone who knows only one culture knows no culture. In coming to know a second or a third culture, one discovers how much that was taken to be reality is actually an interpretation of realities that are seen in part and known in part. One begins to understand that many things assumed to be universal are local, thought to be absolute are relative, seen as simple are complex; one finds that culture shapes what we perceive, how we perceive it, and which perceptions will be retained and utilized; one realizes that culture defines both what is valued and which values will be central and which less influential.[15]

I encourage students to explore their own roots, working on a genogram[16] across at least three generations and then filling in as much data as possible about family, culture, values, rituals, patterns of relating across generations, important sets of relationships within the extended family, customs around holidays, belief systems, rules for behavior, issues avoided, scapegoats or ghosts in the family closet, secrets that everyone knew but never talked about, family image that was important to protect, and so on. It is also important to see the family in its broader social context, including an understanding of the culture that defined and shaped you and its place in the even larger society.

Looking deeply into our own heritage, as well as meeting and coming to know persons of diverse backgrounds, leads inevitably to a fuller appreciation of our common human experience as well as what differentiates us. We will then be in a better position to understand our parishioners' or clients' situations, both personal and social.

As we have seen in the brief historical overview of several ethnic groups, persons are embedded in social milieus that often need transformation. Thus pastoral care will often have to move beyond the personal, and even the family, context if it is to be effective. Archie Smith has helped me to see that "the critical point is to recognize how personal life and social structure intersect in society and to heighten awareness of what role the individual can play as a passive subject or an active agent in social transformation and change."[17]

Churches and pastors are strategically located in the community and have the potential not only to bind up the wounds, but also to be the go-between, the mediating link among the structures of society. The church can be the context for meaningful dialogue, interaction, critical interpretation, and when necessary advocacy between individuals and groups in the community. Pastoral care across cultures cannot afford to operate exclusively in a traditional fifty-minute office setting. It needs to be operative in the marketplace, the city hall, the town meeting, and wherever the rules governing persons' lives are being negotiated.

The caregiver's faith plays an important role in the dialogue called pastoral counseling, but for faith to operate effectively, we must be aware of how ethnicity and cultural background, skills, and political savvy can deter or assist our efforts. Care and counseling reaches its liberating potential as it helps to raise consciousness of the link between the stories of the oppressed, the hegemony of those in power, and the requirements for social transformation.

Augsberger asserts that cultural encapsulation becomes a useful word for human sin. He explains that such encapsulation is a sort of fusion to the culture of origin, "with no distinct boundary between self and society."[18] It may stem from a desire to reduce the complexity of the world, or it may simply be the result of cultural isolation and insufficient experience with diversity. It certainly involves a degree of bondage to a culturally limited world view.

How do we escape or liberate ourselves from such encapsulation? Paulo Freire's pedagogy of "conscientization" points us in the direction of attaining a clearer understanding of our own situation, including our historical relationships to the world's peoples as well as our own cultural roots, values, and basic assumptions.[19] It involves a hermeneutic of suspicion about our own systems of values and interpretations of history and sets our experience in a context of relativity and pluralism. It is movement toward joining the world family. It is not an easy pilgrimage. Getting acquainted with persons who speak a different language, behave differently, and perceive the world through an entirely different set of lenses requires great patience and a willingness to be open to diverse opinions and attitudes.

Gaining expertise and sensitivity to minister across cultural boundaries may require setting aside the theories and techniques with which we are comfortable as well as acquiring some new approaches that may be more relevant. I am not aware of any counseling theories that are politically neutral or value-free. The newer systems approaches have, in my experience, more potential for application across cultures than many of the earlier individual models; but here, too, every particular theorist's style is likely to be laden with that theorist's value assumptions, which reflect the enculturation of the theorist.

We are on more solid ground when we work across disciplinary lines. Education has been compartmentalized into fields, or disciplines, each yielding an incomplete picture of social reality and often obscuring the connections between the person and the system. This tendency has led inevitably to reductionistic theories—that is, viewing an individual's symptom as merely an intrapsychic conflict. An interdisciplinary approach helps us to view personal behavior in its context, and this view of the larger "gestalt" may radically alter our understanding of the person and the meaning of his or her behavior. To the extent that we believe that any one theory of human nature is universally true or that any one approach to helping is applicable to all groups, there is a high likelihood of ineffectiveness and even exploitation. We have seen that nearly all minority groups in the United States have historical reasons for not trusting white Americans. Establishing rapport and facilitating disclosure rests on our ability to create a climate of trust. Our attitudes and behaviors will either enhance or diminish our credibility, and effective care rests on the level of our credibility.

Once we have some credibility with the persons we are attempting to assist, we have to develop appropriate goals and strategies. I learned in my Central American travels that pastoral care in that context was concerned more with survival, making it through the day, than with serenity or happiness or self-fulfillment. Central Americans needed and wanted immediate, concrete help. Persons from lower economic levels in the United States seem to have similar concerns—job interviews, specific skills, filling out unemployment forms, dealing with government structures, child care, and so on.

It is important not to generalize from the scant information and understanding we may have about any group. There is great diversity within groups. A little bit of knowledge may be dangerous if we don't bear in mind that there are numerous factors that differentiate persons within groups. Degree of acculturation, language ability, educational level, and economic level are only a few factors involved. Research shows that Asian Americans, African Americans, Hispanic Americans, and Native Americans terminate counseling after only one contact at the rate of 50 percent.[20] This figure contrasts with a 30 percent rate for Euro-Americans.

Effective care and counseling rests heavily on compatibility between caregiver and care receiver. Transference issues are usually heightened across cultures, and cultural stereotypes must be cleared before there can be a mutual meeting of persons.

This analysis of the promise and the pitfalls of a ministry of care and counseling across cultures is overly brief. There is a sense in which all ministry contacts are cross-cultural. At least thinking about them in this manner may heighten our sensitivity to the distinctive historical situations out of which we all come. It will be especially helpful to develop cross-cultural sensibilities to groups other than ethnic cultures, such as male-female, gay-straight, and hearing-deaf. Space has not allowed for development of these perspectives here.

I have attempted to set the problem in historical perspective, identifying some of the issues and pointing toward some ways we can continue to develop our potential for effectiveness. I recommend that you see your place of work as an opportunity for learning through experience.

The image that I like for my ministry of pastoral care and counseling is one of the "hope agent" who is about the business of "human liberation." "Doing" theology in this context involves my attempt to understand the individual's story in the light of the family's history and to understand the family's story as an expression of the community's history. The freedom that is given by God reaches out to those caught in the concrete and often oppressive structures of the human family. And the church through its ministry of care and counseling is there, representing God's liberating hope.

CHAPTER SIX

Cultural Collisions: A Perspective from Africa[1]

Masamba ma Mpolo

In Africa cultural changes shaped by political, economic, and social aspects of life preoccupy both governmental and religious proceedings. There is, in addition, a crisis of fundamental values concerning the institution called "family." Polygamy, once one of the social structures actualizing the values of African people, has become a crisis factor in the family and society of post-colonial Africa.[2] Western and Christian values have become the norms by which marital sexual unions are validated and legalized.

Case 1. James is a Christian. He lived with Harriet, who is also a Christian, for several years. When he completed the payment of brideswealth, they were married in church. They had no children. Years passed, and in accordance with the custom of their people, Harriet's family suggested to James that he should marry Harriet's sister Lucinda, so that she might have children for James. For some time he refused because he had been told that as a Christian he must not have two wives. However, the family kept pressing, and eventually James and Harriet agreed. He continued to go to church, but not to Communion. Today he is living with both Harriet and Lucinda. Harriet still has no children, but Lucinda has seven.

Case 2. Musoke is not a Christian. He has two wives, and he, his wives, and their children all live amicably together. For many years he was married to one woman only, and his children by her are all over the age of ten. His second wife, whom he married six years ago, is younger, and they have three children. He wants very much to become a church member, and so do both of his wives. His children have all been baptized. He does not want, and does not think it right, to put aside either of his wives.[3]

Case 3. Lukandu is a schoolmaster in a Christian secondary school. He has been a very faithful deacon and a member of the board of trustees of the Baptist church's Bible college for many years. He has five daughters with his wife Nsilulu, who is also a Christian. They have badly wanted a son. Though respected by the church and members of the community for her active involvement in women's groups, Nsilulu has been mocked by other women because she has been incapable of giving a son to her husband. Even though the couple had decided to limit their family to five children, they tried again, and had another daughter. Secretly, Lukandu began an affair with one of his former students, also a Christian, eventually having three sons and one daughter. Afraid that he might lose his job as a schoolmaster, Lukandu sought counseling—alone at first and then with his wives. The two wives agreed to stay together with their husband, even though the second marriage was never legalized. The church authorities refused a second Christian wedding, and Lukandu was excluded from church responsibilities. He was allowed to continue as a schoolmaster.

These three cases illustrate the significant dilemma of the Christian church in Africa regarding polygamy and family life. The church has the difficult task of devising models for pastoral care and counseling in relation to polygamy as a type of marital union and to polygamists as individuals. Until some twenty years ago, the African church was very much within the Puritan tradition introduced by missionaries. The church not only advised its believers to be strictly monogamous but also condemned polygamy and polygamists. Sometimes the church even excluded from baptism the children of polygamists.

Traditional pastoral theology, as understood by the missionary church, did not give adequate attention to African cultural values. The church too often imposed ready-made solutions and values that were sometimes contrary not only to African values but also to biblical teaching. As a result, pastoral counseling in the missionary church was, in general, authoritarian. Now the church is becoming aware of the fact that it has often contributed to the creation of irregular and unjust situations in which a number of Christians find themselves. The church is becoming aware of deficiencies in pastoral preparation for understanding marriage in the African context and for understanding the social aspects of evangelism. It is becoming aware of the lack of synthesis between pastoral care and social change. In a spirit of confession, pastoral theology should receive help from exegesis, sociology, ethics, cultural anthropology, economics, and politics.

The first part of this chapter briefly reviews the traditional African concept of marriage, and the second part discusses church and pastoral positions regarding polygamists. The third part briefly proposes a psychosocial pastoral approach based on the analysis of social systems and the psychology of the individual. Through such a synthesis, with an earnest attempt to apply the gospel in daily life within a particular context, it should be possible to develop a meaningful, constructive approach to polygamy in Africa.

Traditional African Views of Marriage

The African family does not present a uniform system or ideology. Some groups have made a transition from matriarchy to a mixed matri-patriarchal system since the colonial times; some groups are still rigidly matriarchal or patriarchal. Even so, there are constants that should be recognized. In Africa, marriage has served two broad social functions.

First, marriage is an alliance uniting not only the man and

the woman who are married, but also the families (clans) of the two partners. The woman's clan gives the woman as wife to the man's clan. Second, marriage serves as a contract joining the man and the woman in conjugal union, fixing the demands and duties of each toward the other. This contract defines the purpose of marriage for the man and the woman. The specific expectations vary, of course, according to the specific culture, and are sometimes negotiable. For example, among the Efik the setting of bride-price depends on whether the husband acquires the domestic services of the wife and rights on the offspring, or also acquires exclusive sexual access. If the last is included, he can charge any adulterer a heavy fine while maintaining exclusive claims on all offspring of the woman. The children "belong" to the husband's clan, but as long as they need care and financial support, it is the wife who is responsible.

Polygamy[4]

The wife and the children are part of a man's wealth, or in a matriarchal system, of the family's wealth. Because land is only in very few places a limiting factor, more wives and more children mean for African agriculturists the ability to control and develop a greater farming area, to increase social prestige, and—through direct control and alliances—to gain political power, at least within the community. Polygamy is seen by most Africans (including women) as desirable for their families because marriage is an alliance of clans, and because in an agricultural society with no shortage of land, wives and children add to wealth. Indeed, it should not be forgotten that because of the very nature of the technology used in most African agriculture, the number of hands available is an important factor, especially at peak times, such as harvest.

Polygamous marriage creates a complex series of interactions and relationships between the spouses and leads to a multitude of social roles: man-wife, wife-wife, father-mother, siblings, uncle-nephew, and others. All these relationships are codified within a given culture to try to limit ambiguity and satisfy affective, sexual, and socio-cultural needs. "Concerning these relationships by marriage, the Mukongo (for example) is 'husband' of all the sisters of his wife, 'son-in-law' to all her mothers. On her side, the wife is spouse to all the relatives of her husband, those of the same descendence."[5] Because the clan includes the whole family of ancestors who have died, as well as all the family now alive, maintaining harmony must be the basis of all the activity of individual members.

SOCIO-CULTURAL FACTORS IN POLYGAMY

The most frequent reason for polygamy is sterility of the couple, ascribed most universally to sterility of the woman. This practice of marrying a second wife because the first has not produced offspring has been very widespread all over the world. The Old Testament gives us many examples of it, the best known being the case of Sarah (Gen. 16:2). With the high mortality rate in Africa, fertility remains central to the clan's survival, and the practice of second marriage because of sterility in the first is still very common.

Another frequent reason for polygamy may be that the wife has become a widow and has been inherited by a brother of her husband. Most cultures in Africa have a version of the Levitical law (Deut. 25:5) both for the protection of widows and children and as a way to ensure that the dead man's lineage is continued even if vicariously. The Old Testament describes in touching terms how two women protected that right, Ruth (book of Ruth) and Tamar (Gen. 38:6).

Polygamy as a system of confirming and strengthening alliances was widespread in Old Testament days and is still practiced among traditional chiefs in Africa, although less so than when they had more power and, therefore, more need for alliances. In the nineteenth century in Congo (now Zaire), the conquering chief used to impose upon a conquered ethnic group the addition to his harem of a young wife from that group as one means of bringing peace between his tribe and the tribe he had just conquered.[6]

There is yet another important driving force behind the practice of polygamy in African societies: the survival of the human race. The immortality of the clan is central to the thought and actions of any given ethnic group in Africa, and the individual can only contribute to it through procreation.

> For the black African, procreation is a natural necessity. This necessity is, for him or her, a moral obligation. Indeed, the black African owes it to himself or herself not only to assure his or her sense of identity, pride, and continuity, but also that of his or her lineage.[7]

Traditional society respected the man who had a large number of children. On the day of his death, he would be surrounded by the glory of his children. For this reason, the man took several wives in order to have many children. A plentiful progeny has been the most ardent and most widely avowed desire, despite its contradiction with the average individual's economic capacity.[8]

In African cultural psychology, a man or a woman believes that he or she attains full personhood only by becoming a father or mother; men and women define their wholeness in terms of their children.[9] The child is the honor of the parents. It is through the child that a man becomes a father and a woman becomes a mother—not only father and mother of the child, but also and above all father and mother within the whole clan. Both sterility and celibacy are factors of alienation and isolation, which cut off the individual not only from the immediate members of the clan, but also from the ancestors, who continue to preserve their prestige as ancestors only through the children who are born after them in the clan.

Celibacy due to a shortage of partners is a practical result of war. During the past five centuries, Africa has seen many wars, including those due to the slave trade and the two world wars. Not all wars fought on African soil involved men alone, but until recently, wars tended to decimate primarily men of marriageable age. Women and children became booty, prizes of war. Particularly in the victorious societies, the new supply of women would be used to increase the population through new marriages; in the defeated societies, the "surplus" women would also be wedded in polygamous unions to ensure the survival of the clans.

These practices have created in the mind of the modern African elite the impression that there is a permanent surplus of women. The Yoruba, in Nigeria, commonly say that for every man there are seven women. Sexual politics and other social factors do conspire to create an artificial surplus of women by forcing the age of marriage for girls down and postponing the age of marriage for boys through high bride-prices, special demands on their performance, and so on. Such practices no doubt had a high survival value at earlier times. Women were put to the procreative task from the earliest possible time. Young men were given a time when they could be busy on community matters almost exclusively (unfortunately, this was too often warfare), while older, "successful" men contributed disproportionately to the genetic makeup of the next generation.

Polygamous marriage in Africa obviously gains some of its meaning from the total context in which it is practiced and from specific marriage customs. Marriage is not only a phenomenon of the biological relationships between two people of opposite sexes, but it also represents a whole series of conscious and unconscious feelings, both secular and religious. Polygamy is part of the socio-cultural dynamics of the African people. It is a manifestation of the way in which Africans in the traditional society approach not only the practical problems of life, but also the deeper dimensions of the human person. It is the reflection of the traditional African's psychology.

NEGATIVE CONSEQUENCES

Clearly, polygamy, like all social systems, carries its own myths and unfulfilled promises, and its own negative consequences. A common myth is that polygamy favors the fertility of a community. This is untrue. The number of women is not changed by polygamy, and their number of children is fairly constant, given that they marry at the same age. The polygamous union as a solution to barrenness or widowhood in many ways is protective of women, but the elevation of polygamy to an ideal creates other problems for both women and men. No society, unless ravaged by war or predation by surrounding communities, can at any point satisfy more than a small percentage of its men with a polygamous union. Divorce becomes common as a means of circulating the limited number of women among the men and as the women's strategy of realizing some upward mobility. Girls are pressured by family and friends into very early marriages to much older men and are not given a chance to mature before embarking on marriage and procreation.

Polygamy in the African context is clearly a response to perceived problems. To outlaw or condemn the practice does not help to solve the problems or change the perception. From a Christian perspective, however, it is deeply disturbing to see communities drift into an attitude in which women are the major consumer item to be accumulated, particularly as labor and reproductive units. The marital instability that follows the elevation of polygamy to an ideal entails suffering, especially for children, but also for the women, who can never consider themselves to be through with reproduction or sure of their marriage. But it is clear that a blank condemnation of polygamy does not solve these problems either.

The Church's Response to Polygamy

Numerous societies throughout the world have at some point in their history accepted polygamy as a moral relationship and accorded it a socio-bio-psychologic importance in the well-being of their people. Polygamy is in fact a very ancient practice.[10] It was known to the ancient inhabitants of India, China, and Japan, although it was reserved for the rich and for kings. The Code of Hammurabi authorized monogamy but allowed polygamy as an exception. Christianity, however, was greatly influenced by Roman and Greek law. Besides monogamy, the ancient Greeks also accepted concubinage as a social system of sexual satisfaction, although children resulting from it were considered illegitimate, but Roman law recognized only monogamy. At the time of Emperor Diocletian (A.D. 284), bigamy was punished by penal servitude. According to the Jewish and the African traditions, the crime of adultery was always committed by the wife. The law recognized that the husband could not commit adultery, which would justify the existence of a partly polygamous system. In the later Judeo-Christian tradition, polygamy was considered unholy sexual union. It was said to contradict, by analogy with the ideas of the Old Testament, the relationship uniting God with God's people, and with the ideas of the New Testament, the relationship uniting Christ with his church. Christ's teaching on marriage had a new element that challenged the Jewish tradition and challenges the African tradition: Both spouses are equal partners and as such are responsible one to the other as they are bound together in a covenant of fidelity, unity, and permanence. Jesus introduced this element of equal rights in husband-wife relationships and sexual behaviors, and only on this basis can we imply that his teaching spoke against polygamy.

Biblical Background

The plurality of wives is noted in the Old Testament without moralizing or condemnation. Sarah, for example, could not give children to Abraham because she was barren. Abraham took an additional wife as a means of accomplishing God's purpose of becoming the channel of blessing to many nations (Gen. 16:3ff.). Later in life, Abraham took still another wife, Keturah (Gen. 25:1). Jacob, the son of Isaac, in whose seed the "salvation of humankind was to be realized" was tricked into polygamy by his father-in-law, Laban.[11] He married not only Leah and Rachel, who were sisters, but also Bilhah, Rachel's servant, who bore children for Rachel, who was barren (Gen. 29:31–30:7) before God heard her prayer and she gave birth to Joseph (Gen. 30:22-24).

Moses, instead of abolishing polygamy, issued instructions that regulated it in a proper manner. Leviticus 18:18 and Exodus 21:10 make it obligatory for a polygamist to treat his wives with equality, and require that the husband provide the essentials of life to all his wives. We are also told that David and Solomon practiced marriages of alliance in order to consolidate and extend the kingdom (I Sam. 19:11; II Sam. 5:13; II Sam. 11; I Kings 10; I Kings 11:1-13; and Chron. 16:3). After marrying an Egyptian wife, Solomon returned to Jerusalem (I Kings 3:1-3), where he had a harem of more than one thousand wives. First Kings 11:1-3 tells us that Solomon had to build sanctuaries to these wives' gods.

Sad incidents resulting from polygamy are also recorded in the Old Testament: incest (II Sam. 13:1-22), when Amnon, one of David's sons, sexually abused his half-sister Tamar, the sister of Absalom. Second Samuel 16:20-23 tells us how Absalom, after killing Amnon, slept with his father's concubines.

The Old Testament does not make polygamy the rule, however. It was only authorized in order to solve certain social and family problems, such as succession, inheritance, and establishment of alliances between different ethnic groups. In Deuteronomy 25:5, Moses establishes the law that authorized the brother, who might already be married, to take the wife of his deceased brother who did not leave any offspring.

Adultery was prohibited and punished in the Old Testament (Lev. 20:10; Deut. 5:18; Deut. 22:23; Exod. 22:16), and it seems certain that polygamy was not equated with adultery. There is, however, an indication that unfair practices within a polygamous marriage (see Deut. 21:15-17; Lev. 18:18) and the influence of polygamy and wealth on one's relationship to God (Deut. 17:17) were mentioned in the Old Testament. It is curious to note that Ezekiel, who was primarily concerned with calling people to repentance, used the allegory of the two sisters, Oholah and Ohilibah, as God's wives, who bore sons and daughters for God (Ezek. 23:1-4).

The prevalent ideals of the Old Testament resemble those of traditional African culture. Fertility was the profound motive for marriage. This changed at the time of the prophets, however, when the ideal of the couple and the personalization of marital union reappeared in the image of God as the bridegroom, faithful to Jerusalem, the wife of God's youth. In the context of God's love, Samaria and other cities of Palestine ceased to be rivals or to act as co-wives; they became daughters of Jerusalem, the only "wife" of God.[12]

It is by analogy and not by any specific teaching that monogamy may be associated with the relationships of a monotheistic God with people. This basic element of the faith has given every Christian culture the characteristic of monogamy. Man's relationship to woman, which is part of the biblical creation, was referred to by Christ in his reply to the Pharisees:

Have you not read that he who made them from the beginning made them male and female, and said, "For this reason a man

shall leave his father and mother and be joined to his wife, and
the two shall become one flesh"? So they are no longer two but
one flesh. What therefore God has joined together, let not man
put asunder. (Matt. 19:4-6 RSV)

This saying, as well as that reported by Mark (10:11-12), has
been used to justify monogamy and to condemn polygamy. A
closer examination of both texts indicates that Christ dealt with
the question of divorce, not the issue of polygamy. He taught
that the husband cannot divorce his wife, nor the wife her
husband: "Whoever divorces his wife and marries another,
commits adultery against her; and if she divorces her husband
and marries another, she commits adultery" (Mark 10:11-12
RSV). The silence of Jesus on the subject of polygamy could
also mean, of course, that he took monogamy for granted.

The strong emphasis on monogamy among Christians
probably has sociological roots. Christianity was for the first few
centuries a movement of commoners and slaves, hardly the
people to romanticize polygamy; they could not afford to practice
it. Still, when Paul specified that a bishop should be a man of
good character with only one wife (Tim. 2:3; Tit. 1:6), one could
surmise that among the early church membership some had
more than one wife and were not forced to divorce them before
joining the Christian community.[13] These texts have been used to
argue against polygamy. Exegetes, however, indicate that the
Greek used by the apostle in these two passages is very
ambiguous and could lead to at least three interpretations:

First, polygamous men could not become church leaders.
Nobody knows exactly what sorts of positions are referred to in
the texts.

Second, after the death of the first wife or after his divorce, a
church leader could not take another wife. By so doing, he
would enter into a polygamous state. This interpretation may
also mean that if a man divorced his first non-Christian wife
and married a Christian wife, he could not take church

leadership. This, however, was permitted by Paul (I Cor. 7:15). If such a man then took a Christian wife, it would perhaps cause a scandal (I Tim. 3:7) in view of what Jesus had said (Matt. 19:9; Matt. 5:39; Luke 16:18; and Mark 10:11). If this interpretation is correct, the apostle was concerned with divorce and remarriage, and not with polygamy.

Third, church leaders must be faithful in their monogamous marriage. The New English Bible translates the phrase: "faithful to his one wife."

In view of the widespread adultery in the Hellenistic world, where Timothy and Titus exercised their ministry, this last interpretation may seem more probable. Paul instructed his followers that a church leader must be a good husband as well as a good father (I Tim. 3:4; Tit. 1:6b). The principle is that the church leader should not have extramarital affairs. The problem is in knowing whether a polygamous marriage is a valid marital union or not. If the answer is yes, then the principle of being a good husband is as valid in choosing church leaders in a polygamous culture as it is in a monogamous one.

In reference to the Pauline teaching of such concepts as one wife (I Tim. 3:2) and the church as the body of Christ (Eph. 5:28-33; I Cor. 5:15; 12:27), Hillman says that they should be understood in the social, economic, and historical contexts of the New Testament world, and not be taken literally: "A bishop with one wife would be less of a financial burden on the Christian community than one with two or three wives. The concept of corporate personality and kinship justify St. Paul's referring to the marital union of wife and husband as 'two becoming one' " (I Cor. 6:16-17).[14] The expression "one flesh" (Gen. 2:24) does not necessarily imply monogamy, and Jesus' reference to it (Matt. 19:4-5) need not necessarily be taken seriously as a condemnation of polygamy. "One flesh" could be regarded as a "reassertion of the holiness of marriage as an indissoluble union which was implied in God's creation will."[15]

In a culture traditionally built on bargaining, communal covenanting, and mutually agreed social ethics, should agreed upon polygamous marriages be accepted as a valuable expression of love, respect, and fidelity between spouses, including Christian couples? Such an option would not negate Christ, the head of the church, and would not make the African church an unfaithful servant. After all, Christ is one, but the church is legion. We have used the Bible to argue against polygamy, but while the Old and the New Testaments condemn adultery, there is no clear evidence that they address themselves clearly against polygamy or against polyandry. Polygamy and polyandry were never equivalent to adultery in either Old Testament culture or African societies. The ground for challenging polygamy should be argued on other bases than the Holy Scripture.

A Systemic and Pastoral Approach to Polygamy

There are basically four possible ways Christians can regard polygamous marriages:[16]

1. Polygamy is simply a sin, little different from adultery.
2. Polygamy is an inferior form of marriage. It is not sinful where it is the custom of the people, but it is always unacceptable for Christians.
3. Polygamy is a less good form of marriage than monogamy. It does not enable people to receive and enjoy the full blessings of Christian marriage which God offers. But in some circumstances individual Christians can put up with it, just as they put up with slavery, dictatorial government, and many other unfavorable conditions of life. In such cases the church could accept polygamists as Christians.
4. Polygamy is one form of marriage, and monogamy is another. Each has its good and bad points, which suit the conditions and customs of different sorts of society.

According to the fourth position, it is possible to say that, fundamentally, polygamy and monogamy are equally conventional forms of marriage and that both call for bargaining, covenant, fidelity, unity, and permanence. Pastoral psychologists should help the church to understand the complexity of marital unions and relationships between women and men in the context of world ethics, economic systems, and the use of power.

In its pastoral approach, the church cannot dissociate the problem of traditional polygamy from the general situation of contemporary sexual morality, which it must consider as a newly formed social system. At a time when the church and some African governments have been trying to pass laws abolishing polygamy, contemporary morality has questioned the institution of monogamous marriage, which was imposed in the colonies as the only valid social system. If monogamy remains today the official institution of marital sexual union in many countries, it presents, in reality, only an outer façade of a reality of new sexual relationships. In the popular structure of marriage, in which only two people are joined by a contract, fidelity seems no longer to be the only norm.

New attitudes and pastoral approaches to the problem of polygamy are absolutely necessary if the church wants to be able to play an innovative role in social and personal changes in Africa. The church will fail if it concerns itself only with the problem of polygamy when polygamists who have converted to Christianity request baptism or when Christians who have become polygamists wish to participate in the Communion. Polygamy, as one of the traditional values of the African world view, can be understood or modified only when it is analyzed within the total context of the system of social values and attitudes toward self and others. The church's solution cannot be made in the interests of the preservation of the sanctity of baptism and Holy Communion. It must be made for the salvation of a system of status, of attitudes, and of persons.

It is right that the church should be concerned with the preservation of the values and norms of the Christian faith.

The diverse interpretations of biblical texts with reference to polygamy do not help us to defend with much conviction certain Christian values that are in many cases Western cultural values. There is a lack of unity of conviction, which induces the church to involve itself with individuals while neglecting societies and cultures that are often the source of the depersonalization of individuals. It is high time that the church, in its evangelistic efforts, became aware of addressing the gospel not only to individuals but also to social systems. The individual application of the gospel without its social application often becomes a weapon for imposing old values devoid of meaning for today's society.

The gospel is a message addressed to persons. The church must proclaim the gospel to every person, including polygamists. But the message must not become a means by which one proclaims ready-made truths without becoming involved in the pertinent social and personal problems. Individuals and society are both in need of salvation. The gospel that does not concern itself with the individual is irresponsible and is inclined to manipulate the individual to accept dogmas of the faith without studying them and accepting them personally. Such a method diminishes human capacity to understand itself, to analyze itself, and to constantly correct itself. The gospel is not a monologue; it is a creative dialogue in which the evangelist, the individual, and society are constantly shaped and renewed by God's message.

The monogamist and the polygamist each belong to a social system with ideology and values that reflect the conscious and unconscious inclinations of a people. It is in developing a pastoral approach to social systems that the church may become a factor for the healing of societies and for the continual renewal of individuals. The analysis and understanding of the psychological dynamics of the value system would help not only individual polygamists but also society.

Such an approach would allow the polygamist to withdraw from the system in order to analyze and judge it.

In developing the capacity to analyze social values that have been imposed or accepted unconsciously, persons will learn to examine themselves. They will create their own personal moral values when they have understood the reasons for the existence of certain structures and existing social values. They will become aware of the necessity of becoming attached to their culture, to select from it the values they judge to be important for the preservation of society and for the satisfaction of their personal needs. They will develop a sensitivity toward their independence from social structures and cultural values as well as their dependence on them. They will create for themselves the ability to live in a creative tension. They will live as individuals and as social beings without the one aspect completely dominating the other. They will learn to decide, not because they are not free to do otherwise, but because they wish it. They will marry, not to support a socioeconomic system that provides satisfaction for a minority of privileged people, but because they wish to do so. They will marry not because it is desirable culturally, but because they judge it to be necessary personally.

In such a pastoral perspective, the church will help individuals to situate monogamy and polygamy within the framework of personal and social values and to create personal values about marriage and about persons of the opposite sex. The church will know and will make known to others the reality and possibility of various forms of marriage, monogamy being the one that corresponds most closely to God's revelation and to the teaching of the gospel. The role of the church is not simply to give baptism and Communion to monogamists and refuse them to polygamists, but rather to help persons to understand themselves as individuals and as social beings.

Polygamy or monogamy will be the choice of all persons in

the fulfilling of their responsibilities and in the development of their image of man and woman. Polygamy is as much an economic and social system as it is a psychological reflection of one's self-image. In modern polygamous practices, the woman too often becomes an economic tool; she is looked at not as an important equal partner, but as a necessary instrument in the process of social and personal economy. The woman, in this context, loses theoretically and psychologically the status of being an equal partner with the man.

Men should listen to the emerging voices of African women[17] who do not just condemn such practices as excision, infibulation, and polygamy, which militate against women. They are dreaming of a community built not on inequality and rivalry, but on a mystical partnership of women and men, so that both sexes can more visibly participate in the creation of a new humanity.

PART TWO:

THE PRACTICE
OF PASTORAL CARE
AND COUNSELING

INTRODUCTION

William M. Clements

Having examined some of the foundational issues from the perspectives of theology, ethics, and the social dimensions, we turn our attention to many of the pragmatic situations involved in the implementation of an effective pastoral care and counseling ministry. Part two presents a distillation of some of the best and latest ideas and insights—concepts and sensitivities already tried and proven from the ministries of these knowledgeable and proficient authors. The most common concerns raised by parishioners form the framework for this section. We move from the deeply interior dimensions of imagination and prayer in an outward direction that encompasses broader family and social dimensions of issues, such as marriage, grief, and chemical dependency. Theoretical and practical insights that arise from an in-depth introduction to the topics enrich our lives as well as our ministry of pastoral care and counseling. The roles of prayer and imagination are considered in the first section. These two topics have been among the most important themes in pastoral care and counseling over the past decades; yet, they have been frequently neglected.

123

Imagination and Prayer

The traditional divisions between theologically conservative and liberal ministers, when it comes to the role of prayer and meditation in pastoral counseling, are cogently set forth for us by Merle Jordan. Pointing to inadequacies in both positions, with conservatives neglecting the behavioral sciences and liberals disregarding scripture and prayer, Jordan places us on a new stage for understanding this topic. Object relations theory and insights from the faith tradition are combined in a new synthesis in which prayer and meditation are seen as "modes of communication with the perceived ultimate authority in one's life." Jordan shows that prayer and meditation are alive and well, but sometimes "live under an assumed name" in the work of many pastoral counselors. He draws from supervision and therapy in helpful vignettes that concretize prayer as a loving, knowing intimacy. A considera-tion of Jordan's points reduces the previously existing vacuum in the ministries of both liberals and conservatives.

Christie Neuger compellingly argues that images within the psyche have the power to bring together disparate elements for integration because they exist developmentally and functionally prior to words. She discusses the pastoral use of therapeutic imagination in the action of healing in terms of several cases that resonate with themes common in much of our pastoral work with persons who have been wounded along life's journey. Neuger concludes that imagination can "open clients up to experiencing that presence in the quietness of their own souls and in the presence of the pastoral counselor, who names and claims the centrality of God in the healing process."

Grief and Depression

Taken as a whole, the middle section of Part two provides us with an extensive discussion of grief, depression, and career burnout. Howard Stone provides a comprehensive introduction for a single issue, depression, which can range from mild "blues" all the way to total functional disability in its most severe forms. Unfortunately, many completed suicides occur among people who have a severe form of depression, and countless people who are not suicidal suffer crippling pain in all aspects of their lives. Stone leads us as pastors through a thorough existential, historical, and assessment process for the recognition of depression. Therapeutic interventions suitable for the pastor and for the specialist pastoral counselor receive a full discussion. Knowing how to recognize and help the depressed person needs to be at the top of the list of our pastoral care skills. Stone's chapter points us in the right direction and helps us to recognize the subtle differences between depression and the common experiences of loss and grief.

Scott Sullender expands our awareness of loss and grief, pointing to the reality that "every individual loss has a systemic dimension to it. . . . The relocation of an active family to another state forces the congregation to adjust and re-balance its equilibrium." Sullender observes that people who cannot grieve tend to experience more physical and emotional difficulties than would otherwise be necessary. While the loss from death was ritualized from the earliest of times, the newer forms of loss—such as from divorce, the relocation of residence, or retirement—have not yet received the same liturgical and communal recognition. Sullender concludes with the powerful image of the church as the family of God, where it is safe to cry, with ritual as a powerful vehicle for the expression of emotion.

Normal grief is a process that most people manage to move through in some fashion, with a combination of resources at their disposal; however, there are those who have pathological, or unresolved, grief. David Switzer leads us in a more detailed consideration of this condition of unresolved grief.

Switzer's discussion of the psychodynamics of unresolved grief—the repressed but intense ambivalence, the reactivation of latent self-images of low self-esteem and helplessness, and the cognitive disruption that is the characteristic reaction to premature, violent, or sudden death—presents pivotal concepts on which to base our pastoral responses. It is encouraging to share in the vision that persons may be saved from years of chronic distress if "the early signs of potential pathological grief are responded to quickly and effectively."

Recognizing our own impending career burnout, the common sources of stress in ministry, and what effective steps to take for prevention and healing are all discussed by Charles Rassieur in his enlivening chapter. Rassieur identifies some of the common causes of stress among ministers, such as the unstructured work routine, the absence of clear work objectives, vocational uncertainty, and social isolation. Fortunately, he does not leave us with just the diagnosis, but points the way toward revitalization with concrete, achievable objectives that can be put into practice whatever the setting and context for ministry happen to be.

Marriage and Family

Marriage and family issues are spotlighted in the concluding section of the *Handbook*. Harold T. Kriesel provides a helpful road map of many of these current issues, coupled with an introduction to the family systems model, family communication, and the family life cycle. His discussion of context and circularity is particularly rewarding from the perspective of pastoral care and counseling. His thesis that "we are all one with and depend on each other as a living human system . . . [that] . . . speaks to the heart of pastoral care and counseling as a function of the church's ministry" turns systems theory into practice.

The existence of sexuality in pastoral care and its role is

brought out of the shadows and into the light of faith in a most helpful manner by Carolyn Stahl Bohler. Incarnation, revelation, grace, salvation, forgiveness, and confession are theological issues identified by Bohler as touched by sexuality. These themes from the Christian tradition are identified and discussed in the context of our human sexuality with helpful pastoral examples that are easy to identify with from professional experience. Her conclusion that "it is the imperative of ministers to do all we can to affirm our bodies and sexuality, yet to do that in a climate in which we and others will find viable norms that can really be followed" presents a challenge for the decades ahead that must be met more successfully than in the past if we are truly to encompass more of God's vision for humanity.

In his discussion of marriage in the second half of life, Robert Wohlfort has opened up a new dimension in the pastoral care ministry of the church. The role of remembering within reconciliation has implications far beyond middle-aged marriages, as do the concepts of healing and the telling and creating of the story. Wohlfort cogently reminds us that healing "generativity and integrity and caring and wisdom come in many forms." These points are particularly relevant in an aging society, in which more and more couples are surviving well beyond the golden anniversary. Wohlfort's refocusing of our attention on middle-age and beyond anticipates the many significant changes that church and society are destined to undergo in the decades ahead. His openness to this aging dimension of existence points the way toward the twenty-first century.

The issue of pastoral care in the recovery from addiction is surely one of the most common and pressing needs in the pastoral ministry. How are we to assist and facilitate a person's entry into treatment for addiction? Even more important is the critical role that pastoral care may play in the reentry process for the person recovering from addiction. Robert Albers provides a positive overview of this crucial issue. His emphases are particularly relevant in the *Handbook* because Howard Clinebell's first book was *Understanding and Counseling the Alcoholic,* published over thirty years ago. Albers has moved forward yet again our understanding of the pastoral care of those afflicted by addiction, either directly or indirectly.

CHAPTER SEVEN

Prayer and Meditation in Pastoral Care and Counseling

Merle Jordan

"But prayer becomes true only as the distortions affecting our image of God are corrected."
Robert Llewellyn, *Love Bade Me Welcome*

The dialogue about the place and use of prayer and meditation in pastoral counseling has often been polarized as a conservative versus liberal issue. Conservatives have tended to minimize the use of the behavioral sciences in their clinical practice and to maximize the use of prayer and scripture. Liberals, on the other hand, have tended to minimize the use of prayer and Scripture and to maximize the use of the resources of the behavioral sciences. A liberal pastoral counselor might turn to this chapter and think some of the following thoughts.

"I don't want to read one more thing about prayer and meditation in pastoral counseling. There is so much stuff on that subject! I'll skip this chapter and go on to something more challenging and thought-provoking."

"I leave that prayer stuff to the conservatives, and I get on with the real meat and potatoes of the clinical work."

"I haven't prayed with a client in years, so why should I read something that says that I should be praying with my counselees?"

"Prayer and meditation are for the pastor at St. John's by the Gas Station, who is doing supportive pastoral care with parishioners."

"Naturally, there are times when a chaplain prays with a sick patient in the hospital, but that's a different kind of ministry. As a pastoral counselor, I work in depth with long-term relationships that require more sophisticated techniques and more enlightened skills."

A conservative pastoral counselor might retort: "It's time to return to the basics of the faith in pastoral counseling and stop worshiping at the altar of the gods of psychology and psychiatry."

This chapter proposes that we incorporate both the insights of the faith and the resources of object relations theory in understanding prayer and meditation in pastoral counseling. Prayer and meditation are here defined as modes of communication with the perceived ultimate authority in one's life. This dialogue may be with the true Absolute, or it may be with some false mental representation or image of God. In any event, that deeply intimate communication with the central authority in one's psyche, whether it be with the true God or with an idol or false god, is the realm of prayer and meditation under discussion here.

The Trick of Denial of Prayer and Meditation in Counseling

As a pastoral counselor becomes a member of the professional guild of pastoral counselors, he or she is more likely to emulate those experienced counselors who have become less and less interested in spiritual disciplines and resources for their clinical work and more and more baptized into secular psychotherapeutic theories and practice. One's sense of belonging is often more related to the assurance of clinical competence in the psychotherapeutic perspective than to the integration of the pastoral/theological/spiritual into one's counseling practice. There is often a loss of the theological and spiritual grounding of one's clinical work. The inherent danger is akin to C. S. Lewis's idea that the devil's favorite trick is to convince people that the devil does not exist. Likewise, pastoral counseling has sometimes functioned under the illusion of the premature death of prayer and meditation, at least as they relate to its practice. Scientific knowledge and clinical techniques have been the pallbearers for a traditional understanding of prayer and meditation in pastoral counseling.

Prayer and Meditation Are Alive and Well in Pastoral Counseling, but Are Sometimes Living Under an Assumed Name

Meditation and prayer are part of every therapeutic encounter, whether the counselor or the client is aware of them or not. Both the client and the therapist bring their implicit patterns of communication with the perceived ultimate(s) into the therapeutic relationship, whether they talk formally about prayer or not. While some pastoral counselors would not be caught dead using prayer and meditation in any formal sense in the therapy hour, nevertheless they are involved in the depths of their own psyches and in the depths of their clients' psyches with the communication patterns and the imaging of ultimate reality that are at the heart of prayer and meditation. The question is not whether the pastoral counselor is using meditation and prayer in her or his counseling practice; it is whether the pastoral counselor is aware of the implicit meditation and prayer that are already occurring in the therapeutic relationship on both sides of the encounter.

This phenomenon of the counselor's inattention to the

meditative and prayerful dimensions of the therapy is reminiscent of Ana-Maria Rizzuto's comments on counter-transference in regard to analysts' neglect of investigating their own mental representations of God.

> In their training our generation of analysts have not received the detailed understanding I think is necessary to appreciate the specific contribution of the God representation to psychic balance. As in many other areas, if the analyst's personal analysis has not helped him come to terms with his religious beliefs or lack of them, there is a risk of unchecked countertransference reactions in this realm.[1]

Likewise, if counselors are not aware of the mental representations of God in themselves and in their clients—and of the communications, dialogues, prayers, and meditations that are in process between the person and the perceived absolute in both the client and counselor—then the counselor is caught in a countertransference bind of overlooking key material in the case.

A primary task of the pastoral counselor is to diagnose the nature of the fixation of the client to an intrapsychic object of the past and to note how the object of that fixation functions like an idol or false god in the client's psyche. It is helpful to understand that the communication between oneself and the object of fixation is of the nature of prayer, even though the dialogue is with an intrapsychic idol. Some may prefer to distinguish this communication as *secular prayer*.[2] It is worthy of note that the secular prayer to the idol tends to reinforce the power and status of the idol itself. In the fixations of persons with neurotic problems, the prayerful reaction of those suffering with a neurosis of submission is to say "Amen" to the dictates of the false god. Those who struggle with a neurosis of opposition tend to react to the idol with a "Hell, no!" response to the false god's directives and values.

The dynamics of the secular prayer patterns are derived

basically from the experience of the child who attempts differentiation and individuation from the key authority figures of childhood. For example, imagine that one child's attempts at differentiation were met with disapproval, criticism, anger, and the withdrawal of love. Such a child may respond to this threat of separation by giving up his or her freedom to be in order to hold on to the significant relationship with the parent(s). That child's image of God may become the projection of the judgmental, controlling, or withholding parent to whom one reacts with a submissive, obedient "amen," even though the drums of mutiny are rumbling silently within. The child believes that it is safer or better to pay the price of crucifying some parts of his or her personality in order to retain a lifeline to that key authority instead of facing the terrifying possibility of being rejected and "orphaned" that would come from challenging that authority. This in turn is translated into a prayer life that essentially says, "I'll do what I am supposed to do, and I'll be what I am supposed to be, but I'll be resentful as hell inside. However, I'll hide it so that I can have a continuing relationship with you."

On the other hand, another child, responding to the same parent from an adversarial and rebellious point of view, would sacrifice his or her need for love and closeness for the I'll-do-my-own-thing stance. This child may deny the loss and grief over the conditionally loving parent, who is also projected onto God, but the child does the exact opposite of the rules and desires of that authority figure. This child may believe that she or he is really free through the rebellion, but the inner dialogue or prayer communication is still with the same false ultimate authority. The child is still reacting, only rebelliously instead of submissively. On the surface, the child may operate with the idea that the authority figure has no power, and there may even be a complete break in overt communication with that authority. Underneath, however, a covert communication is going on, in which the essence of the prayer is "I am still attached to you by doing the exact opposite of what you want me to do. I will try to deceive you and myself into believing that I am really free, but I will still be orienting my life around you by taking my cues from you and then doing the opposite of what I think you want me to do." Yet, deeper still are thoughts and feelings of sadness and loneliness over missing the loving affirmation of the parent figure: "I miss you and your unconditional love. I wish that you could love me for *me* so that I could have both my freedom and your precious love."

Persons are created for their personality center to be in communion with God.[3] If they are not centered in the true Absolute, then some other psychic object assumes the divine power. If a person is living with a "god who is too small" or with a significantly distorted mental representation of God, then that person also has a distorted sense of self. There is always some tie to the central object of devotion in one's life, and the processes of communication are continuously happening, whether we are conscious of that fact or not. Thus the communication with the ultimate that we may think of as prayer and meditation is always present. Whether or not the pastoral counselor believes in dealing with meditation and prayer in the therapeutic context, they are present and functioning.

A Case Illustration

A corporate executive who was an active churchgoer sought pastoral counseling as a result of burnout in his job and an involvement in an extramarital relationship. He was unusually open to exploring how his childhood experiences had affected his present circumstances. He had been married for thirteen years, and he had two sons, aged ten and five. His own father had died when he was five years old, so as the oldest of two brothers, he had become the "man of the house."

His mother had suffered the loss of her mother when she was only three, and so the death of her husband triggered off the terrible fears and anguish of her childhood. The oldest son was anointed to replace her husband as well as her mother. So he literally walked in his father's shoes and fulfilled the fatherly tasks in many ways, including trying to provide comfort for his mother in her grief and loneliness. The mother had never remarried. The son felt queasy when his mother would ask him to "keep her company" when she was sad, tired, or sick by staying with her in her bedroom and cuddling with her. He also felt great inner conflict and tension when his very puritanical, but also seductive, mother would ask him to come into the bathroom sometimes to wash her back when she was taking a bath or to come into her bedroom if she needed help tying her corset. He was caught in the excitement of seduction and stimulation and the prohibition of his sexual feelings at the same time.

He carried his parentified child role into his schooling. He functioned like the "little professor," with an intense seriousness about succeeding in his studies. His objective to perform and to succeed carried over into his adult life, and he climbed the corporate ladder rapidly.

In the therapeutic process, he became aware of his fixations around the time of his father's death. He had suffered many losses at that time as a result of his father's death. He had lost not only his father, but also his mother's functioning adequately as a parent, and he had lost his own childhood. He had never grieved any of the losses. His instinctive prayer had been "Please, God, make me strong so that I can take care of my mother, my brother, and myself. Don't let me become sad, weak, or out of control." His mental representations of God included the absent, abandoning father who could not be trusted to be there as well as the image of the needy and dependent mother for whom he had to be the rescuer and comforter.

He was able to see how his secular prayers were focused around his erroneous images of God, which had grown out of his unresolved grief experiences at the age of five. He realized that after spending thirty-six years as a parentified child, he had at last run out of gas and his true inner child was crying out for love and affirmation. The fact that his youngest son was five played a part in his crisis, as did the realization that he had married a sickly wife whom he had to take care of and from whom he received very little nurture and support. He had truly recreated in his marriage and in his work the same conditions that were operative in his family of origin after his father died. His reaching out in an affair, for which he had considerable guilt and emotional pain, was a convoluted way of trying to connect at last with someone who would love him for himself.

At the same time, however, he was compelled to reenact an intimate relationship that was fraught with guilt and tension. He needed to pray: "O God, help me to move beyond my replaying of my exciting, but taboo, relationship with my mother. Enable me to deal with my anger at my father for leaving me to become the man of the house in ways that were just too much for me. Help me to seek and to find healthy intimacy, including being able to be free to be me in relationship with you."

Persons who come to us for counseling are generally involved in prayers of the heart, filled with distortion, self-destruction, and depression. Their ultimate allegiance and loyalty are usually given unconsciously to inner psychic objects that function as divine authority and power. Gerald May suggests that at the root of addictions there is

a deep-seated form of idolatry. The objects of our addictions become our false gods. These are what we worship, what we attend to, where we give our time and energy, instead of love. Addiction, then, displaces and supplants God's love as the source of our deepest true desire. . . . Addiction sidetracks and eclipses the energy of our deepest, truest desire for love and goodness. . . . It is addiction that creates other gods for us. Because of our addictions, we will always be storing up treasures somewhere other than heaven, and these treasures will kidnap our hearts and souls and strength.[4]

Pastoral counselors need to be aware of the misdirected prayers of the heart, which are maladaptive and idolatrous. They need to be aware that the deepest desires of the heart are truly meant for loving communion and conversation with the true God.

Training and Supervision

Howard Clinebell has suggested that the disciplines of prayer and meditation "have three uses in pastoral care and counseling. They are important resources for the minister's own spiritual preparation; they can be used by the counselor on behalf of the counselee; they are skills that the counselee can be taught for use in self-healing."[5] I propose to highlight the fact that in the training process the counselor becomes as conscious as possible about the modes of his or her prayers of the heart to various images of God and the need for transformation of those patterns of communication. Because I believe that idolatry underlies much pathology and that the repetition compulsion just continues the relationship with the false gods and the self-destructive communication (prayer) patterns with those idols, I believe that it is imperative for the counselor in training and supervision to investigate as fully as possible his or her own idolatrous prayer relationships and to develop healthy and creative patterns of dialogue with the true God of love as revealed in Jesus Christ. In addition, the supervisee needs to be helped to look at clients' false mental representations of God and the various destructive patterns of communication with those false gods.

It should be noted that collusion can readily take place between the psychic idols of the client and the counselor. They may be locked into a destructive belief system together, and their prayers of the heart may be to the same false god, which would block any opportunity for healing and transformation in the counseling relationship. On the other hand, if the counselor has a loving and creative relationship with God, that may allow for a new world view and a map of reality to occur for the client via the therapist's mediation.

Naturally, the dynamics and patterns of the prayers of the supervisor's heart play a profound role in the life and therapeutic work of the supervisee. Let us turn to an example of a common issue with a parentified child who is now the pastoral counselor under supervision, but still operates with the world view, belief system, and roles from her family of origin.

A Supervisory Example

The pastoral counselor under supervision was an adult child of an alcoholic father. She fit perfectly the profile of the typical ACOA (Adult Child of an Alchoholic) who followed the fundamental rules of her home: Don't feel, don't share, and don't trust. She was a parentified child in her family of origin, and she carried that role and its functions into her care-giving ministry. At the unconscious level, she functioned as though her messianic rescue missions for people in pain were a divinely inspired calling.

She had been sexually abused by her father, especially when he had been drinking. She had been threatened by him never to reveal their secret, or something "terrible" would happen to somebody in the family. Her mother was a co-dependent, and she was not emotionally available to help her abused daughter.

The supervisee tried to make sense of her world, as so many incest survivors do, by blaming herself for "being bad" and for not being able somehow to set limits on her father. She was unable to hold anyone else responsible for her predicament, nor could she ask for help with her dilemma. She could only live with self-blame and guilt that she was a bad person who had caused all the terrible things to happen and was at fault for not stopping them. In her unconscious, she was frightened that she would literally be orphaned if she told anyone what was happening, and she would not tolerate the threat of separation anxiety.

She thus brought a lot of emotional baggage into her care-giving pastoral work. She tended to repeat the same patterns in her counseling ministry that she had developed in her family of origin. She would try to fill the emptiness in her clients' lives. She would be overly supportive in trying to be a problem solver, or what she later came to name as her "Ms. Fix-it" role. When she couldn't get her clients to change and get better quickly, she would dip into her deep reservoir of low self-esteem and blame herself for not being good enough, bright enough, or helpful enough. She would try to get the supervisor to agree with her and to reinforce her "aren't-you-awful" denigration of herself.

In the supervisory process, it became evident that she was using a number of self-defeating secular prayers in her clinical work. On the one hand, she prayed to an absent and impotent God (a projection of her inadequate and passive mother, who was a co-dependent in the marital collusion with her alcoholic husband). The prayer to the idol was "Since you are so weak and ineffective, I will take this on myself. Make me strong so I can do superhuman things. Make me the saviour and rescuer so that I can save my family, other people in pain, the church, and the world." To the image of her alcoholic and abusive father, projected onto God, she was unconsciously praying, "Keep me in my head so that I do not feel. Keep me away from closeness because I need to be protected from the terror of what intimacy brings."

While there were a number of dimensions to her fixations around these parental objects masquerading as the divine, it was important in the supervisory process for her to look at the gods to whom she was praying, at how she was praying, at the content of her prayers, and how her idolatrous attachments and erroneous belief system were affecting her clients. She gradually began to realize that her psychic idolatry and the resulting self-sabotaging prayers that had helped her to survive in childhood were now becoming a problem to her and to her counseling work instead of being a solution. Again and again she found herself in collusion with clients for whom she would take too much responsibility and for whom she would reinforce an unhealthy dependency on her. She would be implicitly praying, "O God, give me the strength, energy, love, time, wisdom, and patience to heal this person. Help me to fill her emptiness so that she will know that she is loved by you and by me." It took her a long time in supervision, her own personal therapy, and ACOA groups to transform her prayer into "O God, help me not to try to save this person all by myself. Help me to let you, and not me, be God. Help me to enable this person to grieve over her losses and her emptiness. Help her to gain ego mastery through facing her pain and anxiety. Help me to stop trying to carry her to Easter without her having walked via the sorrow and pain of Calvary in her own life."

Training and supervision need to take into consideration the following facets of prayer and meditation in relationship to the prayers of the heart: (1) that the counselor seek to be aware of the maladaptive modes of communication with the false representations of God, which impede the counselor's own growth and block the counselor from facilitating the healthy development of clients; (2) that the counselor examine in supervision, personal therapy, and other growth experiences the possible countertransference implications that may result in collusion, stalemate, and resistance; (3) that the counselor be conscious of the patterns of repetition compulsion in himself or herself and in his or her clients, which involve idolatrous fixations and addictions and the resulting maladaptive prayers of the heart; and (4) that the counselor experience the affirmation, validation, and support in himself or herself and in his or her clients of the creative modes of prayer and meditation, which are centered in the loving nature of God and reveal the ultimate reality of the true God, focused in the life, death, and resurrection of Jesus Christ.

Prayer as a Loving, Knowing Intimacy

The behavioral sciences have taught us that there are many games, rituals, and other defenses that keep us from enjoying the experience of intimacy. Intimacy is often seen as the goal of mature relationships. Open and vulnerable communication is usually one of the signs of such loving intimacy. As we facilitate a client's or a supervisee's ability to be more intimate in creative ways in interpersonal relationships, we are also affecting their mode of communication and their pattern of intimacy with their own inner Ultimate Authority, whether we or they are conscious of the transformation in the experience and dialogue with God that is happening to them.

True intimacy involves a sense of a loving knowing that is shared reciprocally in a relationship. A metaphor for such intimacy comes from Psalm 139, which focuses on God as the Loving Knower who is intimately involved with us from our existence in the womb through all the stages of life. Kohut's self-psychology has highlighted anew the centrality of empathy and mirroring in the healing, growing process.[6] A therapeutic holding environment is understood as involving a caring, empathic, mirroring communication process that is essential to healing and growth. This loving, knowing, and mirroring process in pastoral counseling can become not only a corrective to the person's relationship to self and to others, but also a transformation of the inner prayers of the heart in relationship to God. As this metanoia takes place, there is a deepening of intimacy with God as the communication becomes sacred prayer between the heart of the person and the heart of God, between the mind of the individual and the mind of God, and between the spirit of the human and the Spirit of the Divine. The identity of the self is then in communion with the identity of God.

An important goal of pastoral counseling is to enable a person to move into a more authentically loving, intimate relationship with the true God. This experience has been poignantly described by David Jacobsen:

> Prayer is rooted in love.
> The experience of prayer is the experience of love.
> Prayer is the means by which we develop the intimacy with God which is love.
> Prayer is love.
> Love is prayer.
> What we yearn for in life is the certainty that God is and that he loves.
> To know that with our minds or to hold that as a belief is important but not complete.
> When we experience prayer, we experience that certainty.
> The experience is movement toward completion of our knowing that certainty.
> The more we experience the communication of prayer, the deeper is the sense of intimacy which comes.
> Our "chief end" (that is, our primary purpose in life) is to "know God and to enjoy God forever." That is what the old catechism says.
> We get to "know God" in prayer. Intimacy comes in that experience.

To "know God" is to enjoy God. To truly know God is to experience God's love.

Prayer is the gift of grace which offers us an opportunity to develop intimacy with God. This intimacy is the experience of the love God has already given us. It is a high privilege.[7]

Pastoral Counseling as Encouraging Wrestling with God

Let us take one issue in the overt or covert prayer life of a client or a supervisee and explore it in some depth. That issue has to do with the individual's mental representation of God as inviting an assertive and self-differentiating stance in prayer or as being repressive and condemning such an open and assertive mode of communication in prayer. The issue can be stated constructively as "The will of God is to wrestle with the will of God."

Passive compliance rather than assertiveness is often seen as a guiding principle of prayer. Submission rather than wrestling is thought of as the will of God for the prayerful state. The throne of grace is considered approachable only with the submissive, passive side of ourselves. The gentle and receptive side of personality is acceptable for prayer, but assertiveness is often considered taboo and evil in the life of prayer. We have believed that we should be obedient in a passive, compliant way to the will of God, and we have not been aware of God's call and invitation to be obedient to God's will by wrestling with that will. The need to assert vigorously the depth and breadth of one's authentic self with all the relevant emotions and human needs is all too frequently believed to be unacceptable in communication with God. The expression of assertiveness and autonomous strivings is suppressed or repressed in favor of an attitude of passive submissiveness.

The dynamics of such passive compliance and submission in prayer are often rooted in our early childhood relationships with significant authority figures, usually parents, with reinforcement from other quarters, including the institutional church. The patterns of interaction between a child and authority figures in regard to assertiveness and submission can become transferred to the relationship with God. The early experience with closeness and intimacy in the family of origin tends to condition our perception of and relationship to God. Misconceptions about the nature of God based on faulty learnings growing out of our early interpersonal relationships can be the basis for experiencing God as being in opposition to or indifferent to our thrust for individuality. For instance, if a child has perceived that closeness to an overly coercive, controlling, and dominating parent means that the child should be compliant and submissive, then it is very difficult for that child in growing up to experience closeness to God as anything but a threat to individuality and autonomy. Thus God can be perceived either consciously or unconsciously as an autocratic or controlling authority who demands submission just as the earthly parent did. In another kind of family situation, a youngster may experience a parent as emotionally distant or absent. Such a parent does not enter the child's world with empathy and concern for the child's needs, including the child's need to take some risks and to make some mistakes in the struggle for growth and autonomy. The child can take that emotional distance from the parent and transfer or project that negative learning experience into an erroneous image of God as a detached and non-affirming Being.

Children can also develop negative self-images in their human relationships, which they replicate in their relationship with God. The negative, self-defeating values and attitudes that children learn about their own worth, individuality, emotional feelings, and need for autonomy tend to continue into adult life and to become automatically a major part of the values and attitudes incorporated into the relationship with God. Such negative learnings about oneself, based on the "bad news" from childhood authority figures concerning one's personhood, can cause a poor self-image and low self-esteem to become so entrenched that these powerful patterns block the experience of the corrective "good news" of God's love. For example, a person who was raised in the atmosphere of "a child should be seen and not heard" is unlikely to feel that God is open and receptive to the feelings and needs of that person even as an adult.

When a child's feelings are squelched and that child's assertiveness is labeled as bad or sinful, then that child may have difficulty in perceiving God's graceful acceptance of his or her whole person. Such persons often grow up believing that God can only care for the pious façade, the "good me," and that the "bad me" and the "not me" (the parts of ourselves that we hide even from ourselves) are totally unacceptable to God. Being "nice" or "good" are thought to be conditions we have to meet in order to influence God to approve of us. Unfortunately, we have often been taught and conditioned by well-meaning parents, religious leaders, and other teachers in the community that we cannot really be ourselves, have our identity and own our own feelings and needs if we are to have approval and acceptance by significant others. So we learn early to manipulate our own personalities, to repress and bury major parts of our personhood, and to sacrifice central elements of our genuine identity in order to have a better chance of being accepted, of belonging, and of receiving some needed strokes of approval. We learn to be inauthentic and to live by "shoulds, oughts, and musts" in order to merit our acceptance.

Passive submissiveness and sacrifice of authentic selves are not the will of God, however. God is saddened that we believe God requires us to destroy divinely given dimensions of our personalities in order to be loved. God caringly struggles on our behalf to lead us into that free space of joyous autonomy, where we live by trust in God's love and grace. God lovingly struggles on our behalf to help us to find our individuality and to express our unique autonomy. The Creator deeply desires that we, as God's children, experience the divine love that calls us into the freedom to be our whole selves. God's love calls forth our strength, our individuality, and our autonomy. God loves us all and all of us; God rejoices in our freedom; God celebrates our emerging autonomy; God validates our individuality. God knows that we do not feel truly accepted until the all in us, including the "bad me" and the "not me," are experienced as accepted by God.

Some of us have experienced this affirmation of our autonomy and assertiveness on the human interpersonal level, but we may not have transferred that learning to our relationship to God. The relationship of parents to children may help to clarify this point. Parents often delight in seeing their children move into and through the various developmental stages of human growth toward individuality. There may be joy over the first word spoken or over new phrases that are articulated, and parental "oohs and ahs" over a baby's first steps. Parents can offer a variety of affirming expressions for the growth and development of the child's personality and individuality. Human parents are so often enthusiastic and pleased with their children's unfolding. How much more does the divine parent celebrate our steps into our freedom and autonomy as God's beloved children.

Likewise in giving spiritual direction or counseling, the director or therapist will often feel aligned with the part of the person that is struggling for the freedom to be, even before the person can fully claim that desire for his or her own life. The counselor's caring is concerned for the individual's fullest expression of personhood, or for the unfolding of the image of God in that individual. How much more is God's love involved in the struggle for our autonomy and individuality! If we can experience such an affirmation for others' autonomy in our caring, so much more does God's love seek to validate our unique personhood.

None of the above is to be misconstrued as saying that God is blessing a new kind of narcissism in terms of idolatrous self-actualization. God is not placing a benediction on the self-actualizing person who puts his or her own self at the center of the world without reference to the Creator and to bringing love and justice to the neighbor. Personal growth and development are not to be misinterpreted to say that we are the savior or messiah for ourselves. God is not placing a benediction on a psychological and/or spiritual hedonism that says, "You do your own thing, and I'll do mine." That is not the gospel. Rather, God is affirming the depth of individual personhood in the context of our relationship to God and in terms of love and justice with our neighbors. In fact, the deepest acceptance of our own individuality and autonomy is to be experienced only through the knowledge that the ultimate Source of being is also the Divine Affirmer and Guarantor of indestructible identity.

Devotional literature dealing with the theme of assertiveness and autonomy in prayer has been sparse. In a little-known book entitled *The Soul of Prayer*, Peter Taylor Forsyth devotes his last chapter to the subject of the insistency of prayer.[8] In his emphasis on the importunity of prayer, Forsyth maintains that it is the will of God for persons to wrestle with God in prayer out of their strength as well as their weakness. He is critical of the popular theme that acquiescence, submissiveness, and passivity should be dominant in the life of prayer. He points out that the phrase "Thy will be done" appropriately reflects an attitude of submissiveness only after an assertive struggle, as Jesus had in the Garden of Gethsemane. Jesus initially prayed that the cup of suffering might be removed from his lips, and it was then and only then that Jesus said, "Nevertheless, not my will but Thine be done."

There is much biblical support for the view of prayer that God seeks us to encounter and to address God out of our strength and our assertiveness, and not simply out of our submissiveness or weakness. Jesus encourages seeking, knocking, and asking. There is the parable of the unjust judge, who responds finally to the request of the importunate widow. There is the incident of the Syrophoenician woman, who encountered Jesus forcefully and apparently changed his intention by the manner of her approach. The struggling cries of the psalmist, the confessions of Jeremiah, and the protestations of Job are but a few biblical examples of bringing assertiveness and strength into the life of prayer.

The encounter of Jacob's wrestling with an angel of God is a helpful paradigm for this theme of God's desire to engage God's people in strenuous and vigorous encounter on their behalf. Divine love and caring initiated the wrestling, not as an opponent of Jacob, but as one who sought to enable Jacob to discover his true identity and then his mission in life. God was not simply there to celebrate the gift of identity that Jacob wrestled out of his experience. Rather, God was present to help to initiate for Jacob that struggle to discover his true identity and to affirm Jacob's uniqueness, his autonomy, and his freedom to be.

Wrestling with God in prayer in a strenuous and vigorous way is not done in the spirit of competitiveness or as antagonists. Rather, the wrestling can be more closely compared to the passionate embracing of two lovers who seek to affirm each other in sharing their love. God is an assertive and affirming God of love, initiating for our own good the struggle for the freedom of our personhood and our individuality. As we experience God's nature in that lovingly vigorous and dynamic way, we may discover that God is calling forth in us that same kind of vigor, strength, and assertiveness of our total beings in order to fulfill our lives.

A prayer that summarizes this theme of assertiveness and autonomy in prayer might contain the following thoughts and feelings: "O God, who is divine love, inviting forth all of the potentialities in us, how great you are. Your loving strength initiates and calls forth the freedom in us to be ourselves, even when we doubt that it is all right to assert our needs and our feelings. We are grateful that you are not a fragile or a touchy God who cannot accept us and relate to us out of our strengths. We are grateful that you seek us out that we may be fully human and experience the widest spectrum of our feelings. Enable us to bring all of ourselves to you, that we may know the full acceptance of your love, and that we may exercise the depth of our powers in your loving service. Amen."

God is ever seeking to bring us into life by inviting us with all our strengths, our assertiveness, our individuality, and our total personhood into loving and prayerful encounter with divine love. We could speak of our ministry as a crusade to free persons from the demonic and self-destructive patterns of their existence so that the authentic image of God that is buried in each person can be free to live, love, have meaning, and be in intimate relationship and dialogue with God. As a part of that ministry, we are to help persons become free from their fixation to false absolutes and their idolatrous prayers to those idols. We seek to enable persons to live in the new reality, the new creation, where their communication with God is freeing, liberating, loving, and justice-seeking.

As C. S. Lewis was fond of saying, "May it be the real Thou that I speak to; may it be the real me who speaks."

CHAPTER EIGHT

Imagination in Pastoral Care and Counseling

Christie Cozad Neuger

Sarah sat on the couch, tears running down her cheeks. "I let myself reimagine the dream that I have had for so long, and it went just as it always does. I tried to let myself be open to newness in it, like you said, but the dream began to unfold in the same way it does every time I have it. Then, I got to the part where I went to comfort the child, who could not be comforted, and something amazing happened. As I reached for the child, all of a sudden I became the child, and God entered the scene and embraced me, just as if God were the mother, not me. I can't tell you what it was like. All this time I have felt that God was telling me in the dream that I'm not good enough, but all of a sudden I knew that God had been trying to comfort me and that I haven't allowed that to happen. I could never have believed that this could happen—nothing you could have told me about God's love would have made me feel that I was the one who needed care. But I experienced God's care in doing this redreaming, and it changes everything."

What Sarah described in this experience came through the use of imagery and imagination in a pastoral counseling relationship. It came in the midst of counseling that had been going on for four months in which Sarah had been stuck in a cycle of self-negation and destructive guilt. She was trapped between a longing for God and a need to live up to an ideal of self-sacrifice that she thought was her only path to God's care. She lived a life that was devoted to caring for and giving to others, even when she was so empty that she had nothing left to give. Like Sarah, many of us become blocked in our lives without knowing what resources will help us to move on. The purpose of this chapter is to talk about one resource, imagination, that can be a valuable ingredient in pastoral counseling.

Imagination has played a significant role in our theological tradition. Both the Hebrew and the Christian Scriptures are filled with metaphorical, image-provoking language and stories. Particularly in the parables of Jesus there is rich metaphorical language that calls out for the imaginative participation of the hearer. Jesus seemed deliberately to put together images that conflicted in such startling ways that the hearer had to become deeply engaged in order to find new order and new meaning in the stories. As Belden Lane put it, "As people listened to the stories of Jesus, they never knew exactly what he meant. In fact, he was reluctant to speak with a clarity that might forestall the listener's thought and participation."[1] For the people of God, trying to understand God's message, imagination was and is a necessary resource.

As the Church evolved, imagination continued to be important in the attempts of the faithful to participate in the holy. Familiar examples can be found in the writings of Julian of Norwich, John of the Cross, and Ignatius of Loyola.[2] Each found that imagination was a unique path, especially if disciplined and guided, to deeper and richer spiritual insights and experiences. Julian of Norwich found profound new images for God and for Jesus that allowed her to connect with the holy in radically different ways. John of the Cross, in his spiritual direction of people in religious life, found striking metaphors for the process of spiritual development. His metaphor of the "dark night of the soul" is one that people today still find meaningful when in the midst of spiritual doubt and despair. Ignatius of Loyola developed a set of spiritual exercises that encouraged the use of all five senses to explore with the imagination a variety of dimensions in spiritual life. These three persons and countless others in the history of Christianity who found ways to use the imagination in spiritual direction and devotion paved the way for effective imagination in pastoral counseling.

Contemporary theologians and spiritual directors continue to offer us insight into the use of imagination in developing our theological positions and in enhancing our spiritual lives. For example, Sallie McFague uses metaphor, rich in conflicting imagery, as a central vehicle for theological formulation. She points out that a metaphor always contains the message "it is and it is not."[3] The metaphor helps the hearer to grasp the reality that language and imagery about God and the experience of the holy are always only partial. Belden Lane says, "Metaphor, then, with all its suggestive incompleteness can point us toward that semantic humility which may be our salvation."[4] Other theologians who find imagination to be central in the development of theological viewpoints include Gordon Kaufman and David Tracy.[5]

Many people working in spiritual direction find that using the imagination provides a spiritual resource unavailable through verbal approaches. Avery Brooke offers a four-step meditation structure that uses imagination to find pathways to hearing God's voice through a focus on everyday objects, such as a leaf or a verse of Scripture.[6] In his guided imagination fantasies, G. Michael Cordner uses particular contexts that are also central biblical themes—such as the movement from darkness to light and the movement from the riverbank to full immersion in the river—to help people move more deeply into their spirituality.[7] In similar ways, Ira Progoff uses "twilight imagining" as a way for people to let themselves be fully open to the spiritual richness available to them through the imagination as they attempt to connect with personal and communal images of spiritual wholeness. Progoff's goal is to touch the wellspring of universal spirituality through a series of structured and unstructured exercises done in a relaxed, "twilight" state.[8]

It is clear, then, that the use of imagination in both theological formulation and spiritual direction has enriched the traditions of the Church, and continues to do so today.

Imagination and Psychological Tradition

Imagination has also been a part of the psychological traditions. In the nineteenth century Sir Francis Galton, an English psychiatrist, formulated the theory that there are two primary modes of thought: visualization and verbalization. He believed that each person is either a visualizer, who thinks in images, or a verbalizer, who thinks in words. He developed projective tests to discover to which category persons belong. His tests are still used today in studying certain dimensions of imagery.

American psychologists William James and Edward Titchener, in the late nineteenth and early twentieth centuries, believed that the image was a fundamental concept in psychology and focused considerable research on its characteristics. Titchener developed the structuralist school of thought, in which imagery was foundational. Around the same time, however, the behaviorist school was taking hold. In its eagerness to turn psychology into a "hard science," behaviorism sacrificed the realities of psychology that were not external and visible. Imagery and imagination became redefined and discredited, and introspection was dismissed as unmeasurable and, therefore, irrelevant. Although this psychological emphasis left out much of human experience, the study of imagery was ignored in America for many years.

The Europeans, meanwhile, were following a different path. Sigmund Freud took imagery and imagination very seriously in his early work, but he abandoned imagery for words, convinced that images, in the form of fantasies, provided an escape from reality rather than a constructive exploration of it. Most psychoanalytic thinkers followed Freud's lead. Carl Jung, one of Freud's early followers, was an exception to this early psychoanalytic tendency to negate imagery. He developed a process he called "active imagination," which he valued as a positive therapy experience focused on the imaginative and creative growth processes. Jung helped people to connect with their personal images as well as with the images of what he called the "collective unconscious," the universal images transferred through human evolution. Jung's emphasis was a passive openness to the images that already existed deep in the psyche. Many European psychologists followed self-consciously in Jung's footsteps in their development of techniques for therapy.

Jerome Singer, a well-known American researcher in the field of imagination theory, has explored reasons for the reemergence of imagery research in America in the late 1960s. He has suggested that it can be attributed primarily to the emergence of information theories and computer methods that allowed for conceptualizing the complexity of human thought; important research in the field of sleep and dreaming; investigations into the dynamics of hypnosis; the emergence of cognitive psychology; Singer's own research on daydreaming and its relationship to other forms of thought; and the widespread use of a variety of image and fantasy techniques, especially in the European-based approaches.[9]

Other theorists tend to agree with this analysis, often placing emphasis on the rise of the cognitive psychologies as a major factor. Jean Piaget, the founder of cognitive psychology, felt that both imagery and verbal skills are necessary and parallel in early development, but that imagery becomes an auxiliary function in later development. One of his greatest contributions to the understanding of imagery was his concept of the dialogue between the internal image and the external reality.

Contemporary Imagery Therapies

Today, there is a wide variety of therapeutic approaches that have imagination theory and technique at their center. Although Jungian therapy is not an imagery-focused approach, it does include a strong imagery component and was the precursor of many of the imagery therapies. Jung's active imagination therapy, developed more fully by his followers than by him, is still in use in much Jungian-oriented therapy. In it the person is encouraged to take a symbol and make it dynamic. Out of this process, new images and symbols emerge. These are then interpreted in the therapeutic dialogue in order to gain new insight. This approach encourages a passive waiting in which the unconscious provides the clues and directions to the evolution of the imagery and symbols, in contrast to some other approaches in which the images are more actively manipulated and redirected.

Psycho-imagination therapy, developed by Joseph Shorr, has focused entirely on the diagnostic and therapeutic uses of imagery. Shorr developed his theory out of a neo-Freudian background that emphasizes the interaction between the therapist and the client. A variety of imagery approaches elicits repressed emotion and provides a sense of cognitive clarity about conflicts.[10] In Jerome Singer's "Daydream Methods for Psychotherapy," the therapist guides the client in an imagery situation in which dialogue takes place so that the therapist can intervene in the imagery to promote certain ideas or possibilities.[11] The Directed Daydream Method of Robert DeSoille elicits intense imagery, but the therapist does not engage in significant interpretation of it. The images are effective in promoting insight and change without significant external interpretation. Hanscarl Leuner's very successful Guided Affective Imagery maintains the vivid and autonomous qualities of the image as the client is guided through a series of five standard fantasy motifs over a series of weeks. These motifs progressively encourage clients to move more deeply into themselves, and in the final image clients find their unconscious.[12]

Despite a common commitment to the healing powers of the image, there are differences between the various theoretical approaches. They differ in their understanding of the primary nature of imagery work. Psychoanalytic theorists, for instance, tend to focus on the uncensored access that imagery gives to the unconscious and the ability that the image has to be integrative in working with the unconscious conflicts that emerge. Imagery primarily uncovers and interprets. Behaviorally oriented theorists see the image as a means to redirect behavior. Fearful and anxious reactions can be modified, new approaches to relationships can be envisioned, and alternate patterns of responding can be rehearsed. The focus, however, is always on behavioral change. Cognitive theorists see the primary use of imagery as the ability to redirect unhealthy thinking. Imagery allows the client to experience in fantasy what the client's thinking would not allow in reality. In the safe setting of the counselor's office, this fantasy experience creates new possibilities in thinking and feeling. Finally, theorists who are more growth-oriented see the primary role of imagination and fantasy to be the exploration and integration of deeper levels of the self in the service of personal and communal growth.

Benefits of Imagery Therapy

These imagery therapies have a number of benefits in common, one being that working with the imagination in counseling has both explorative and healing possibilities that other forms of counseling do not. Working with the imagination bypasses both the censorship and the linear logic of the verbal therapeutic mode. It allows a client to connect with and to describe experiences for which there are no words. Experiences that carry powerful affect—such as terror, rage, transformative joy, and transcendent connection—often can only be communicated through the symbols and metaphors of the imagination. As we know, naming an experience often facilitates healing. The ability to name what has no name must come through the imagination. Imagination can often help people to work with experiences that they have not been able to name, either because they occurred prior to language formation (such as early childhood abuse) or because they have been too powerful for words. Often these experiences have been outside of healing because of their wordlessness. It is not so much that they have been avoided as that they have been unavailable. Using imagination approaches can make these life history events available again. In a sense, this ability to name and to process otherwise unnameable events and experiences returns a sense of control to the client.

Other benefits of imagery counseling are related to this sense of control. The imagery theories emerging out of cognitive psychology have demonstrated that imagery can be used to help redirect the thinking and feeling that has caused the client to be out of control in her or his life. Particularly in depression, much of the spontaneous imagery in the client is negative and self-defeating. By using imagery guided by the therapist, new options for thinking can occur, and a sense of control is returned to the client. K. David Schultz conducted a study with ninety men who were hospitalized for depression in order to see whether the use of guided imagery would be helpful in alleviating depression and, if so, whether particular types of imagery experiences were especially healing.[13] His results indicated that guided imagery (as opposed to free association imagery) did, in fact, help to reduce depression. Only one ten-minute imagination session with each person caused brief improvements in his depressed affect. Aggressive and social gratification imagery worked best with depressed men who had themes of dependency in their depression, and social gratification and positive nature imagery worked best with people who had primarily self-critical themes in their depressions. This study demonstrates that imagery work can be beneficial to depressed people if care is given in choosing the type of imagery that will best fit the themes of the depressive patterns.

Another benefit of imagery work involves control in the face of anxiety and fear. Control can be returned to the client through the use of imagery in rehearsing future behavior, in reducing fears and phobias, and in coping with stress. Imagining the situations that are most stressful and devising strategies to address them in the safety of the counseling room gives considerable reassurance to people who struggle with intense anxiety.

One of the primary reasons that imagery is so helpful in counseling is the paradoxical reality that images are autonomous in and of themselves, having a life of their own, while still being under the control of the imager. This autonomy is one of the most powerful characteristics of imagery. Even in the process of induced or guided imagery, an image takes on a life of its own, tapping into knowledge and perceptions through a nonlinear, nonintellectual route. Experiencing the power of this autonomy in imagination work can have a profound effect on the client; yet, even in the intensity of this process, the imager knows that there is choice. The therapist and the imager can manipulate the image in terms of setting and process. They can watch the imagination process as if they are standing outside of it. In fact, it is the very safety of this control, the "I" being able to observe the "me" in the image, that allows the imager to participate in the almost inescapable power and novelty of the fantasy experience. It is the responsibility of counselors both to reassure clients of the controllability of the image experience and to invite them to participate in the autonomy of it.

With the wide variety of theoretical approaches to imagery and imagination, it becomes important to understand how the image functions in therapeutic imagination work. For our purposes, I am defining the image as an internal experience that integrates perception, feeling, and meaning into a new whole. The induction of images through spiritual guidance or pastoral counseling enhances the potential to do the integrative work needed to ground ongoing spirituality in tradition and to transform it through creativity. The use of imagination unleashes each person's creative, integrative power to find out what symbols open up a more meaningful connection with God, with self, and with creation.

When it is defined in these ways, it becomes clear that an image is much more than an internal or mental picture. It is, instead, an experiential reality in and of itself—one that integrates thought, feeling, and meaning inside the self and in the social context. As Thomas Droege states, "The imagination is a natural resource that we all have for a fuller, more effective life. Rather than escaping reality, the imagination has access to the inner world of our experience and can give a deeper-than-intellectual expression to that reality."[14]

One clear point of agreement among all the theorists is the *power* of the image and the imagination process. When it is used in spiritual direction and pastoral counseling, this power must be respected and treated with care. Imagination work in which the power of the image is not taken seriously can cause considerable damage. Because of its ability to both reintegrate and disrupt, there are times when it should not be used at all (for example, with people who are psychotic or with people who have difficulty differentiating reality from imagination). Imagery techniques, particularly extended fantasy techniques, *should not be used.* Imagery should probably not be used with people who have strong mood changes due to organic damage, who have low motivation due to personality disorders or to lack of imagery ability, or who are intellectually impaired in such a way that imagery techniques would be frustrating. The effectiveness of imagery use in the counseling plan should always be evaluated during the counseling.

The powerful impact of the image and of imagery-based counseling raises an important issue for the counselor. The counselor who works with imagination counseling must be able to connect with her or his own imaginative resources. It is important for the counselor to be aware of her or his inner life and the nature of the symbols residing there. The process of being with someone in a guided fantasy experience means that a counselor must walk the fine line of being able to participate in the imagery for reasons of empathy, of assessment, and of timing, while at the same time being able to stand apart while the client works with her or his own autonomous processes. This requires counselors to be familiar with their own inner lives and with the power of imagery work for clients.

Despite all these caveats, pastoral counseling calls compellingly for the use of imagination. As G. Michael Cordner says:

> Religion and psychology encounter one another on the stage of the imagination. Each has grappled with and continues to attempt to define and describe clearly the significance of imagination and its products. Fantasy is always to be considered whether religion is dealing with the person's relationship to the divine or psychology with the person's relationship to his or her own depths. Perhaps that is because

ultimately—at the last—those questions are essentially the same.[15]

Through the use of metaphor and imagination, we can help people to explore and to express more fully their experience of the holy. Through the use of metaphor and imagination we can also empower people to engage in their own quest for meaning and for the integration of spirit and psyche. While I have separated the healing traditions of spiritual direction and psychotherapy in this chapter, people's problems do not separate along those lines. Sarah's story, with which I began this chapter, was not the story of a woman with a psychological problem, although her problem manifested itself in the perfectionistic and compulsive behavior patterns that lay behind an ongoing depression. Neither was it the story of a woman with a spiritual problem, although her problem manifested itself in a stunted relationship with a false and idolatrous single image of God, which kept her from realizing and connecting with the divine power of God's reality. Sarah's story was that of a woman who, in all her complexity, was afraid to live life—afraid of not being good enough in her own eyes, in God's eyes, and in the eyes of the world. It was the story of a woman who was conscious of judgment in her life, but not of grace. It was the story of a woman who could not afford to risk making new mistakes and so could not try new behaviors. It was the story of a woman whose problems were human problems; therefore, they had spiritual, psychological, behavioral, and social components.

Imagination is a place where these various dimensions can come together in their complex interrelationships. Images, because they have an integrative power and because they are developmentally and functionally prior to words, can bring together a variety of disparate elements. Not only can they bring together the various dimensions of a problem, but they can also bring together the problem, as it exists, with potential new options for resolution out of the wisdom of the self in connection with the Spirit. Since images tend to flow together in a storylike way, new solutions can emerge as the fantasy progresses. In that process, the three resources of the psyche are brought together: reason, feeling, and choice-making. New possibilities emerge as the imager releases old ways of addressing the issues and begins to imagine new ways.

There are a variety of contexts in which imagination can be helpfully used in pastoral counseling. In each of them the balance between direction and non-direction, between control and giving up of control, and between personal history and future possibilities shifts according to the counseling needs and contexts. Some of the most important applications for imagery theory come in working with people who are depressed, in transition, in grief, looking for help with spiritual growth, and in certain anxiety or crisis situations. The following case illustrations demonstrate the use of imagery in pastoral counseling in three of these contexts: depression, transition, and grief.

Depression

Anna sought pastoral counseling because her depression had become the sole focus of her life. She had experienced numerous mini-failures and had entered seminary hoping to find new direction. Unfortunately, she was beginning to experience again what she had always experienced—social isolation, loss of self-esteem, and barely passable work in her classes. She came to counseling depressed, with no vision for change in her life. She felt that she was a victim of her own shortcomings.

Anna and I worked together to construct a history of her experience. In the midst of that, she brought me a series of drawings demonstrating her images of herself. They showed Anna curled in a fetal position within a cave-like room without doors or windows. She felt trapped and helpless, and yet also very comfortable. We used this image as a vehicle for exploring herself and her choices, combining relaxation exercises and guided fantasies into the experience of this image and, consequently, of Anna herself. Anna began to get in touch with three new thoughts. One was how safe it felt to be able to predict her patterns in any new situation, even if those patterns meant failure. The second was how constrained she was in this womb-like existence. The third, and this was the thought that brought a transition into new possibilities, was that she had some choice about where she had located herself.

After this assessment work had been done, we began to try to change the image. Eventually, we put a door in the image through which she could come and go from this comfortable, but constraining, womb. With the addition of the door Anna, began to seek new images for life outside the depression. We began to explore some of her assumptions. When I asked her to imagine a social situation and explore her feelings and behavior in it, she made clear self-negating assumptions about how others saw her. We practiced, first in the image and then in reality, checking out those assumptions and acting "as if" she were acceptable. She had increasing success with this. More important, she began to use self-guided imagery as a resource for herself.

In the midst of our counseling work, we looked at why Anna had entered seminary. She was unable to come up with a verbal answer, so I asked her to locate God in the image of herself in the womb. To her complete surprise, she found that the womb was in God and that her image of God's will for her was to be enclosed in this restricting womb. It was important for her to see both the positive and negative ramifications of "resting in God" so literally. Coming to seminary had been, in many respects, a real way of being enclosed by God. However, as she began to experiment with other scriptural images for

God and for God's relationship with and call to creation, Anna let new possibilities for her relationship with God and for her vocation emerge. The womb of God became one of many important images for her, and the diversity of images allowed her to carry her relationship with God into other dimensions of her new life.

Anna and I counseled together for sixteen weeks. Our work ended when she was no longer experiencing depression, had viewed her entrance into the womb as her choice, and had developed new patterns of relating to herself and to other people. She decided that she did not want to be in ordained ministry, and she left seminary to work in an artist's studio. She became involved in a volunteer capacity with the music program of her church, which was where she felt the most comfortable.

Imagination played a variety of roles in this case, working with depression as a psychological, spiritual, and behavioral problem. It was used in assessment and to express what was inexpressible in words. It allowed for a context in which to try out new possibilities. It also allowed for identification of thought patterns and rehearsal of new behavioral options. Finally, Anna's use of imagination to explore her relationship with God and to help her find access to God in new ways was a powerful experience that had life-changing results.

Transition

Probably all people who come to counseling are in some form of life transition. However, there are varying intensities of transitions, and imagination work can be helpful in empowering a client to move through them constructively. Jinny, a thirty-year-old woman, came to my office on the recommendation of her boss, who had given her a poor annual work review. She had been asked to do some personal and vocational exploration in counseling in preparation for making some choices about her career.

Jinny was unsure of herself and feeling wounded when she came to the office. She had chosen to see a pastoral counselor because her relationship with the church was very strong. During her youth she had wanted to be a priest and had been disappointed when it was made clear to her that in the Roman Catholic tradition women could not be priests. She currently was working for an organization that coordinated activities between ministers in specialized settings and the national office for the denomination. It became clear as we talked that for her this had been the closest she could come to being in ministry.

There were many issues from her life history that Jinny had not addressed. Her mother had died young, and her father was a practicing alcoholic. Consequently, she had become a parent to her father and to her siblings early in life. She was very responsible within her family, but she had a pattern of running away from responsibilities outside of her family—in her job, for example. Jinny was very controlled in her discussion of these issues, quite verbal and self-possessed. She wanted to let go of her control so that she could move through the transitions that were facing her; yet, she wanted to hold on to that control for the safety and security of her already bruised self-esteem.

Jinny seemed most creative in her verbal use of images and metaphors, which were often startling or poignant. This helped me to see that she might be a good candidate for imagery counseling. I asked whether she would be willing to do some imagination work to explore, first, who she really was and, second, what she needed and wanted at this point in her life. She agreed.

We began by learning the relaxation procedures that are central to all imagination counseling. Through a process of progressive muscle relaxation and focused breathing, Jinny learned how to relax enough to allow images to flow into her mind. Then we practiced a guided meditation to help her become familiar with the methodology. After this preparation, we negotiated what she wanted in this experience. She felt that she needed to know parts of herself that had been hidden to her for a long time. She was worried that she would not like what she found, but she felt that it was important to explore because those parts of herself were operating outside of her conscious choice. She also hoped that new options for her life would become clear to her. I wanted her to stay open to whatever emerged in the work and to be patient. The danger was that she would try to control the images in order to receive the answers she wanted. This would subvert the imagery process. She agreed to be patient, and we negotiated a twelve-week contract.

In the next session I asked Jinny to go through the relaxation process and then to let herself in her imagination descend a set of stairs slowly. I counted down the stairs for her as she descended. When she reached the bottom, she was instructed to look around and describe what she saw. She found herself on a pathway. Upon following that path, she discovered a cave in which there was a central cavern with a series of rooms around it, most of which were not clearly visible. She reported considerable anxiety at being in the cave, surrounded by all this uncertainty. I asked her what she needed to make that exploration safer for herself. She asked me to stand at the entrance to the cave, and I agreed to that. She also added a dog for company in the cave and a lantern to shed a little light in the central room. With these additions to her image, she was able to tolerate the process of the fantasy.

Over the next few sessions, which were spaced one week apart, Jinny explored the rooms. She found in one a playroom in which she seemed to gain energy. Jinny had never had a play life, either as a child or as an adult. Exploring that room thoroughly gave her options for relaxation and pleasure that she had never before considered. She also found an office environment, which upon investigation turned out to be a set of church offices. She explored, first imagistically and later in reality, the possibility of being associated with the professional ministry of a local church. She found one room closed by a steel door, securely locked, that she did not want to explore. However, after several weeks of these explorations, she found the door unlocked and was able to begin to touch the childhood hurts and griefs that had been locked behind it. There were other doors—doors leading to friends' homes, doors still shrouded in mystery (to be explored some time later), and doors leading to places just to go and sit for a while.

She found pictures on the wall next to every door. They helped her to know whether she was ready to go into that room and gave her clues about what she needed in order to cope with what she would find. At the doors where she felt a great deal of anxiety, particularly at the locked door, she found pictures of Jesus on the wall. This gave her both a new image of God as being present with her in times of stress and also the confidence of that presence in doing her exploration. Her previous images of God had tended to be of the one who is distant and "helps those who help themselves."

At the end of each session, I would escort Jinny back up the stairs so that she could leave the fantasy and move outside of the image and reflect on it. Occasionally, she would reenter the image on her own at home, and she learned to do some self-directed imagery work.

We concluded the twelve weeks of imagery work and spent three more weeks looking at what the experience had meant to her and how she was putting what she had learned into practice. She obtained a position as coordinator of volunteer services in a large local church. She began to incorporate relaxation and play into her life, and she did some work with her family of origin in order to process some of the insights she had received about her own griefs and longings. What was most exciting was her new ability to have access to her inner life through self-guided imagery and introspection.

The extended fantasy trip is a very helpful approach for people in transition and for people who are seeking to enhance their own potential for growth. It is common for people to find unexpected dimensions of themselves and unexpected possibilities for their lives in an extended experience such as this. The counselor should encourage description, but not interpretation, during the imagination time; interpretation calls on cognitive resources that tend to disrupt the imagery process. The counselor should also monitor the degree of anxiety being experienced and explore what will help the client to cope with that during the fantasy time. If the client has to face too much anxiety, tension results, and the ability to produce imagery freely tends to be reduced. In the face of that anxiety, the client may begin to manufacture imagery instead of letting it spontaneously emerge. If the manufacture of imagery seems to be happening, it can be helpful to take the client through the relaxation procedure again.

Grief

Imagination can be helpful in working with "frozen" grief—grief from the past that was never fully explored or integrated. John, a man in his early fifties, came into counseling with a sense of emptiness in his life. He thought that this was related to the fact that his wife had gotten more involved with her career at a time when his was winding down. This issue was important, and we spent considerable counseling time, both in individual and couple work, addressing it. However, John continued to feel the emptiness and a nagging sense that something was wrong.

One day he told me about how his father had died. John had always tried to be a dutiful and thoughtful son. In fact, he was very close to his parents as he moved into adulthood. When he was twenty-four, he decided that it was time to move out of his parents' home and build a life of his own. He had recently gotten a job in a city about thirty miles away and decided to take an apartment there. His parents supported the move. After moving away, John began to develop interests and relationships of his own. One summer he decided to go to Europe with a group of friends. When he reported this to his parents, his mother was supportive, but his father did not want him to be away for the six weeks he was planning to be gone. John spent a long weekend with his parents just before he was to leave the country. He helped his father do some painting and maintenance work. Each time John was ready to leave, his father came up with one more thing that needed to be done. Finally John left for his apartment, saying that he would come back to visit as soon as he returned from Europe. As he began to pack for his trip, his father called and asked him to return for one more day. John, taking an unprecedented step, told his father that he was busy and needed to prepare for his trip. Two hours later, John's mother called. His father had just died suddenly from a heart attack. John was devastated, but did not know how to cope with his intense and ambivalent feelings. He returned home to comfort and support his mother for a day and then left, as planned, for his trip to Europe. He did not attend the funeral.

John related this twenty-five-year-old story in a mechanical and very controlled way. He reported that it had been a long time ago and the details were hard to remember, despite the fact that his narrative had been rich in detail. I asked him if he would be willing to do some imagination work about the death of his father. We had used imagination in some of his other previous work. He agreed.

We proceeded through the relaxation exercises, and then I asked John if he could bring the image of his father to mind. He was able to do this with startling clarity. I asked him to describe the image: what his father was doing, where he was, and so on. John's father was on the porch at their home, and John was sitting on the steps with him. I asked John to focus on that scene and just let the image unfold as it would. We did not discuss the image as it occurred; instead, this imagination process went on entirely inside John. After a while, John began to cry quietly. We continued to sit together in silence. Finally, he told me that he and his father had spoken together. John's father had asked John why he felt so guilty about living his life. John had begun to respond that he didn't feel guilty when it dawned on him that he did indeed feel very guilty about living a satisfying life when he had not fulfilled his father's last request. He told his father how badly he felt about not coming out to see him and about going off to Europe instead of to the funeral. At that point in the image, John's father, who had never been very demonstrative in his affection, put his arm around John and hugged him. He said that John had been the best son he could ever have had and that he loved him. John expressed his own love to his father, and then the image receded.

As John described this process, he was unable to put the fulfillment and the power of it into words. He was only able to say that he had been released and was now able to let go of having failed when he was most needed. The grief and guilt that had been reawakened and addressed were no longer dominating his life. The sense of emptiness was gone.

The use of imagery in grief is often very powerful, especially if the client is dealing with grief frozen from some earlier time in life. When the grief is more recent, it can be hard for the client to separate the imagination from reality because intense images and hallucinations are common in recent grief. To use fantasy in pastoral care with recent grief may be confusing to the grieving person, but imagery is a helpful resource in reconnecting with past grief and is often the best way to accomplish the unfinished business of frozen grief.

Imagination in Pastoral Counseling

There are many other uses for imagination work in pastoral counseling: rehearsal of anxious situations, such as job interviews, so that potential problems and creative solutions can be generated; rehearsal for women in abusive situations so that they can devise a more comprehensive plan for escape should they be threatened with violence; assertiveness training through the use of imagined situations; healing images for psychic, and even physical, wounds; and imaging new ways to relate to God and to one another.[16]

In all of these uses of imagery in pastoral counseling, the potential for spiritual enrichment exists. God is always a part of every pastoral counseling encounter. Imagination can open clients up to experiencing that presence in the quietness of their own souls and in the presence of the pastoral counselor, who names and claims the centrality of God in the healing process.

CHAPTER NINE

Depression

Howard W. Stone

I am lost in an immense underground cavern with tangled, unending passageways. What distant light I could once see soon shrinks to a glimmer and now is gone. Earlier I tried mightily to get out, to find the light of day again, but it is no longer possible and I no longer care. I'm very, very tired.

I don't have energy to turn back, to find my way out. It would be futile anyway. I have no real hope for the direction I am going. There is no real reason to continue, but I am afraid to stop; I might never move again.

I am very cold. My hands are numbed by the cold, scarred and caked with blood from my falls on the dark uneven floor.

People (those who wish me well and those who don't) are irritants. They want something from me, or they want to do something for me (which I do not want). I shudder at a knock on the door, the sound of the telephone. I wish all of them would be gone. There is nothing I want to do. Nothing excites me.

God is absent. Perhaps God has more important things to do elsewhere. . . .

Sharp words are now dull aches. The thoughtlessness of others is hardly discernible. I stumble on. Cracking my head against an unseen rock brings fresh blood mingling with my tears. I hardly feel the pain. What was once acute now is only a dim, pervasive ache. Nothing matters.

Why should I go on? I see no light, no end, no way out. No one beckons me. All that exist are cold, damp walls closing in on me. Ahead is a useless journey, exhausted step followed by

172

exhausted step, leading deeper into the unknown. Why not throw myself on the ground and let numbed sleep peacefully overcome? I blunder on.

These are my own words, penned in the middle of the night some seventeen years ago. While I sat in bed beside a sleeping spouse, my hand moved almost automatically. Thoughts became words became movement in my fingers, and I was merely an observer. The "cavern" was so vivid that the bedroom was a blur.

I was depressed. I had been so for several months and had several more to look forward to. I was not greatly incapacitated. I functioned in my job, gave service to the community, visited my friends, stayed married. But there was little joy. The images and the despair of that cavern dominated my inner world for a long time. I was one of the six million people in the United States who, at any given time, are depressed.

The Depressed as Church Members

During any year, according to a recent study for the National Institute of Mental Health, 15 percent of all people in the United States between the ages of eighteen and seventy-four will have significant depressive disturbances. In addition, 75 percent of all those hospitalized in a psychiatric hospital will report depression as part of the total cause of their treatment.[1] Since it strikes especially during the adult years, when vocations are important and children are being reared, depression not only affects the individual but also has a major impact on the marriage, the family, the church, even society. It is the "common cold" of mental and emotional disorders.

Depression can also be a spiritual disorder. It seems to me that the "dark night of the soul" described by Christian mystics is akin to, though not necessarily the same as, what today we call *depression*. The expression of the absence of God, the doubt, and the loss of meaning in religious ritual and service are much like many of the symptoms of depression. For the melancholic, depression leads to disturbance of relations with significant others.[2] For the mystic, it is the most important relationship that is changed, the relationship with God.

Further insight into depression as a spiritual problem comes from a study of the vice *accidie,* one of the seven deadly sins now frequently translated as "sloth." It may help our understanding of the melancholy that creeps into one's relationship with God and ultimately causes some to leave the church. The term *accidie* (also known as *acedia* or *akedia,* but essentially a lost concept today) has gone through considerable transformation of meaning throughout the centuries. At first it was used to describe something that affected only hermit monks; in the Middle Ages accidie was applied to all Christians.

Accidie, at least as it was understood by the Egyptian desert monks, was a form of melancholy that affected their relationship to God. A staleness in this relationship and in religious practices frequently led the monk to avoidance of the ascetic observances, to a feeling of general malaise and sleeping away time, or ultimately to escape from the community and sometimes from the church.

I do not believe the states described by mystics as the dark night of the soul or by the ascetics as accidie are radically uncommon. They are not the exclusive problems of another age or of the full-time monastic. They are common to human experience, albeit magnified by their concern with absolute reality. So accidie does indeed appear to be depression, but with unique characteristics arising from its association with the absolute. It is, to use Morton Bloomfield's definition, a "dryness of the spirit" that can affect one's whole being.[3]

On an average this dryness of spirit will be felt by fifteen of every one hundred adults in churches this year. How will the depressed worshipers respond to the sermon I am preparing for Sunday? Will they sense any hope? Will they even be in church? Is a depressed church member able to experience hope or only despair? Is depression tantamount to lack of faith and, therefore, sin? When I speak in the sermon of the trinity of virtues—faith, hope, and love—how can the depressed individual (who has little faith in God, others, or self, lacks hope, and feels as if no one cares) make sense out of my words? Even more, what do these words mean when the very person speaking them is woefully distraught? How can a depressed minister speak of faith and hope?

What Is Depression?

We have seen that melancholy, or depression, did not appear suddenly on the scene in recent times. Throughout recorded history one can find descriptions of depression and explanations (both psychological and environmental) for its cause. The book of Job tells of one man's immense melancholy. In the depths of his despair, Job could not imagine that his life would ever improve. He turned his anger from his parents toward God: "God's onslaughts wear me away" (Job 6:4). He described his agony: "My eyes are dim with grief, my limbs wasted to a shadow. . . . My days die away like an echo; my heart strings are snapped" (Job 17:7-11 NEB).

From the earliest recorded descriptions of depression to the present, there has been considerable confusion concerning what depression is and how it develops. Under some circumstances (such as bereavement), depression appears to be a normal—and very natural—response. Just as there is normal and pathological grief, so also there is normal and morbid depression. In seventeenth-, eighteenth-, and early nineteenth-century Britain, for example, it was rather fashionable, not "bad," for one to be overcome with melancholia. There have always been "tortured" artists and melancholic poets. In fact, depressive episodes may be actually beneficial for those who are unhappy with the way they are living their lives; depression may be the signal that something is wrong, and may provide the impetus needed for positive change. For the grieving person, it is a necessary stage in the healing process.

Melancholy, the historical word for depression, literally means "black bile" (one of the chief humors, or body fluids, that in ancient Greece was believed to come from the kidneys or spleen and produced depression, irritability, or gloominess). Hippocrates talked of depression some 2,500 years ago, writing that it arises from particular dyscrasias of blood and humors: "Melancholics develop their illness when the blood is contaminated with gall and mucous; their mental state is disturbed, many even become mad." In his discussion of one patient, Hippocrates stated: "Stupor accompanies her continuously; loss of appetite, sleeplessness, loss of initiative, attacks of rage, discontent, expressions of melancholy affect." He did not equate momentary bouts of loneliness or feeling blue with melancholy, but suggested only "if a feeling of fear or sadness continues for a long time, the suffering is melancholic."[4]

Debate over the cause(s) of depression—whether it is based environmentally (on psychosocial factors) or physiologically (especially on genetic, biochemical, and neurological predispositions)—has continued for centuries. It would be difficult to argue successfully that environment alone, or physiology alone, causes depression. In my estimation, it is the most organically or physiologically based emotional disorder. Many persons who seek counseling cannot identify what has triggered their dysphoria, a generalized depressed feeling of ill being, the opposite of euphoria. Still others may report physical symptoms, such as sleep disturbance and fatigue, without knowing why they have these symptoms, without being aware that they are depressed, or even without feeling remarkably sad or "down." In other cases, a seemingly minor environmental event will set off or be associated with a deep depression. One woman I counseled had to be hospitalized for depression after her husband announced that he had bought a dirt bike. (She had been wanting a new sofa.) Furthermore, it appears that some people are more physiologically biased toward depression than others. For them, it seems, a less potent precipitator is required to trigger melancholy than for others. You or I may respond to a scowl and angry words from a colleague with the thought, "He is just out of sorts today." But for another, the same event can be the beginning of a downward spiral of self-recrimination, self-doubt, social isolation, and pervasive despair. The difference is not necessarily one of relative mental health.

The question may be raised: If depression is organically based, shouldn't the individual be given antidepressants rather than counseling? The answer is an equivocal yes and no. Beck's research suggests that various forms of antidepressants are at least somewhat helpful for 60 to 65 percent of individuals, but that leaves 35 to 40 percent who cannot be helped by drugs and many others who are unwilling to take medication or who suffer from side effects that preclude their use. Counseling can be of benefit regardless of whether one's depression is due to environmental factors or a physiological predisposition, and whether or not antidepressant medications are used.[5]

Characteristics of Depression

Depressives as a group report a number of typical symptoms. It is highly unlikely that anyone would exhibit all of these symptoms. One individual may experience ongoing exhaustion and difficulty speaking with others, and yet have no headaches or sleep disturbance. Another person may feel immense sadness, a loss of satisfaction in what previously had been desirable activity, and frequent bouts of crying—but no other signs of depression.

It is important to keep in mind that some of these symptoms

are also characteristics of physical diseases. For example, a client I saw several years ago described low mood, constant exhaustion, diminished appetite, weight loss, and ongoing marital strife. He had a history of depressive episodes, but the rapid weight loss and his general "out of sorts" feeling suggested to me that his problem might be more than just depression or marital difficulties. I recommended a physical examination, which revealed that he had cancer and needed immediate surgery. I was fortunate to have made a medical referral! The minister is not in a position to diagnose physical illness; therefore, it is suggested that any individual with more than a mild depression be referred to a physician for a thorough medical checkup.

The characteristics of depression fall into four categories: affect, or emotions; behavior; physiology; and cognitions. Accidie is not a fifth category—it is the whole of which the four are the components.

Affect. The depressed often feel dysphoria, a pervasive state of feeling sad, "blue," or "down" most of the time (except in the case of manic-depressives, who can have wide swings of mood from euphoria to depression). They may suffer guilt and anger, although the anger is usually at themselves. They think of themselves as failures. They feel helpless to do anything about their situation; everything seems hopeless. Their spiritual life may become stale, and it may seem as if God no longer has interest in them. Joy is replaced by melancholy.

Depressed persons lose satisfaction in doing things. A person who previously enjoyed sailing, eating out, or riding a bike no longer gets a kick out of such activities. They even lose motivation for undertaking the mundane activities of life. They may find themselves crying frequently and for no apparent reason.

Behavior. Depressed individuals experience a generally lowered activity level. Put in fewer words, they do less. They engage in fewer spontaneous activities (like calling a friend to go out to a movie after dinner). They may spend more time sitting, staring into space or idly watching TV, leafing through magazines, or napping. When they do practice spiritual disciplines, such as worship and prayer, they do so without vibrancy. They often abandon spiritual activities altogether.

Associated with a lower level of activity is the tendency to avoid or escape from the usual pattern or routine of life. When I am depressed, all of my daily activities seem useless, boring, and devoid of meaning, and I have my "Volkswagen van" feelings. I want to throw a sleeping bag and fishing tackle into a van and take off for the lakes or mountains. I do not want any constraints. I want to get up when I want, fish when I want, sleep when I want, and do whatever I feel like at the moment.

Many depressed persons experience increased dependency. Those who feel helpless and hopeless rely more on others for what they feel unable to provide themselves. At the same time, they frequently experience a loss of emotional attachments—both the desire to be related to others and, because they have withdrawn from people, the actual opportunity to be related. When depressed persons do interact with others, they tend to have interpersonal problems. They may find it difficult to be assertive, or, at the other extreme, they may erupt easily in a destructive rage.

Depressed individuals have impaired abilities to cope with practical everyday problems. One who normally can replace a washer in a faucet, find a lost mitten for a child, or deal with a mixed-up order at a catalog store, now finds these tasks insurmountable.

Physiology. Physiological retardation can accompany depression. The person's movements are slowed. (The severely depressed individual may sit in a corner and not move all day!) For me, an early indication of the onset of depression is my racquetball game. I simply cannot move my body around the court to hit the ball as fast as I ordinarily can.

Retardation of speech patterns is a common sign. Depressed

persons may speak slower and at a lower pitch, and the severely depressed may speak in a flat, lifeless monotone (if they speak at all). There is often a general feeling of exhaustion or fatigue, even after periods of rest. Those who are depressed tend to feel tired all the time; they lack the energy to do the things that would help them combat their melancholia. Some have difficulties with headaches, constipation, or diarrhea. There can be a loss of appetite; the joy has gone out of eating, and, in fact, food may seem tasteless. There can also be a loss of interest in sex. The severely depressed often totally lose the sexual drive and experience sex as an intrusion into their private world.

Finally, many depressed persons experience sleep disturbances. Insomnia is one form, especially waking up early in the morning and being unable to get back to sleep. On the other hand, there are depressives who sleep more than usual, as much as fourteen to sixteen hours or more each day. I have counseled several people who would fall asleep at one or two in the morning, wake up just long enough to get their children off to school, and then sleep again until moments before the children arrived home.

Cognitions. Depression affects thinking, causing one to tend to distort and misinterpret reality. In this regard, Beck speaks of "the primary triad," or the three major disturbed thought patterns of a depressed individual: viewing events, self, and the future in an idiosyncratic manner.[6] The depressed perpetually interpret events in a negative way, conceiving of their interactions with the world—and with God—as defeat, disparagement, abandonment, and deprivation. Neutral, or even positive, transactions with other people are seen as failures. Cognitively, the depressed evaluate their own *selves* lower or of less value than when they are not depressed (lowered self-esteem). They commonly indulge in self- or other-blame and self-criticism, followed by feelings of guilt. When comparing themselves to others, they find themselves wanting. They also tend to be indecisive and may spend immense amounts of time trying to make a choice, often looking for the "perfect" solution or the "right" path. They view the future negatively. They have a sense of hopelessness, of a future that will bring only continued suffering and pain, of being trapped. To them, time most emphatically does *not* heal all wounds.

It is my experience, both personal and clinical, that depressed persons also experience God and religion in the same negative and hopeless manner. Although faith is not based on cognition alone, the depressed tend to be especially troubled by doubts or to lose their faith in God entirely. They have difficulty saying with the psalmist, "My hope is in the Lord." A steadfast faith that could not be pried loose by many earlier adversities, even tragedies, can crumble under the weight of depression.

The cognitive "set" that has been described can sometimes lead to thoughts of suicide. If it seems that life consists of unending and unabated suffering, and that suffering is due to his or her own defects, a person may view suicide as beneficial not only to self but also to friends and family.

Prerequisites for Helping

Depression is not a momentary bout of sadness, but a response that can affect the total organism—cognitively, physiologically, affectively, and behaviorally. Because it is not a simple phenomenon, it is rarely easy to care for. It seems to have a multiplicity of causes and a number of ways in which it shows itself. Therefore, the helping response must be tailored to each person's particular situation and grouping of symptoms.

Let us say that a person who claims to be depressed or who has many of the symptoms of depression has walked into the minister's office for the first time, asking for help. At the outset, it is important for the pastor to discern whether the person is in fact depressed or has some other configuration of emotions, or possibly a physical illness. Since both the experience of depression and its precipitators vary considerably from individual to individual, the minister must learn the specific ways in which the client is experiencing the dysphoria and what might be causing or exacerbating it.

It is also necessary to determine the extent and severity of the depression. Degrees to which melancholic persons are depressed are quite variable. We have already noted that the episodic and transitory "blues" that most of us experience, lasting a few hours or a few days, are not depression. Uncomfortable as those moments are, they are not of significant scope or duration.

The extent of a true depression customarily is categorized as mild, moderate, or severe. In a *mild* depression, the individual may feel sad or blue, a feeling that fluctuates considerably. It even may be absent at times, and the person may feel quite cheerful. Or the individual may be unaware of feeling especially sad, but may experience a loss of interest in work or hobbies, some insomnia, and/or relatively moderate but uncharacteristic fatigue or restlessness. The dysphoric feeling can be relieved temporarily or permanently by outside stimuli, such as a compliment, a joke, a vacation, or a piece of good news. Other symptoms are often relieved by such things as regular strenuous exercise, a reevaluation of one's goals, and appropriate dietary changes.

The *moderately* depressed person's dysphoria tends to be more pronounced and more persistent and is less likely to be influenced by attempts to offer cheer. Any immediate relief of this condition is temporary, and treatment can be expected to take some time. The dysphoria is frequently at its worst in the morning and may lighten somewhat as the day progresses. Cognitive, physiological, and behavioral symptoms are likewise more resistant to simple solutions.

The *severely* depressed are apt to feel relentlessly hopeless or miserable. Persons experiencing agitated depression often state that they are beset with worries. In Beck's study, 70 percent of severely depressed persons said that they were sad all the time and could not snap out of it; that they were so sad it was very painful; or that they were so sad they could not stand it.[7] Severe depression is also more likely to slow people down to an extreme, to cause debilitating exhaustion and passivity, to seriously impede their relationships and their normal functioning.

It is obvious that some depression is so severe that hospitalization and/or medication are needed; yet, the majority of individuals the pastor encounters are only mildly depressed and can be offered skillful and much needed help. Such pastoral care is not second-class treatment, but is exactly the quality of care that is needed with such cases. It occurs not only in counseling sessions, and is offered not only by the pastor, but it also includes the response of the priesthood of all believers, incorporating the depressed into the community of faith.

As a rule of thumb, ministers do best to see only mildly and some moderately depressed individuals, referring the more severely depressed to mental health professionals. However, both minister and congregation can offer considerable support to seriously depressed members who are in and out of psychiatric hospitals throughout their lifetimes.

The first meeting with the depressed client should involve some history taking, establishment of a relationship and rapport building, ventilation of emotions concerning specific problems, and assessment of the depression's severity— especially when the client is so severely depressed as to require medical attention or even hospitalization. The minister who is uncertain about the depression's severity needs to refer the individual for psychiatric evaluation.

The minister should remember that grief is not depression—though a grieving individual will usually be depressed for a time (and inadequate resolution of grief can bring on long-term depression). There are major differences between the depression that is a normal part of grief and a significant chronic or acute depression.[8] Grieving people most frequently describe *bouts* of depression that come and go with decreasing intensity and frequency after a loss. The depressed, especially the moderately or severely depressed, are less likely to have episodic bouts and are more likely to find no relief for days, months, even years.

Early in the counseling process, it is helpful to communicate that the pastor and the parishioner are a pair of sleuths who must investigate the depressed person's thinking, emotions, and behavior. This investigation is the equal responsibility of the client, who in the future ideally will take on the majority of the assessment task. In a collaborative fashion, minister and parishioner ask the following questions of the depression to ascertain its severity and to discover what strengths and coping abilities are available.

What immediate difficulties are impeding functioning? If the person's marriage is disintegrating, the first intervention may focus on this area. If he or she is suicidal, this must be addressed first. Or the person may have been laid off, fired, or passed over for a promotion—a career crisis that seems to have precipitated the depression. If so, that's where intervention can begin.

What are this person's strengths? Each person has many skills, abilities, and resources that may have been temporarily forgotten or undervalued and need to be rediscovered. This can be accomplished by helping the person to remember good or successful experiences from the past and to review how he or she functioned differently in those positive situations.

Are the symptoms primarily behavioral, physiological, cognitive, or affective? When you refer to the four symptom areas discussed earlier, it is valuable for you to identify a clustering of symptoms so that treatment methods can be aimed toward the areas that seem most debilitating.

What practical first steps can be taken to help turn this depression around? Both the minister and the parishioner may have a long-range vision for that person's life, but the complete task often is too much to tackle. They need to come up with some realistic first steps that can stop the slide into deeper depression and initiate the journey out.

In addition to answering those questions, the minister may use a number of standardized inventories to considerable advantage in ascertaining the extent and depth of the depression, such as the Beck Depression Inventory, the Zung Self-Rating Depression Scale, the Raskin Rating Scale for Depression, and the Hamilton Rating Scale.[9]

If, during the process of assessment, it appears that a person is suicidal, some additional steps must be taken. One does not need to be depressed to threaten, attempt, or commit suicide, but a significant number of depressed individuals do all three. One study found that the suicide rate for depressives is thirty-six times higher than for the general population, and at least three times higher than for either schizophrenics or alcoholics.[10] Ideas of suicide occur at one time or another in roughly 75 percent of depressives, and at least 15 percent make the attempt.[11] These statistics reveal a population at risk.[12]

The assessment process may itself accomplish a great deal; indeed, some depressed persons need only this one encounter with the minister to allow some catharsis and problem solving, and will not desire or require further visits. If an individual finds more than one visit necessary, but is not sufficiently depressed to require medication, medical help, or hospitalization, the minister can follow one of two approaches. One course involves one to three additional visits that focus primarily on sustenance, allowing discussion of difficulties and imparting some strength and self-esteem to the individual through the minister's presence and support. During such sustaining sessions, a few relatively small changes in habits could be suggested (such as a change of diet or exercise). The other option is to begin a process of care that will most likely take longer, will strive for more significant change on the part of the client, and will use several of the methods described in the next section of this chapter.

Depressed persons who come to the pastor for help usually do not arrive saying, "Pastor, I feel depressed." People who are depressed tend to go to physicians, describing back problems or sleeplessness rather than depression. They go to marriage counselors, complaining, "My husband is insensitive to my needs," rather than speaking of their melancholy. They likely go to the minister with their guilt or spiritual struggles rather than with a recognizable identification of depression. The minister must listen for depression lurking behind somatic complaints, troubled marriage, or dryness of the spirit. Many of the depressed do not speak directly of their pain. In fact, many depressed persons do not ask for help, and it may be friends or family members who tell the minister of the person's trouble. A visit from the pastor is usually required, and in such situations the pastor's position is unique among professional care-givers.

Counseling Methods

Several methods for the treatment of depressed individuals are presented below. Each method focuses especially, although not exclusively, on one of the four characteristics of depression (affect, behavior, physiology, and cognition). These techniques are derived from a variety of psychological schools, from the field of pastoral counseling, and from the history of pastoral care and spiritual direction. They all, in my experience, have been helpful responses to depressed persons. You will readily observe that a number of these methods can relieve more than one characteristic of depression. A review of "outcome" research studies indicates that the best treatment often incorporates methods that target more than one symptomatic cluster. For example, cognitive methods used alone are typically less helpful than cognitive and behavioral methods used together. In some cases, adding the benefits of antidepressant medications to the treatment plan gives even more effective results.

The list of methods presented herein is in no way complete, and the discussion will of necessity be brief. No minister or counselor would ever use *all* of these. I suggest that ministers choose from the methods available the ones that appear most beneficial for the people they encounter. I do think it is helpful for the minister to have a confident grasp of at least two techniques that apply to each of the four areas of depression.

Methods of Affective Intervention

We know from research done on the process of psychotherapy that significant symptomatic relief occurs between the time a patient enters a waiting room and the time he or she leaves after being interviewed by a clinic secretary; thus, it should not be surprising that some patients with mild depressions can be sufficiently helped through the clarification, catharsis, and hopefulness of an evaluation interview.[13]

Liberman is suggesting that for some people, depression can be turned around simply through the *expression of emotion* and the *discussion of the problem*. The empathy, warmth, and hope that a minister offers may be sufficient to help them with their melancholy. In this understanding environment, they can say what previously could only be thought; they can put into words the feelings that had once seemed too powerful to express. Sometimes, the depressed are afraid to talk with friends or family about what troubles them, and so a whirlpool of ruminations swirls around within them. With mild, but reasonably acute, depression, the expression of such feelings may be not only beneficial but also sufficient.

The *expression of anger* also can be very helpful. Some psychological theorists view depression as anger turned inside. Venting this anger may serve as a motivator and energizer to action. Beck has pointed out, "Being angry is not only more pleasant than being sad, but has connotations of power, superiority, and mastery. . . . Nonetheless, the expression of anger is often regarded negatively by the [person] and may provoke other people; thus it is not a reliable vehicle for improvement."[14] He also states that "talking about how miserable and hopeless they felt and trying to squeeze out anger often seemed to accentuate the [persons'] depression; their acceptance of their debased self-image and pessimism simply increased their sadness, passivity, and self-blame."[15] Indeed, in the name of "love," some very well-meaning Christians have invested many hours listening to depressed individuals and running to their beck and call, and to an extent perpetuating their depression. *Repeatedly* talking with people about their depression and sympathetically listening without urging them to action may amount to offering a stone instead of a loaf. Many melancholic individuals are so preoccupied with negative thoughts that further introspection—though possibly resulting in some short-term good feelings—tends to aggravate the pervading dysphoria. In my practice, the ventilation of feelings has been effective primarily with acute, but not severe, depression, and then only in the initial stages of care.

Resignation is another affective method. One of the tasks of the bereaved in the weeks and months after the loss of a significant relationship is learning to let go, to release attachments to the dead. It is a recognition that one can no longer have what once was precious, that one now must live life within the loss. Resignation is a natural part of the grief process. Resignation, as one resigns oneself to a loved one's

death, is also beneficial for melancholics who are depressed
because they worry about what might happen in the future, or
because their expectations are out of proportion to their own
skills and abilities. These helpless feelings may actually be
realistic; these persons may not have the abilities, skills, or
wherewithal to obtain the outcomes they desire. Resignation
with depressed persons involves finding more realistic
expectations for themselves, for the world, and for others;
changing some of their unrealistic assumptions or expectations; choosing alternative goals to work for; and discovering
new sources for meaning in life. It does *not* involve resigning
to helplessness, however. On the contrary, encouraging
people to acquire whatever new skills they need to cope with a
loss is also important.

Another technique, from the psychological school of
psychosynthesis, is the use of *dis-identification*, or self-iden-
tification, exercises. Roberto Assagioli maintains: "We are
dominated by everything with which our self becomes
identified. We can dominate and control everything from
which we dis-identify ourselves."[16] I have found his technique
of dis-identification to be helpful for people who are very
self-critical. The purpose is to help them to dis-identify
themselves from their negative emotions, thoughts, or
desires, recognizing that they have them but are not defined
by them. They are ultimately to see themselves as infinitely
precious to God—even though they may have difficulty
believing it—and as infinitely worthful persons for whom
Christ died. The clients are instructed to relax (relaxation
techniques can be used if needed) and then to dis-identify with
their body, emotions, and intellect through detailed imaging
of an internal dialogue ("I have a body, but I am not my body. I
have an emotional life, but I am not my emotions or feelings."
"I have desires, but I am not those desires." "I am lonely much
of the time, but that loneliness is not *me*." These are all
examples of the type of dis-identifying statements clients may

mentally say to themselves.). They are urged—first, in the session, and then in practice on their own—to use formulas like these with anything they falsely identify as their *selves,* such as their "role," their depressed feelings, their own self-image, their sins, their misdeeds, and so on. Finally, a positive assertion is introduced, such as "I am a child of God: I am an infinitely worthful person." Clients are to practice these dis- and self-identificatory statements for ten or fifteen minutes, twice a day, in a relaxed position with their eyes closed, imagining the mental dialogue. This ritual dis-identification is helpful only with mildly depressed individuals who are generally healthy but desire greater directedness and control over their lives—especially those who feel they are dominated by particular feelings, thoughts, objects, or individuals.

The affective technique of *diversion* is especially helpful with individuals who find a certain part of the day (typically the morning) or week especially difficult, when their depression seems most pronounced. Clients are urged to plan diversionary tactics for such times. For example, every morning Earl, a retired man who lived alone, felt very depressed and had difficulty facing his work around the house. The method he developed to deal with his depression was to get up early, finish all his chores by 8:00 A.M., and leave the house until noon. Getting out of the house did not always mean going to some other location; it could mean nothing more than pulling weeds in the backyard or sitting in a lawn chair and reading. Earl's morning diversionary tactics were, in my assessment, one of the major aids in his coping with his depression—especially at first, until other methods could also be employed.

Depressed persons are sometimes urged to *tell a friend* about their feelings, a technique that is particularly helpful for those who are not sharing their anguish with anyone, who carry it close to their breasts. Such individuals are urged to express their pain, in small or moderate "doses," to significant other people. By so doing, they may be enlisting the support and sustenance of people who probably were not aware of their inner pain. I have not had much success in helping very shy, depressed individuals to share themselves with others unless I was able to involve them in supportive group situations. Small existing groups within the congregation (such as a choir or ongoing Sunday school class) or specially created "sharing groups" can be beneficial. Otherwise, it can be *very* difficult to help depressed, reclusive individuals to pour out their hearts to others.

The opposite extreme, however, is more common in my experience: those who burn out family and friends with incessant talk of their sadness, irritation, and anguish. These individuals can be helped by setting limits on *excessive* expressions of their melancholy. When sharing their suffering with others, typically they invest even more time focusing on the bad feelings and thus become more depressed. Furthermore, such behavior usually is repellant to friends and relatives who might otherwise serve as a significant support system.

Behavioral Methods of Intervention

Melancholic individuals tend to see themselves as ineffective. It is, therefore, extremely important for them to be *active*, in order that they have the opportunity to see themselves being productive. This usually requires two counseling processes. The first is helping depressed persons to structure into their lives a number of activities in which they can be effective. The second is helping them to look at what they have already done (or are presently doing) and recognize their own competence. The latter calls for cognitive techniques, which will be discussed later. Since most depressed people greatly resent any attempt to prod them into activity, the pastoral counselor needs to be very creative in choosing the methods of assistance and the incentives to be used. At the same time, some depressed individuals see all of life as *either/or*, and their expectations are so elevated that they could not achieve them even if they were not depressed. The minister can use cognitive techniques to help these persons to trim such expectations.

Assisting the depressed to become more active typically requires a series of "homework" tasks. Homework is ideally negotiated between pastor and parishioner rather than "assigned" in an authoritarian manner. (In cases where the depression is quite deep, several of the first assignments may have to be prescribed. Later, such clients can take a more active part in determining the tasks they will do outside of the actual counseling sessions.) It is helpful to have the clients write down precisely what homework they have agreed to do and at what time. I request those who are very withdrawn or who significantly distort reality to read back the assignments to make sure we agree on what the homework is to be.

It is vital for depressed individuals actually to *do* their homework, thus taking the small steps that lead to success. If the depression is advanced, some of the early assignments need to be quite small and easily achievable. These people do not need another failure! Too large a task may become another insurmountable obstacle.

Some of these first assignments may seem inconsequential, even trivial, but to the depressed they can be very rigorous. The minister's task is to determine that clients are not attempting too big a jump, one at which they are likely to fail. For example, the man previously mentioned, who needed to get out of the house every morning, agreed first to weed the garden and then the yard. From lying in bed or sitting around the house all day, it was a big step for him to spend an hour weeding. Successfully accomplishing this led Earl to further, more difficult tasks.

Depression is a vicious circle in many respects: Fewer activities or interpersonal interactions with positive outcomes lead to depression; the more depressed people feel, the less motivated they are to be involved in activities that might have positive outcomes; being less active leads to even greater depression; and so on. This spiral can turn positive, however, and homework assignments are a key to the reversal. Improved performance in activities and interpersonal relationships leads to improved self-esteem and self-evaluation, which now increase the motivation to do even more, which leads again to improved performance, and so on and so on.

Several researchers have described "mood related activities" that can be helpful for depressives.[17] Their research—and my own experience—has found that individuals who do the following types of activities feel better and are less depressed than those who do not do them.

Interpersonal activities in which the depressed individual feels appreciated, accepted, valued, esteemed, and liked. For example, a depressed amateur radio operator shows his equipment to some interested "novices"; a lonely single person makes a point of being among people who are enjoying a mutual good time; or an elderly widower finds others who show interest in his ideas and hobbies.

Activities in which the depressed individual can demonstrate competence, independence, and adequacy. For example, doing a special project at work, beyond the normal requirements of the job, that allows creativity and independence.

"Fun things," activities that contain intrinsic pleasure—or would, when the depressed person is not melancholic. For example, going out for dinner at a fine restaurant, lying on the beach, going to a favorite sporting event, or taking a drive in the country to see the autumn colors.

Activities that give the client a sense of meaning in life. Most depressed persons have difficulty finding any sense of purpose for their existence. Victor Frankl suggested that those who are able to make some sense out of life—even in a concentration camp, as he was—have less tendency to be depressed and more energy for carrying on the tasks of existence.[18] He pointed out that meaning is not something that comes to us, but something each of us has to carve out, seek, strive for. In the concentration camp, those who did not find meaning did not survive. Meaning is crucial for survival.

Unfortunately, many depressed persons, because of their depression, simply will not do these activities. Being pushed too quickly will only strengthen their resistance. It may be useful to explore for activities—however infinitesimal they may seem—the person *can* realistically accomplish.

A purpose of homework assignments, then, is to help people to make some sense out of their existence and to gain some meaning in life. Depressed persons must ascertain what might be potentially meaningful for them, and begin to do those specific activities (like doing grounds work at the church or volunteering to tutor children who have reading disabilities). Sometimes the only way to determine what is meaningful is to begin to act and then reflect on what is done.

Several things can hinder the performance of these activities. Depressed persons frequently exhibit a lack of serious care in picking activities. They just fall into activities in which they have little interest, rather than choosing what might give them enjoyment, meaning, or a sense of adequacy.

The feeling of pressure from tasks left undone can be another hindrance to performing activities. I find this pleasure-destroying anxiety common among depressed students, who have difficulty enjoying a movie or reading a novel because they cannot stop thinking about all the homework that has yet to be done in the semester. During the last few days of the term, this is appropriate, and they should be studying; but four, six, or even eight weeks into the semester, they cannot expect to complete all of the term's requirements before relaxing!

Sometimes the precipitators of a depression (crisis,

significant loss, or change) remove the availability or possibility of high-quality activities. This is especially true of pleasurable relationships with friends. For example, in grief research carried out several years ago, I found that widowed middle-aged spouses immediately lost half of their friendships when their mates died. Those lost friends, frequently other couples, could have been an important source of sustenance.

Anxiety or stress also affect both the performance of activities and the enjoyment of pleasurable events. Persons under significant stress are less likely to experience enjoyment in what they do, especially if they are already depressed.[19]

The following suggestions for the scheduling of activity homework may help to overcome such hindrances. Help the depressed person to recognize that *doing* the activity is most important, not necessarily what or how much the person will accomplish.

Sometimes, what a person is able to accomplish is determined by external factors as much as, if not more than, by internal ones. For example, it may be generally helpful to learn to be assertive, but one's employer may be afraid of such behavior and make things more difficult because of the employee's assertiveness.

Many depressed persons have a tendency toward either/or thinking and believe they have to do every iota that they have planned. If they cannot manage what they have planned, they feel even worse and assume their time and effort was wasted. It is beneficial for the minister to aid in trimming expectations and keeping things in perspective.

It is helpful sometimes to encourage clients, especially the more severely depressed, to schedule their daily activities. Each evening before bed or the first thing in the morning, they write out an hour-by-hour schedule of the day ahead. For those who are considerably depressed, accomplishing a few basic maintenance activities around the house is a giant step forward.

Another behavioral method is *teaching specific social skills*. This is crucial for those who have been depressed on and off for an extended period of time. Research indicates that the depressed tend to seek out fewer social events and interpersonal contacts, initiate fewer contacts with new people, and perform less skillfully in interpersonal and social interchanges than non-depressed individuals do. They also describe themselves as less comfortable in social situations, often sensitive to being ignored or rejected and yet not performing the required social niceties. They also may lack skill in being assertive. Part of the minister's task is to help them to learn whatever social skills they need and to develop the assertiveness they lack.

Such social training may be done in many ways; the minister's approach is really up to his or her own creativity. Some methods that have been helpful for me are:

Role-play specific social events that are especially troublesome to the depressed person.

Model ways of interacting socially.

Give didactic instructions on some of the niceties that are required in social occasions.

Encourage the person to join a church group that will be especially supportive, empathetic, and open to new members. (Be aware that some church groups are closed and unreceptive to new people, especially if the new members are somewhat reclusive and depressed.) Sometimes it is helpful to make contact with one especially helpful, empathetic member who will assist the client's entrance into the group.

Involve the person in a sharing group or group therapy.

Suggest assertiveness training or social skills classes taught at a local community college.

A final behavioral method is asking clients to *keep a journal* of their activities. Frequently, depressed persons are unaware of how many events in their lives *do* give them a sense of meaning, pleasure, and confidence, or some sense of mastery and competence. In addition, the daily record of activities helps the minister to continue to plan new activities and assists in the honing and refining of present ones.

Methods of Physiological Intervention

There are fewer techniques available to the minister to cope with physiological symptoms. Obviously, the major physiologically effective technique is the use of medications, and a few comments on their application might be helpful. Two of the drugs commonly used to treat depression are tricyclics and lithium carbonate. The first is actually a group of antidepressant medications, which includes drugs like Tofranil (imipramine), Sinequan, Elavil. It was mentioned previously that 60 to 65 percent of melancholic individuals demonstrate a definite improvement when treated with a tricyclic antidepressant drug.[20] These drugs do not provide immediate relief, as aspirin does, but have a cumulative effect requiring a period of time, usually one to four weeks, before benefits are observed. Most physicians believe that antidepressant drugs, unlike common tranquilizers, such as Valium and Librium, are not habit-forming (though there is always the possibility that future research will reveal otherwise).

The second drug, lithium carbonate, has had almost miraculous effects with some severely depressed individuals, especially the bipolar types, such as manic-depressives. Lithium, a salt that already exists in the blood of all persons, was first used for the treatment of the manic phase, or "high," in the mood swings of manic-depressives. Research is presently underway to determine its benefits for depression. So far, the results have not been as "miraculous" as with the manic phase, but there is hope for its potential.

Some depression is precipitated or exacerbated by drugs. A number of depressed persons who come to the pastor may be seeing several physicians for various complaints, and obtaining medications from each one. Unfortunately, such people often fail to tell every physician of the other drugs they are taking, and may use half a dozen to a dozen different ones—drugs that may well be interacting with each other. In such situations, it is very important to send these persons to *one* of their doctors to take inventory of the medications they are taking, or (my preference) to a psychiatrist or other physician with whom the minister is in consultation, to evaluate the total constellation of their drugs, to be in contact with the other physicians, and to determine whether there are any inter-drug problems.

Medications like Reserpine, a drug for the treatment of high blood pressure, can produce depression as a side effect. Another such drug is birth control pills. If depression is triggered by a drug, the physician needs to find another medication that will not produce that side effect—or decide whether the benefits of a particular drug are not being eclipsed by the side effect of depression.

Depression is complicated in some cases by the use of some more readily available drugs, most commonly alcohol and caffeine. Alcohol is a depressant and, though possibly giving some short-term relief, will only heighten the melancholy. I customarily urge depressed clients to abstain from alcohol totally or trim down to a couple of drinks each week—and never drink alcohol when they are feeling especially depressed. (This also goes for illicit drugs like "downers.") Caffeine—found in coffee, tea, many soft drinks, chocolate, diet pills, and the like—seems to affect depression in many people. It gives a momentary "up," followed by a greater "down." Caffeine, and even sugar in excess, acts as a drug, causing overstimulation of the pancreas, resulting in higher insulin output, thus causing low blood sugar levels, irritability, and possibly depression.

A number of depressed persons have their most difficult period in the morning. Many people routinely begin their day with several cups of coffee, toast, and a glass of orange juice (which is surprisingly high in simple sugar). At midmorning they may add two or three more cups of coffee or a cola and a doughnut or danish. So in the five hours or more after the deprivation of food during the night's sleep, they have ingested primarily sugar and caffeine. On the other hand, beginning the day with at least twenty grams of protein for breakfast, no doughnuts, sweet rolls or other sugars, and no caffeine beverages can be a way for *some* people to help trim wide mood swings in the morning. For one recent client of mine, these diet changes and the addition of regular exercise were all that was required for a significant change in the depression, and only one counseling session was needed. The client did not have exceptional situational precipitators for his depression—outside of the normal stresses and strains of his life—but he was in need of some physiological attention.

I usually do not use any particular techniques to address loss of desire for food or sex, since neither tends to bother most depressed individuals. A physiological symptom that *is* of great concern to many depressives is sleep disturbance, and it is experienced by a majority of mild, moderate, and severely depressed individuals.[21] Such difficulties may consist of early morning waking, difficulty in falling asleep, or the kind of restless sleep from which one awakens feeling as if one never really slept. Most individuals will regain their typical sleeping patterns after the depression has lifted.

There are some suggestions the minister can make to help depressed persons to sleep better in the meantime. Suggest that they use the bed (in effect, the bedroom) *only* for sleep and sex. It is not a good idea for people with sleep disturbance to watch television, read for long periods of time, or study in bed.

If they are not sleepy, they should not stay in bed. When depressed people lie awake in bed, they may obsessively rehearse their negative thoughts. It is far better for them to get up and do something constructive. The occasional loss of a night's sleep is not harmful and may help them to sleep better the next night.

Encourage them with the fact that they actually get more sleep than they think. Many who believe they were lying awake all night actually gained a considerable amount of sleep, but part of their negative thinking is to believe they are not sleeping.

Help them to become active during the day. Persons who spend most of the day sitting around, reading or watching TV, and taking naps will not be inclined to sleep at night. It is better to be as physically active as possible and not to take naps.

Regular exercise can be very helpful, except in the last two hours before sleep, because it can serve to stimulate and energize as well as relax.

A fixed bedtime routine can cue people that it is time to sleep. One such routine might begin with a warm bath before watching the ten o'clock news, followed by a period of quiet meditation and prayer (possibly using some relaxation exercises), followed by a light snack.

Emphasize that anyone with sleeping problems should always avoid stimulants like tea, coffee, chocolate, and caffeinated sodas, before going to bed.

Train the persons in relaxation techniques. Frequently (though not always), learning to relax physiologically also causes the mind to slow down, and obsessive negative thoughts quiet down as well. Some cassette relaxation tapes can be very helpful in this task.

A final physiological technique is exercise—especially cardiovascular exercise. Long before jogging was in vogue, researchers found that people who performed regular cardiovascular exercise (at least three times a week) had less depression and less anxiety than did those who were sedentary. One difficulty with exercise is getting people—especially depressed people—to do it regularly. Therefore, a crucial step is to help depressed persons find exercise activities that bring enjoyment as well as cardiovascular benefits.

Exercise is beneficial in several ways. It obviously helps people to get in better shape physically and thus feel stronger and more energetic, and it has the additional benefit of giving people a sense of accomplishment. Here is something that they *can* do, and it introduces some discipline into what is usually a haphazard life. Discipline gives a sense of self-control to depressed individuals, who tend to feel they have control over little if anything.

Cognitive Methods of Intervention

Depressed persons sometimes have an ever so subtle shift in their cognitive mental organization. Certain thoughts begin to predominate to the extent that the individuals regard themselves, their experiences, and their futures in a negative way. Misconstructions and misperceptions follow these basic, faulty information-processing efforts. Theorists on the cognitive components of depression have described six typical ways in which depressed persons cognitively misconstrue their experience in a negative way.

1. *Arbitrary inference.* The depressed draw inferences that are counter to supportive evidence or in absence of such evidence.

2. *Selective abstraction.* The depressed focus on one minor detail while ignoring the more crucial features of a situation, and they view the whole situation based on this one item.

3. *Overgeneralization.* As the term indicates, depressives can make conclusions about themselves, their worth, and their ability to perform from a few isolated incidents.

4. *Magnification and minimization.* Melancholic individuals do not accurately perceive events, but tend to blow small, negative occurrences out of proportion, and render almost insignificant their positive accomplishments.

5. *Personalization*. Depressed persons may take responsibility for external events (usually bad) when there is little or no basis for such a connection.

6. *Either/or thinking*. The absolutistic, dichotomous thinking of depressives categorizes all that they do in one of two opposite positions: perfect or defective, all or none, immaculate or filthy, and so on. Since depressives can never fit the "good" (perfect) category, they see themselves as "bad" (defective).

Most cognitive theorists believe that childhood experiences serve as the basis for forming negative beliefs about ourselves, the future, and the external world. These negative concepts, or cognitions, frequently are latent, but are brought to life by some specific external precipitator that is dynamically analogous to the original experiences that created the negative attitude. Most depressives are not negative about everything, but tend to be especially sensitive to certain categories of stimuli, or "triggers," that set the negative thinking in motion.

Techniques have been designed to change the negative cognitions that have been learned by individuals, and to teach them a new set of more reality-based beliefs. In fact, Arnold Lazarus believes that "the bulk of psychotherapeutic endeavors may be said to center around correction of misconceptions,"[22] which may either precede or follow actual change of behavior.

How does one change another's cognitions? It is not easy! Ministers, who are trained in pastoral care and counseling and also have a background in theology and philosophy, are probably the best equipped of all helping professionals to enable people to change their beliefs.

Cognitive restructuring is the name used for the process of helping persons to see the world more realistically and to change unfounded beliefs, misconceptions, and expectations. The recent philosophical emphasis on the conscious objective experience draws extensively from the works of Kant,

Heidegger, and Husserl. The historical church has generally acknowledged (though post-1950s pastoral counseling practice often has not) that our beliefs about the future, self, others, the world, and God greatly affect how we act. Cognitive psychological theorists recognize this as well, but state it in nontheological terms.

The method of changing cognitions, or cognitive restructuring, outlined below is one I have described elsewhere in greater detail.[23] It includes the following steps.

1. *Assessment.* One of the first tasks of the minister (and of clients) is to try to understand the core negative assumptions or misconceived beliefs that the depressed hold about themselves, about God, and about the world.[24]

2. *Teaching/Learning.* The next task is to help depressed persons to change their erroneous beliefs. Exposing cognitive misconceptions is the easy part of the process; relearning is much more difficult. It can be facilitated by an explanation of how people develop faulty information processing mechanisms or irrational beliefs.

3. *Practicing.* The third step is the movement from educating the depressed about their negative misconceptions to the actual practice of catching themselves. Clients need to recognize their own irrational thoughts and to reformulate them in more reality-based ways. They may not catch their cognitive misconceptions right away, sometimes not for several days. When they are suddenly overcome with a wave of depression, they are urged to stop and move mentally backwards to find the trigger of the depression and identify their automatic unrealistic thoughts and beliefs.

Additional methods that can aid in the process of changing cognitions include the following: *Thought stopping* is a method to be used together with other techniques of cognitive restructuring. It teaches clients to mentally shout the word *stop* whenever obsessive and upsetting thoughts come to mind. They begin by vocalizing it (in fact, screaming it) out loud, and gradually work to saying it subvocally. Whenever negative ideas appear, they silently yell, "Stop!"—and the ruminations do stop. I urge clients to practice thought stopping two times a day for ten or fifteen minutes at a time the first week after learning the technique. Frequently, they can gain quicker control over their intrusive negative thoughts by purposely bringing them to the fore, and then practicing their banishment, rather than waiting for them to occur. Once the skill is developed, thought stopping can be used by clients to banish troublesome thoughts whenever they crop up.

Worry time is scheduled for some depressed people who find themselves so overwrought with worry that they spend every counseling session and many hours each day obsessed with their troubles. In a fifty-minute counseling session, I may suggest that ten to fifteen minutes of the session (usually the opening minutes) be given over to the venting of their problems, and the rest of the session to working on changes to be made in their lives. When this technique is used by clients at home, the idea is not to completely avoid thinking about troubling subjects, but rather to gain some control over them, to decide exactly when and how much time will be devoted to them. For example, a client may choose a half-hour period for worrying each day, say from 4:15 to 4:45 P.M., and is not to do anything else during that time except worry. The purpose is to free the remaining waking hours from lugging about this load of worries and problems.

The *blowup technique* asks clients to exaggerate their disturbing negative thoughts to such an extent that they no longer seem so awesome and may even appear ridiculous, ludicrous, or humorous. This method can be enhanced by having clients close their eyes and mentally image a troublesome situation in which such negative thoughts may occur. Then they are to exaggerate mentally the whole situation while describing in the first person what they are thinking, feeling, seeing, and experiencing. (It should be noted, however, both with thought stopping and with blowup, that terminating negative thoughts does not necessarily bring about positive ones—especially with more severely depressed individuals. It is necessary for the depressive to learn new positive, reality-based thoughts.)

The *alternative technique* is especially useful for persons who systematically have biased all their interpretations of stimuli and events in a negative way. The pastor explains to the clients the six cognitive information-processing errors that people frequently make. Then, together they discuss specific experiences, coming up with explanations and interpretations of the events other than the ones previously formed. The task for the depressed individuals is to recognize their negative biases and substitute more accurate interpretations of their experiences. This technique serves as a basis for problem solving. Clients consider and strategize alternative ways of handling problems based on a new interpretation of the circumstances.

In *cognitive rehearsal,* clients mentally image themselves going through all of the steps involved in a certain activity, and then discuss specific roadblocks and potential conflicts that might occur while actually doing the activity. They report all irrational thoughts that occur and attempt to correct these cognitive misconceptions. Clients are urged to pay special attention to every detail, and then to work out strategies for carrying out the activity in real life. They imagine the activity several more times to discover any additional cognitive misconceptions and to begin feeling comfortable with the step-by-step process required for carrying out the act. The minister needs to be aware that individuals who are quite depressed may have difficulty concentrating, and their minds may wander. Patience and gentle urging are called for.

Reattribution, a cognitive method somewhat similar to the alternative technique, helps depressed clients to assign correctly blame or responsibility for negative events that happen to them. Working together with the pastor, the depressed persons discuss selected events in their lives, applying the laws of logic and common sense and a sound understanding of ethics, to a variety of negative incidents, and they try to determine realistic responsibility for them. The goal is not to absolve themselves totally of responsibility, but to note the multitude of extraneous factors that can contribute to any negative event. Reattribution greatly helps individuals to lift the weight of self-reproach, to search for ways of salvaging troublesome situations, and to prevent recurrences. It can help parishioners to accept responsibility for *real* guilt and *real* sin, but not take blame for imagined sins. Reattribution of major negative events (such as a divorce) can be followed by the historic pastoral methods of confession, forgiveness and absolution, and amendment of life. The pastor should be alert, however, for a dangerous pattern that Roy Fairchild suggests many Christians learn: "They [the depressed persons] move from guilty feelings to atonement to attempted redemption by placating and obeying, by overworking, by denying themselves pleasure, and by subtle self-sabotage or clear self-destruction."[25]

The recent tendency of the church to minimize or even ignore sin, except as part of some global social issue, is an immense loss for depressives. Most feel they are very sinful and have done wrong (and indeed they *are* sinful and *have* done wrong). The minister who does not believe in sin or offers grace too glibly does not take the depressed or their experience seriously. To the degree that this occurs, the depressed are left to grapple with their gnawing guilt alone, unaided by the religious professional.

Spiritual direction, not only a cognitive technique but also a historical pastoral care method that is still practiced, especially in the Catholic and Anglican communions—is another useful way to help people change. Depressed persons tend to be very self-absorbed. Most of their thoughts are about themselves or about how they relate to other people or events. Spiritual direction allows them to develop and extend their relationship to God, to focus on something that is Ultimate, beyond themselves.

There are a variety of spiritual disciplines, some of which I have covered in greater detail elsewhere.[26] One that I have found helpful uses certain selections of Scripture (especially Psalms, or certain portions of the Gospels, such as the parables). Clients first read a passage completely, then line by line, reread it several times, focusing and reflecting on what the passage says to them. They may use the passage as in the spiritual exercise *Lectio Divina* and turn the most compelling portions into a litany, which they repetitively pray for a period of time. This method's value for depressives is that they are not dwelling on their own problems, but are concentrating on what the Word is saying to them. With those who are greatly distorting their experiences, I first go over the passages in the counseling session, where we have a chance to talk about them together, and I help them to catch distortions in their interpretations. For example, the person who thinks forgiveness is only for other people is urged to apprehend what is freely offered to all, irrespective of how heinous the sin may appear. For less troubled individuals, this method can serve as an excellent homework task.

One caution to keep in mind about the use of spiritual direction is that some depressives may use spiritual direction as yet another way to pull away from other people. Be careful that the uses of Scripture, prayer, meditation, contemplation, or the offices do not become an additional excuse for people to retreat from their worlds. For the depressed, spiritual direction ideally is a way in which they enter into a positive outside relationship with the Ground of their Being.

Conclusion

As I remember the "cavern" and the pain of my own bout with depression, I am impressed by what impact melancholy can have on a person and those around him or her. Depression usually does not wriggle and squirm, act out and disrupt class, or even rob a bank. It is more likely to sit quietly in the corner, not wanting to be a bother to anyone. In its quietness, it frequently is not noticed until the silence becomes so powerful that problems become obvious—problems like deterioration in job performance, reclusiveness, marital difficulties, even suicide. Understanding that depression can affect feelings, thinking, physiology, and behavior gives the minister a clearer focus on the variety of ways depression can manifest itself.

This chapter has offered a number of methods that can be used to offer care to the mild and moderately depressed persons the minister encounters in the parish. Since depression is so often a quiet phenomenon, the parish pastor, more than any other helping professional, is in a position to see and to offer help. With some pastoral initiative, those who are "down" can be reached before a severe depression occurs.

The church as a caring community can provide the light in the cavern that helps depressed persons find a way out. Its ultimate vision is to return them to a life of meaningful service; as they shed some of their own pain, they are called in turn to assume some of the individual agonies and global pains of this world. Meaning, for the mature Christian, is based on service and on a positive attitude toward life that relies on "the strength . . . through him who gives me power" (Phil. 4:13).

CHAPTER TEN

Loss and Grief

R. Scott Sullender

It became an expected thing. It happened so often that it was a good-natured joke among the clergy staff. The church was a large, downtown church with a beautiful sanctuary. The ministers probably officiated at one hundred weddings a year. The "expected thing" was crying, of course. Nine times out of ten, the couple or their parents would shed tears during the ceremony.

This phenomenon has always struck me as a bit curious. Weddings are supposed to be happy occasions, so why do people cry? Yes, some of it is just the sentimentality and beauty of the occasion, but much more of it is a type of grieving. The parents are saying good-bye to their son or daughter, and the bride and groom are bidding farewell to the adolescent phase of their lives. Both the parents and the newly married couple are moving through passages, and both transitions carry accompanying losses. The passages of life, some poet once said, are lined with tears.

The First Presbyterian Church is a changing congregation in a changing neighborhood. Thirty years ago it was in the suburbs and boasted a membership of nearly 2,000 people. It had a staff of three full-time ministers and a campus that included twenty-four classrooms, a chapel, a gym, and a lovely sanctuary. Now, some thirty years later, it has a membership of barely 250 and most of those people are over 40 years of age. Its Sunday school barely fills one classroom. What happened?

The neighborhood surrounding the church has changed dramatically in those thirty years. The area now consists mostly of Hispanic families, poor families, and aged families. Few people from the immediate neighborhood attend the church anymore. Most of its remaining active members drive from one to ten miles to what is now called "the downtown church."

The mood of the congregation could be described as low and discouraged. They have not been able to keep pastors very long in recent years; they cannot pay them much. But more important, the lay leaders are frustrated, and when the church does not grow according to their expectations, they direct considerable blame and criticism toward the pastor. Each time they go looking for a new pastor, they stubbornly set as their top priority "someone with a dynamic preaching style who will attract people to our church."

One of the most important aspects of a pastor's ministry in a congregation is the pastoral care of grief sufferers. In fact, the clergy is probably the single most important profession when it comes to the care of grieving persons. Pastors more than any other professional group, except for funeral directors perhaps, are in the front-line trenches when hardship and tragedy strike. Pastors are usually readily available when crises occur; they support and guide the family through the maze of procedures; they comfort and uplift fallen spirits; and they officiate at the appropriate ritual event. Some of them even do regular follow-up pastoral visitation. However, the two examples of loss with which I opened this chapter illustrate two kinds of grief work that most pastors largely ignore. One of these areas involves "diverse" losses, and the other the issue of "collective" losses. The two themes are obviously interrelated, and I want to address both subjects in the course of this chapter.

In the years since the first publication in 1966 of Howard Clinebell's *Basic Types of Pastoral Counseling,* we have seen a rapid increase in the professional appreciation of and research into the field of death and dying. The name Elisabeth

Kübler-Ross, for example, is now practically a household word among health professionals, and her *Death and Dying* has been a standard textbook in seminary classes for decades.[1] Thanks to her work and to the efforts of many other early pioneers in this once forbidden topic, ministry to the dying has become a valid and important form of specialized ministry in the church today. However, in recent years the field of death and dying, and bereavement in general, has moved beyond Kübler-Ross and beyond the narrow focus on death as the only type of loss worthy of study. The field of pastoral care and counseling has been, and continues to be, affected by the research of Holmes and Rahe on stress, by the newly formed discipline called life-span psychology, by the study of rituals, and by family systems theory. All of this has led to a significant shift of perspective in the study of loss and grief. No longer do we see everything in terms of death and dying. Now we see many more types, varieties, and degrees of losses in life, and our understanding of death, even as the most intense form of loss, must be placed within this larger framework of understanding.

Such a perspective is not new to hospital chaplains, who regularly minister to persons experiencing a wide variety of losses. Besides the obvious example of the dying patient, there is also the patient who has lost a significant body part or bodily function.[2] Usually, persons experience such a loss as the result of an accident or medical emergency. For most, that event is traumatic enough. Yet, in the following days or weeks, the patient must deal with the lingering and sometimes hidden feelings of grief and sorrow. People may mourn for their lost leg, eye, or bodily function. It isn't just a leg or a breast, of course—it is what the leg means to that individual or what the breast means to that woman. The amputee has lost mobility, independence, and possibly the ability to work. The mastectomy patient has lost a symbol of her femininity and may wonder if she will be sexually desirable again. Such losses are difficult to adjust to precisely because they involve so many complex secondary losses; losses are compounded by losses.

The other perspective that hospital chaplains are keenly aware of has to do with the systemic nature of loss and grief. Each individual is surrounded by family, friends, and a team of medical professionals. Rare are the times when a loss is experienced in isolation. The pain experienced by the patient is also experienced, in lesser forms, by the patient's family, friends, and even health care professionals. And any social and psychological adjustment that the patient must make as a result of his or her loss is an adjustment that will affect his or her system of relationships as well. For example, a person's inability to work because of an amputation will require certain changes in his or her family system, role definitions, and mutual expectations. The supporting spouse may "grieve" not just for his or her spouse, but also for the changes in his or her own life-style. In a sense, grieving is a social activity—and well it should be. The more that caregivers can facilitate the grieving of everyone involved, the easier they will heal and adjust to the new life before them. Conversely, every health professional has seen instances where the patient did his or her grief work well, but the family resisted theirs and thereby blocked the patient's full recovery. We in the pastoral care community must learn ways to facilitate the mourning of not only individuals, but of their support systems as well.

What is true in the hospital setting is also true in the parish context. My pastoral counseling work has led me to serve what is called a bedroom community, one of the many fast-growing suburban areas that surround metropolitan Los Angeles. Many people relocate in and out of these communities with great frequency. The pastor of a church in this community jokes that he does not have to move; he just waits, and every ten years he gets a new congregation.

Moving is one of the most underrated of loss/change events. It involves the loss of many things simultaneously: the loss of a home, the loss of friends, the loss of work or school, and perhaps the loss of income. And when a move occurs in connection with the death of a parent or the dissolution of the family unit, the losses are compounded.

Part of the problem is that most people do not recognize this transition as a type of loss. They may experience depressed feelings, nostalgic feelings, feelings of disorientation, perhaps even anger, and they wonder why. "Why, I should be happy," they say to themselves. "Here I am in a bigger house (or a better job)." These people do not recognize that their feelings are a type of grieving.

Some adults, deeply involved in relocating, can be particularly insensitive to children and their feelings. Unlike their parents, children are not going on to a better job nor do they usually appreciate the value of moving to a bigger house or a better neighborhood. All they know is that they have lost their friends, their school, their favorite bedroom, and maybe even their father or their mother. When children are not encouraged to talk out their feelings, they will act out their feelings. Most counseling clinics are filled with children and adolescents with behavioral or academic problems that began soon after a significant move or change in family functioning.

The Power of Diverse Losses

As researchers have moved beyond the narrow focus on death and dying and have begun to study these diverse losses, they have learned that these so-called minor losses are not so minor when their cumulative effect is considered. The research of Thomas H. Holmes and Richard H. Rahe at the University of Washington School of Medicine in the late 1960s was the pioneering work in this area. Since then, their work has become so well known that one can hardly attend a stress management class without hearing about their Social Readjustment Scale.[3] The Social Adjustment Scale attempted to measure the impact of different loss/change events on people's physical health. Fifty different loss/change events were given numerical values by Holmes and Rahe, depending on the severity of their impact. They found that persons who have more than 300 impact points within the last year have an 80 percent greater probability of getting sick within the near future. This research has been duplicated and repeated in varying forms, in many contexts, and among various ethnic groups. The statistical link between periods of prolonged high stress/adjustment and physical illness is now well established, and the startling fact is that this link is valid not just for stress-related illnesses, such as strokes and ulcers, but for such seemingly unrelated ailments as cancer, the common cold, and even broken bones.

One of the more significant books on grief dynamics is Colin Murray Parkes's *Bereavement,* which reports on the research and thinking about conjugal bereavement that has gone on in England, particularly among those associated with the Tavistock Institute of Human Relations.[4] Parkes's book is significant for two reasons. One, Parkes, with John Bowlby, attempts to present a new theoretical framework for understanding grief using an anthropological model.[5] Two, Parkes's book updates American readers on the extensive research on bereavement that has gone on in England in recent decades. In particular, Parkes reports on several studies that clearly document a link between bereavement and increased incidents of physical and mental distress. He concludes, after an exhaustive review of the literature, that "bereavement can affect physical health."[6] He then documents the fact that bereavement can also have a significant impact on a person's mental health. A significant loss certainly increases the amount of stress on the individual, and in some cases that stress triggers a psychiatric collapse that otherwise would not have happened.

The implications of such research have not been lost on

pastoral counselors and pastoral-care specialists. We now look upon losses, even minor losses, with renewed concern.[7] When parishioners experience several seemingly minor losses within a brief period of time, we must be concerned. Such persons, along with persons suffering severe losses, are more vulnerable to a wide variety of physical and mental difficulties. They are more "at risk." The caring pastor will endeavor to respond to such persons.

What the Holmes and Rahe research did not address, however, and what the Parkes material only hints at, is why certain persons who experience one or several significant losses don't get sick. Why are some people more vulnerable, while others seem to respond to hardship and stress with renewed strength and vigor? One of the key reasons, in my opinion, is the ability of the person to process his or her own feelings—to grieve. People who can grieve easily and freely are more likely to pass through one or several major losses with their family and personal mental health intact. People who cannot grieve, who deny grief feelings, and resist mourning, tend to bring on more physical and emotional difficulties than would be necessary.

This observation has been supported not only by my own professional experience as a pastoral therapist for fourteen years, but also by the thinking that is coming from the family system theorists. I am particularly reminded of Norman Paul, a family therapist who has argued for years that grieving is a family process, not just an individual process.[8] Furthermore, he has found that when families cannot grieve openly and together, a certain kind of family pathology develops that may manifest itself as much as several generations later in the form of behavioral or psychological problems in a particular "identified patient." What the family systems people have taught us is that families, too, can get sick, and that one of the key dynamics that make them sick is their inability to grieve successfully a common loss. In Paul's therapeutic work with "sick" families, he finds that they get better to the extent that they have a "corrective mourning experience"—that is, they complete together their unfinished grief work.[9] When this kind of healing occurs, the family is freed from its bondage to the past and is able to release its identified patient to grow into adulthood. What Paul's work tells us is that it is not just loss and grief per se that make us vulnerable to illness, but that it is *the inability to grieve* that leads to mental and familial problems.

Seeing the tremendous impact that grief, and in particular "stuck" grief, can have on a person's physical, mental, and familial health has given us in the field of pastoral care an increased sense of urgency about the church's grief ministry. Caring for grieving persons is more important than ever. As Howard Clinebell so often says, "There is a virtual epidemic of unresolved grief in this nation," and many of the increased mental and familial problems of our times can be directly traced to our inability to grieve. Now more than ever, the church is called to provide an informed and skilled ministry of caring for those who grieve.

Developmental Losses

Some losses are unwelcome accidents. As such, they are sudden, often dramatic, and very painful. Other losses are developmental in nature—that is, they are predictable losses that occur at approximately the same time in every person's life. These losses may be no less painful than accidental losses, but they do have a slightly different set of dynamics and issues. As we move away from a focus limited to the subject of death and dying and consider the wider perspective and role of losses in life, we find that many losses can be set within a developmental, or life-span, framework. This life-span perspective offers us a different and helpful way to understand the diverse losses in our lives.

Developmental losses may be major or minor in nature. They may include such major events as the death of one's parents or such minor events as the graduation of one's child from high school. What makes them developmental is that these losses are the marker events that signal to us that we have passed from one life-stage to another, from one social role to another. Through such transitions we pass from single to married, from adolescent to adult, from married to widowed, and so on. Many of the diverse, or minor, losses that we have been discussing can be best understood from a life-span perspective.

Losses occur throughout the life cycle. Some theorists have argued that birth itself is a type of loss—the loss of the intra-uterine comfort and security. Others, particularly the early Freudians, pointed to weaning as one of the most significant early losses. The implication of both of these points of view is that if these losses are not handled correctly or are somehow inhibited, then the person suffering the loss is likely to have severe psychological problems later in life.

School and its transitions are often the context for many losses in childhood and adolescence. When children first attend school, both the parent and the child feel a loss as the child passes from the secure home environment to the larger world of school responsibilities and social interactions. Anyone who has ever attended a high school graduation—and we all have—cannot help but notice the abundance of tears that engulf most graduating seniors. They are sad to be leaving their beloved school, their cherished friends, and this special period of their lives. They instinctively know that it will never be the same again. They cannot go back. Neither can we, in spite of the many movies and television shows that have tried to recreate our high school years for us.

In recent years we have seen a wealth of literature on the various losses in the second half of life. The literature on the psychology of aging focuses a great deal of attention on the dynamics of loss and grief in later life.[10] In the public's mind, however, the losses that have received the most attention are those related to the mid-life crisis. The mid-life crisis has received considerable attention, I believe, partly because this transition is the first major loss of the second half of life. Up to this time, most losses have been growth experiences. Now, and from here on, losses take on a finality that gives grief greater intensity. Several subtle loss processes are involved. Most mid-lifers have a keen awareness of their growing loss of youth, manifested so clearly in an expanding waistline, deepening wrinkles, and graying or thinning hair. Many people (mostly men) experience a plateau in their careers and the related loss of dreams and ambitions. Others experience a significant loss when the children become increasingly independent and eventually leave the nest. Women may experience feelings of grief as they pass through menopause and experience the loss of their ability to bear children. The successful resolution of these many losses is a key ingredient in helping a person to pass through the mid-life crisis into a new stage of adulthood.

There are many more losses in later life.[11] In fact, losses seem to come faster and with greater intensity in later years than at any other time in our life cycle. The loss of our parents through death is an underrated trauma in our society, one that affects us more significantly than we might realize. The loss of work through retirement signifies our passage from a stage of life characterized by values of productivity and task orientation to a stage of life characterized by values of simply being. The loss of one's spouse is commonly considered to be the most difficult of all of life's hardships; yet, it is a developmental loss that forces us into a new stage of life wherein loneliness and independence/dependence issues dominate. And as we age further, we experience the gradual, but persistent, loss of our own health in either small increments or sudden declines. All of these losses are significant; many will be difficult as well. All of them are inevitable, and therein lies both their terror and our advantage. If we anticipate these losses and prepare ourselves well, then they will not be as difficult as they might otherwise be. We will pass through them with grace and increased wisdom. If we ignore their coming, however, they will come upon us with greater shock, intensity, and destruction.

When we view losses and grief from the vantage point of a life-span perspective, we see clearly how important grief work is. Without doing their grief work well, persons actually resist moving into the next stage of life. A child who cannot leave home and enter the larger world of school will block his or her social and psychological development. In a sense, the child cannot grow unless he or she is willing to let go of home. Growing always involves some risk-taking. Similarly, parents who cannot let go of their almost adult children not only interfere with their children's development, but also block their own passage into a fuller stage of adulthood. In a sense, parents cannot become friends with their adult children until the parents are willing to mourn the loss of their children as children. Nowhere do we so clearly and dramatically see how interrelated grief and growth truly are as when we look at losses in a life-span perspective.[12] From this perspective, there is no growth without grief, no gain without loss, no maturity without suffering.

The field of pastoral care and counseling now views loss and grief ministry in this larger, life-span perspective.[13] We are now aware that losses are present throughout the life cycle and that pastors must be attentive to the lesser losses, as well as to the larger, more dramatic losses that strike parishioners. In fact, it is becoming increasingly clear that there are common threads between the lesser losses and the more significant ones. How a person copes with the small losses of life is often a paradigm for how that same person will cope with the larger losses of life. Persons who deal with pain through denial will do so in both subtle and dramatic losses. Persons who tend to regress will do so in both situations. Conversely, persons who tend to grieve well will do so in both gradual and sudden losses. Therefore, as pastors help parishioners with the smaller losses, they are also preparing them to cope with the larger losses. In this way, grief ministry based on developmental losses can be a type of education or preventive pastoral care.

The church is still the only institution in our society that deals with the individual in a developmental or life-span context.[14] It is the only institution that pays attention to and has access to the individual throughout his or her life cycle. It is the only institution wherein a professional can see and work with several generations of a family concurrently. Clergy are the only professional group in society that has access to people at the critical transitions from one life stage to another. Many will argue that in this modern, secular, and increasingly urban age, the church's rituals are pale ghosts of their former selves. That is true; nevertheless the church is still the only institution that provides even a bare structure around which we ritualize our life-cycle passages. What potential, then, the church has to be a place where developmental growth is facilitated, encouraged, and celebrated! What an opportunity we have to celebrate the journey! This potential will be fulfilled, though, only as pastors and pastoral care specialists shift perspectives and begin to see the many diverse losses of life in a life-span perspective.

The Changing Face of Grief

What I have been suggesting here is that there has been a significant shift in the theoretical understanding of grief in the last twenty-five years. Initially, all grief was understood in the framework of death and dying dynamics. Kübler-Ross's five stages of dying were (and still are) applied to nearly every kind of loss or change event under the sun. Now, we are seeing that death and dying is not the primary paradigm for understanding grief, but is a subspeciality within the larger framework of loss dynamics. Once this theoretical shift is made, then one can also begin to see a larger perspective on grieving.

In the sudden, dramatic losses of life, grieving is straightforward. It is acute and very painful. It is dominated by emotional release, physical distress, and disorientation, the features that most of us are familiar with. But if we see loss in a larger perspective, then we must ask ourselves: "What does grieving look like in the case of a gradual loss, as in the gradual loss of youth? Or what does grieving look like when the loss is prolonged, as in the case of many divorces? Or what does grieving look like when the loss is subtle, as in the loss of face?" In these circumstances, grieving takes different forms and shapes. The usual dynamics are not so usual. We may not recognize grief.

Grief, or the grief process, varies according to several variables. One factor is, of course, the type of loss that the person in grief has experienced. Sudden losses are more dramatic than gradual ones. Unwanted losses tend to provoke resentment. A death by suicide will often trigger intense feelings of guilt and responsibility in the surviving family members. Another variable is the personality of the grieving person. People tend to grieve in ways that are consistent with their overall personality structure and style. Persons with a tendency toward dependency and helplessness tend to have a hard time with the inevitable depressive periods in bereavement. Persons who feel that the world owes them tend to grieve with bitterness and resentment. People who are workaholics tend to throw themselves more deeply into their work as a way of coping with their inner pain. Seasoned pastors, who have been with a congregation for many years, know their parishioners well and can almost predict how certain individuals will grieve. This is a helpful position to be in. In some cases, the pastor, more than anyone else, knows what is "normal" for a particular individual. Each person's grieving process is ultimately unique and a mirrored reflection of both the nature of the individual's attachment to what was lost and the type of loss that has occurred.

The idea that grieving includes expressions other than crying is not a totally new concept in the pastoral care and counseling literature. Some of the earliest writers in the field, such as Granger Westberg, attempted to delineate several phases of grieving. Westberg's book *Good Grief* continues to be popular some thirty years after its initial printing, partly because it is so easy to read and because it has this larger perspective on loss and grief.[15] The idea of the stages of grief is not as simple nor as clearly sequential as Westberg described it. Yet, the idea that grieving includes periods of depression, of anger, of fatigue, of physical distress, of guilt, and so on, is both well documented and an invaluable insight for the grief-sufferer.

Today's pastoral care specialist should realize that grieving, or the lack thereof, can take many forms and expressions. Parishioners with a sarcastic attitude or a prolonged depression or with an increased use of alcohol may be in need of pastoral intervention as much as (maybe even more than) the widow who cries her way through worship every Sunday. Such varied expressions of grief are particularly evident when the more diverse losses that I spoke of earlier are involved. Grieving has many faces, and if we are to be effective caregivers and facilitators of healing for our flock, we must have this larger perspective on grief.

Can Congregations Grieve?

Recently I was involved with a congregation that had gone through an unfortunate and painful process regarding its pastor of fourteen years. About six months ago, the pastor was forced to resign by the denomination's higher judicatory because of gross malpractice. Apparently, this man had been having regular sexual relations with several women parishioners. These covert affairs had been going on for about three years and, as is often the case, were clouded in secrecy and false promises. None of the women knew that there were others, and each was bound by threats and shallow promises of love not to tell anyone. In time, one woman did tell her husband. After attempting unsuccessfully to confront the offending pastor, they took their complaint to the higher judicatory for action. All of this was not known by the majority of the congregation, so when the pastor was forcibly removed by the denomination, the news and the related explanation caught most of the congregation by surprise. Shock and disbelief prevailed. People just could not believe this to be true, but there was little opportunity to process their feelings directly with the pastor. He disappeared from the church and from the community virtually overnight.

The assistant pastor, who was also taken by surprise, was left to manage the parish and its reactions as best he could. He was relatively new to the professional ministry, so the denomination in its wisdom employed several specialists, myself included, to help minister to the collective grief wounds of this community of faith. Through one church-wide meeting and several smaller group meetings, we attempted to process the congregation's feelings and responses to this shared pain. At least three losses surfaced again and again in conversations: the loss of a particular individual, their pastor, who in spite of his recent sin had cared for the church through thick and thin for many years; the loss of face, or honor, as the congregation felt that the pastor's immorality reflected on the people and their church; and the loss of innocence or purity, as they now felt that they were "dirty" and that no new pastor would ever want to come to their church. The emotional responses to these losses covered the full gamut from overt weeping to outrage to depression and even to relief. Some individuals, as many will do, looked for someone to blame—the pastor, the tale-telling women, the higher judicatory, or themselves. Others just left the church and took their membership elsewhere (or nowhere).

Congregations do experience collective losses. This was an extreme and complex example of such a collective loss. Most of the time the relocation of the church's pastor is not so sudden or so laced with mixed feelings.[16] Other examples of collective losses might include the destruction of the congregation's building, the slow decline or aging of the congregation, the rapid change of a congregation's identity or mission, the loss of face when significant leaders in the congregation fail, and the death of a pastor or significant lay leader. Each of these losses will trigger a grieving process for the congregation as a whole as well as for individual members of the faith community.

Collective losses are difficult to deal with for several reasons. First, there are few prescribed rituals in our society or in the church for dealing with collective losses. The normal rites of parting, such as good-bye parties, retirement dinners, installation services, or gift-giving, seem weak compared to the heavy load of emotion they sometimes must carry. When groups of people experience a common loss, they often want and need to be together. Yet, without prescribed rituals, people often mill around, unsure and uncertain about how to process appropriately their pain as a community. Second, collective losses can be difficult to work through just by virtue of the mechanics of getting the whole community together at one time and place. Segments of the community often refuse to participate and remain isolated from the collective healing process. Those segments then either drop out or resurface later, still in an earlier stage of grieving than the majority of the congregation.

Denominations have begun to recognize the fact that congregations, like individuals, go through a grieving process when a beloved (or not so beloved) pastor leaves. This is one type of a collective loss that every congregation experiences repeatedly. Congregations need time to grieve, time to process their feelings, and time to reorient themselves around a new leader and a new direction. If congregations do not grieve well, then life for the new cleric can be difficult at best. He or she can be subtly resented, and his or her program initiatives may be resisted and constantly compared to the glories of those of the predecessor (which can get more glorious every year). Conversely, if congregations do grieve well, they can be "ready to go" when the new leader arrives and ready to move into a new stage of growth and vitality. The question now before many denominational shepherds is how best to help congregations do exactly that.[17]

What are the rituals, the structures, and the procedures that can facilitate collective grieving? We have been considering collective losses, losses that strike at the heart of a community. I also want to suggest that every loss in the family of God is, in a sense, a collective loss. Or better said, every individual loss has a systemic dimension to it. The death of any member of a congregation, for example, affects the entire church family, much like ripples in a pond. The relocation of an active family to another state forces the congregation to adjust and to rebalance its equilibrium. A bitter divorce of a couple in the church can divide an entire congregation much like the particular nuclear family is divided. Every loss is experienced both on an individual plane and on a collective or systemic plane. No loss in the body of Christ is a completely private affair; all members are interrelated. When churches are at their best, they do indeed "Rejoice with those who rejoice and weep with those who weep" (Rom. 12:15). The Creator has designed grief to be a social process, and for good reason.

The family systems perspective, as noted earlier, focuses on the family as a system of relationships and interactions. Unlike individual-oriented psychology, family systems theory sees the primary patient as the system, not the individual. The individual's well-being is interrelated to the group's well being and, I would say, vice versa. A healthy individual can help a grieving congregation to heal, primarily by sharing his or her own pain. This dynamic is particularly true of pastors. Yet, the reverse is also true. Congregations can help individual members by giving them permission to grieve and a structure within which they can express appropriately their feelings of mourning. Unfortunately, the negative cycle is equally possible and too often true; an unhealthy pastor can block a whole congregation's healing, and a closed and rigid community of faith can stifle the grieving processes of its individual members. In short, we must understand that health and illness are both individual and systemic entities.

This understanding of illness and health has grown rapidly in recent decades and is having a major impact on the field of pastoral counseling, and in particular on how we do grief ministry.[18] In the past, most pastors and pastoral counselors were trained in individual psychology and in the skills of individual counseling. The task now before us is to retrain ourselves to provide pastoral care and healing for congregations as well as for individuals. Grief ministry includes not just a ministry to the individual grief-sufferers in a congregation but to the congregation as a whole. As we develop this perspective into new programs, I suspect that we will discover that just as some pastors have gifts in individual counseling, so also others will be gifted in the care and feeding of congregations. In the years ahead, I hope that such gifted pastors will come forth and teach the church how best to help congregations to heal.

Rituals as Vehicles of Healing

Rituals serve many functions in the life of the church. They celebrate commonly held beliefs and values. They teach younger generations the tenets of the faith (and did so long before there were Sunday schools). They help us to process changes in social status and roles, such as occur at weddings and funerals. They provide us with a structure within which we can process our feelings, both as individuals and as a congregation. At their best, rituals facilitate mourning. This particular function—to facilitate grieving—was not widely appreciated by the leaders of the recent liturgical renewal movement, who tended to favor the theological and educational functions of rituals. My hope, however, is that the church might look again at its rituals and the impulse to ritualize as a natural therapeutic tool for grief ministry.

It is easy to see how the funeral and its related ritual should be vehicles for mourning, but few people see the link between grief and other ritual events—until they begin to see the larger perspective on loss and grieving that I have been arguing for in this chapter. When loss is understood in a broader, life-span perspective, it becomes clear that every life-change event has an element of loss to it, and therefore an element of grieving. Every life-change event involves some element of letting go of the past as well as a moving into the future. The manifestations of this letting go may be varied; not all grief is crying. Yet, grief and grieving are almost universally present in all of the losses and change events of life, and pastors are the primary professional group that cares for persons and families in times of loss and change. Ritual is one of the main pastoral tools for helping people to deal with their feelings, particularly their feelings about a loss.

Anthropologists have been studying rituals for years, mostly among so-called primitive peoples.[19] Primitive cultures are filled with rituals. Rituals, in my opinion, are primitive people's group therapy, being a means of processing an individual's and a community's feelings associated with a particular loss or change event. Modern people, particularly those in highly individualistic and pluralistic settings, have few prescribed rituals. Furthermore, what rituals we do have are not as meaningful nor as powerful as they were to our forebears.[20] They are often shallow forms, empty of meaning. They do not satisfy.

There are many reasons for the decline of rituals in Western, "civilized" societies, and many would not mourn their passing. Yet, I think that it is safe to say that ritual was a major channel for expressing grief in former times, and that without clearly prescribed rituals that can give structure to our grief work, modern humans find it harder and harder to grieve effectively and easily.

Thus in these times when there are fewer rituals and what rituals exist are devoid of much of their traditional meaning, pastors are often left with the task of creating new rituals to minister to new losses or of tailoring old rituals to fit new uses. One highly mobile congregation where I occasionally worship has created parting and welcoming rituals for its members who move away or join the church as new members. The brief rite includes a set statement and prayer that touch on the theme of union in the body of Christ and the singing of the first line of a hymn, "Blest be the tie that binds. . . ." The ritual is always done after the sacrament of the Lord's Supper, which is celebrated once a month in this congregation. The sacrament's emphasis on the communion of saints is a fitting setting for this brief grief ritual. The ritual's power is in its repetition and in its structure, which gives people the opportunity to express inner feelings and to adjust to new realities.

One of the prevailing questions in our times is what rituals to develop for the new losses that have come with this modern age. The most obvious type of a new loss is divorce. Nearly one-third of marriages will end in divorce. Divorce is, of course, not a uniform experience. For some it is a tragedy; for others it is a new growth experience. All will affirm, however, that it marks a transition into a new stage of life. Thus there are many both in and out of the church who have called for the development of a rite for the ending of a marriage. They have argued that such a ritual would help people to facilitate their grief and accept the change in social reality before them. They have also argued that such a ritual might help divorcing couples to remain in the church rather than to feel that the church has abandoned them in their time of need. Yet, the church for the most part has not developed such a divorcing ritual. There are many reasons for this, not the least of which is that the church has been so overwhelmingly pro-marriage and pro-family that many worry that such a rite might be construed as giving encouragement or license to persons looking for an easy divorce.

Another new loss or transition that has received the attention of churches concerned with ritual development is retirement. Retirement, like divorce, is really a product of twentieth-century industrial societies. In earlier, more primitive cultures there was no such thing as a prescribed period of leisure at the end of one's life. Yet, affluence and excellent medical care have enabled us to look forward to a period of leisure or semi-leisure as the last stage of our lives. The transition from the stage of work to the stage of leisure can be difficult, however. Some people make the passage easily, but others do not. There has been great interest in how to help people make this transition smoothly and with good psychological adjustment. Toward that end, some church scholars are suggesting that the church should develop a ritual of retirement as a way of easing this passage.[21] Such a ritual might also be an opportunity for the church to affirm that a person has worth apart from his or her work, a belief that industrial societies have great difficulty hearing.

I do not know whether the church will, or even should, develop new rituals. The widespread discussion of such issues is encouraging, however. More church leaders are beginning to see the wider perspective on losses in life and are beginning to see the role of the collective losses of congregations. These circumstances lead pastors and pastoral care specialists to turn their attention to the ritual life of the church. My hope is that there will be greater dialogue at the seminary level, the denominational level, and the local congregation level about how the ritual life of the church may be revitalized and strengthened to serve the pastoral care function of facilitating people's grieving. I believe that this is the growing edge in the ongoing development of effective grief ministries in the church today.

A Place to Cry

When I work with bereaved people in counseling, they sometimes embarrassingly tell me that they cried during a recent worship service when they sang a favorite hymn or heard a touching prayer. At such occasions, I am fond of saying, "Well, if you can't cry in church, where can you cry?" Most of my clients are mystified by my remark. Nonetheless, my prescription for such clients is to keep attending worship and to keep crying.

As we move into the late twentieth and early twenty-first centuries, my hope is that the church will indeed become a place to cry, that we will affirm the function of ritual as a vehicle of expressing emotion, and affirm the importance of the family of God as a context in which we can find healing for the losses in our lives.

CHAPTER ELEVEN

Unresolved Grief [1]

David K. Switzer

Anyone who has been in pastoral ministry for even a brief period of time is well aware of the amount of physical and emotional energy that is required in the pastoral care of the bereaved. In some parish settings there may be only a relatively few deaths and funerals, but in a majority of congregations and communities such occasions are quite frequent, and the minister finds a large amount of her or his time taken up in the emergency calls immediately following a death, preparation for the funeral, the funeral itself, and follow-up calls with the grief-stricken. Few responsibilities are more demanding, and few situations present greater opportunities for clergy who are genuinely committed to the personal growth, including growth in faith, of the persons and families they serve. Such opportunities for growth are detailed by Sullender, both in his book[2] and in his chapter in this volume.

It is rare to find a text that is in any sense an introduction to one's functioning in pastoral care that does not include the pastor's role with person in grief.[3] In addition, several entire books dealing with grief have been written by clergy and for clergy.[4] Still other books, chapters in books, and journal articles are available to assist ministers in understanding grief and to give guidelines for their functioning with persons and congregations in bereavement. The emphasis of all this material is on assisting persons to move through the grief process in such a way as to minimize long-term difficulties; to grow in insight into oneself, in sensitivity to others, and in appreciation of God's gift of life; and to become more deeply committed to God and to the community of faith.

Although such pastoral ministry is by no means easy, it can be rewarding as we see people moving through the process, however slowly, observe their growth, receive their heartfelt appreciation (most of the time), and often grow in certain ways ourselves.

But what about grief that remains unresolved? For the purposes of this chapter, *unresolved* refers to the grief that, after a time, exhibits no noticeable changes in the direction of resolution. Other terms are often used to refer to the same condition: *abnormal, pathological, morbid,* and *atypical* grief. Unfortunately, clergy have very few resources to help them identify such reactions with reasonable confidence, understand the underlying dynamics, and respond in constructive ways. Clinebell, for example, speaks of such situations in only two pages.[5] A number of otherwise useful books have even less information. Exceptions are Jackson, Parkes, Rando, and Switzer, who each have a whole chapter devoted to the topic.[6]

There are a number of questions for the pastor. What is pathological, or unresolved, grief? How can we identify the reaction? What do we do then? What difference does this make to us in our ministry in this congregation and community? It makes a difference because these are people in pain—chronic pain and unhappiness. Because of the particular nature of their suffering, they are not able to respond fully to the invitation to "have life and have it abundantly." The Word is hindered. The work of the minister is both to proclaim the Word by several methods and to relate to people both in groups and one-to-one so that they can be more open to the Word and more capable of assimilating it. People with unresolved grief are in our congregations and are on our boards and committees. The specific form of their suffering, or their attempt to cover up or reduce their suffering, may interfere not only with their own responses to God's gift of life, but also with their relationships with others in the church, with the quality of their work with others on church boards and committees, and with their Christian witness to those outside the church. The fact that they are often difficult for us to identify and work with does not remove them from the arena of our pastoral responsibility.

Understanding Normal Grief as a Process

One of the major contributions to an understanding of grief, and thus to ministry to the bereaved, including those whose grief remains unresolved, has been the clarification of persons' normal reactions to loss as being a process. Process is clearly defined by Parkes as a "succession of clinical pictures which blend into and replace one another," rather than merely a set of behaviors that occur "after a loss and then gradually fade away."[7] The concept assumes that the various behaviors (including thoughts and feelings) are a function of intense intrapersonal and interpersonal needs. As these needs are relatively well met, the person *moves through* the process, in various stages, to a reasonably satisfactory resolution or readjustment. The assumption is also that if none of the needs are glossed over or left unmet, the person then can be expected to reach a satisfactory outcome. These needs include those that are common to most persons following a serious loss as well as those that are unique to a particular person who has lost another particular person and with whom he or she has had a unique relationship.

Stages of Grief

Stage theories of grief have been criticized by some, often with validity. Some of the inadequacies are magnified in those formulations that attempt to define the stages too narrowly and thus present schemes with eight or ten stages. Among these are inevitably those that present as a stage merely a single emotion or behavior, such as anger, guilt, or fear. Such so-called stages are not sufficiently comprehensive to contain the complexity of human feelings and motivations that are interacting at one and the same time. On the other hand, some formulations of stages are far too general and may have only three stages, such as shock, emotional disruption, and resolution. Such a scheme, while accurate, really offers no useful guidelines at all. Another flawed scheme is the attempt to understand the grief following a death by reference to stages of dying, such as those of Kübler-Ross.[8] Some writers present these as stages of grief without critical discussion.[9] Yet, the fact is that stages of dying are in several ways not at all comparable to stages of grief following the death of an emotionally significant person in a survivor who is attempting to readjust to her or his continued living.

It should be self-evident that an awareness of grief as a process with certain stages, however formulated, can be misused. The pastor can confuse the bereaved persons, put undue pressure on them to fit a prescribed pattern and/or to move at a pace more rapid than what is possible for them, and thus thwart the process, actually harming the persons. The warning by Mitchell and Anderson that "generalizing about grief is likely to inhibit the full expression of grief because it cancels our particularity"[10] has to be taken seriously. While they do not absolutely deny that there might be relevant formulations of stages of grief, they emphasize "the unpredictability of grief" and the need for broad definitions of the stages. I concur with their point, but also firmly suggest that some knowledge of grief as a process can provide at least some flexible guidelines for a pastor as she or he is a companion to a person or a family following the death of one with whom they have been closely related emotionally.

For example, it seems self-evident that a large percentage of persons respond initially to severe loss with some sort of shock, numbness, and denial (*Stage One*).

When this first reaction is not maintained, and it rarely is, there follows a complex set of feelings (the pain of sadness, guilt, anger, anxiety, and so on), disruption of usual cognitive processes at least to some degree, usually some physiological symptoms, crying, overactivity or withdrawal, the triggering of certain mechanisms of defense. Within this reaction is the need to come to terms with the reality and finality of the death (*Stage Two*).

When the acceptance of reality is being approached, it is absolutely necessary for the bereaved's well-being that her or his emotional relationship with the deceased be revised or transformed. Such a process involves withdrawing emotional energy from the physical, *external* presence of the person, so that some amount of that energy gradually becomes involved in the *internal* identifications with the other that have been made and that, of course, remain as a part of oneself. As this is taking place, there is usually some reduction of the number, the frequency, and the intensity of the most distressing experiences mentioned in the previous paragraph. At the same time, there is also usually a more effective and satisfying engagement on the part of the person with others, with work, and with other activities (*Stage Three*).

It seems clear that if one doesn't move from shock to some feeling, that if acceptance of the reality and finality of the death does not take place, then inner renewal is impossible, and if that does not occur, genuine resolution and adaptation are impossible. Since these needs and tasks of the bereaved are in fact somewhat chronological, although overlapping, we are obviously talking about a process with several stages, however named.[11]

An Introduction to Pathological Grief

The beginning point for an understanding of unresolved or pathological grief is a very precise knowledge of the usual behaviors in each stage of the normal grief process. It is necessary for a bereaved person to go through all the stages of the whole process in order for there to be, in a sense, new life. To have such a picture of normal grief is to provide the basis for understanding pathological grief, since the latter is not different in its appearance from the former except in terms of the selectivity of the behaviors and their rigidity and duration. Pathological grief is the fixation on a particular symptom or a particular segment of a specific stage of the normal grief process, with the adoption in a rigid and inflexible manner of one or a small number of mechanisms or behaviors of that stage. This fixation contrasts with the usual grief process in which there is experimental testing of various behaviors over a period of time, discarding those that are not functional in the maintenance and restructuring of the self, and then going on to utilize in a constructive and adaptive way several of the behaviors that facilitate self-maintenance and growth.

Examples of Unresolved Grief

Now that the concept of pathological or unresolved grief has been introduced, what does it actually look like?

I visited a sixty-five-year-old woman in the hospital. She had a mild heart disorder. It was not surprising that in this condition she would be somewhat depressed. At one level she seemed to appreciate my visit, but there was an underlying resistance to engaging herself fully with me. There was a mistrust, along with several negative comments about the church and its ministry. On my subsequent visits, she revealed the story of her hospitalization some three years before, following an automobile accident in which her husband was driving the car and she was rather seriously injured. Not until the fourth day in the hospital did a doctor and a minister come to her room together to tell her that her husband had died as a result of the accident and that his funeral had already been held. The doctor had thought it best for her own physical recovery that she not be told earlier.

As I visited her at home after her hospitalization for the heart disorder, it became clear to me that she had been depressed, angry, bitter, desperately unhappy, since the time of her husband's death. The attempts on the part of the minister and the numerous offerings of themselves by a Sunday school class had not been effective in helping her move through the grieving process. She had rejected invitations to be active in the class, yet spoke of her aching loneliness and how no one had done anything for her. She had not had the opportunity to receive the shock of her husband's death when it occurred and had not been able to attend his funeral. Her anger at not having been told interfered with her relationships with doctors and ministers who were trying to help her subsequently, and continued to be a barrier to her moving on to experiencing anger over the accident itself, the death of her husband, and the terrible sadness of her loss.

A genuine tragedy! Someone was lost—lonely, torn apart, yet resistant to numerous people's efforts to enter her life and to bring her into theirs, a brokenness in the fellowship of the church.

Margaret and Ed had two children, Robert, age sixteen, and Betty, age ten. Margaret was happily and productively employed during the hours that the children were in school, giving her the opportunity to see them off every morning and to be home to greet them when they returned from school. Ed had a very responsible job that required many hours of work but paid quite well. The children did well in school, had numerous friends, and enjoyed many activities. The family got along well together as a whole and in individual relationships with each other. They were committed Christians and active in an independent conservative church. They had many friends in the congregation, including a close relationship with the pastor, a very well-educated and competent minister.

One day, as Betty was crossing a city street, she was struck by a speeding car and was killed instantly. The driver of the car had alcohol in his bloodstream at a percentage just above the minimum legal definition of intoxication. The family members were devastated. Their pain was inconceivable. Over a period of months, the ministry of their pastor, faithfully and competently done, and the continued support of numerous church members individually and their Sunday school class as a whole, seemed not to lead to any change in their feelings and behavior. Ed could not concentrate, did not sleep well, had times of excessive anxiety, lost interest in his job and in sexual intercourse. He claimed that he was not aware of any anger at the driver, saying that he just felt dead inside. Margaret became very depressed, very bitter about the accident, so enraged at the driver of the car that she wanted him to suffer like she was suffering, and did not really see any hope that she would ever change. Robert, the son, was saddened by the loss, disturbed by his parents' condition, and felt devalued by the parents' withdrawal from him.

After about eight months, they began to see a specialist in grief therapy but were erratic in their keeping of appointments and were so preoccupied with the trial of the driver, set many months in the future, and their desire to see him punished that they had a very difficult time focusing on Betty's death and their loss of her. Even though their theological position was that God had a hand in everything that took place in this world and they raised questions as to why God had not saved Betty, none of them were able to identify in any significant way their anger at God. They seemed to be very afraid of doing so. The therapy was not successful in helping them make any noticeable movement through their grief. Each was turned inward, withdrawing from the others. Some two years after Betty's death Ed tried to kill himself but was discovered and taken to a hospital emergency room. From there he entered a psychiatric hospital and was released later with some amount of improvement. However, it seemed clear that Margaret and Ed were headed for divorce.

Just observing these two tragic situations, we can see some of the variety of appearances that unresolved grief may take: depression, bitterness, complaining, confusion, a lack of close friendships, pushing people away, inability to work well, anxiety attacks, strong suicidal impulses, the breakdown of family life, a loss of interest in one's sexual life, general irritability, outbursts of anger, demanding a lot of time from ministers and physicians. There may even be hallucinations and a sense of the unreality of the world. Unresolved grief may range from any of the manifestations of normal grief to quite extreme and bizarre behavior.

What can we ministers do for such people? If we mean how can we function effectively so that a person who has developed a set pattern of pathological grief can be restored to a happy and effective life, we may often not be able to do very much. This is not meant to be a discouraging statement, however.

Identifying Chronic Sufferers

The first and most important step is to be able to identify the persons who are suffering from unresolved grief. Sometimes they are persons who have come to be looked upon as chronic complainers in the congregation, thorny to be around, standing in the way of church programs, highly dependent upon the minister or others in the congregation, and becoming emotionally draining to us. They may have problems that are troublesome not only to themselves but also to others and to us and which seem to be intractable, sometimes embarrassing to the church, such as an excessive use of alcohol and/or other drugs. If it can be determined that these persons' personality characteristics and behavior date from the time of a severe loss, we get a different perspective from which to view them and relate to them. If we can experience them and then react to them not primarily as just plain troublemakers, but as people who hurt desperately and who are trying to protect themselves against their pain, then our relationships with them may change. Only at this point do we become capable of allowing them into our lives, thereby gaining some possibility of being allowed to enter into theirs. Only at this point can true ministry begin. Understanding the source of their behavior and their suffering can enable us not to take what they say and do personally, reducing our own sense of threat, our hostility toward them, and often the tension between us. We can also help others to understand and respond to them in the same way.

With the source of their difficulty identified, we are in a position to extend to them the pastoral care that we offer to others who suffer. As ministers, we are fortunate to be the recipients of the great gift of initiative-taking with people we see to be our responsibility. The frequent visits and the conversations that we now have with the persons who are experiencing unresolved grief begin to focus on the relationship of their present unsatisfactory lives to their uncompleted grief.

The Psychodynamics of Unresolved Grief

A critical question presents itself: Why is it that most people move on through the stages of grief, albeit with varying intensities of feelings and with differing lengths of time in each stage, while other people are unable to move through the process? Several researchers have pointed to certain distinguishing dynamics of pathological grief. If these dynamics are not different in kind from those of normal grief, they certainly are different in the power of the conflicts involved.

Volkan specifies the universality of a love-hate ambivalence in the persons with pathological grief whom he has treated.[12] In fact, such ambivalence is involved at least to some degree in all or almost all grief, although obviously quite minimal in some. It is the presence of *intense* or *exaggerated* ambivalence that seems to be involved in the psychogenesis of pathological grief. Volkan's point is that this ambivalence has been repressed because it is intolerable. It continues as a live force that is a barrier to the person's accepting the reality of the other's death and to the conscious feeling of the sadness that must be experienced to move through the grieving process.

Volkan considers the diagnosis of pathological grief reaction:

> [Six] months or more after a death, we observe an attitude toward the loss indicative of intellectual acknowledgement of its existence, accompanied by emotional denial. We find the pathological mourner clinging to the dead person in the *chronic hope* of his return, while at the same time, dreading this possibility. . . . The contradiction in this fearful but eager and absorbing search reflects the ambivalence with which the dead person has been regarded in life.[13]

On the basis of Volkan's observations, theory, and specialized psychotherapy of persons in pathological grief, I began to work with persons, primarily psychiatric hospital in-patients, whom psychiatrists suspected of having unresolved grief as a primary or exacerbating dynamic in the etiology of their particular disorder. Usually, but not always, those persons were suffering from severe depression with suicidal impulses. With much of Volkan's therapeutic approach, to be briefly summarized later, most of these persons improved significantly. The majority of these distressed persons were women whose spouses had died.

After a period of time, I experienced a very painful failure in my attempts to help one person with the methods I had been using, a woman whose daughter had been brutally murdered. Since then, I have had the opportunity to be the pastoral counselor to several other people whose spouses had died or whose children had been killed in accidents in which the repressed ambivalence that Volkan emphasizes seemed to me either to be absent or insignificant and thus not the major dynamic factor. I then began to try to conceive of other major sources of the reaction of unresolved grief and to adapt procedures to these situations. Confirmation and helpful elaboration of some of my developing ideas were later discovered in another writing by Horowitz and three colleagues, who have observed in grief, as others have in depression, a "learned helplessness" exhibiting itself sometimes in persons in whom such a sense of helplessness had not been observed before the present loss occurred.[14] The process seems to be something like the following. In infancy and early childhood, we take into ourselves the perceived attitudes of significant others toward us. This self-image becomes a dominant organizer of our mental life, how we tend to screen experiences that we have of ourselves, of others toward ourselves, and of the larger world. In some cases, this self-image tends toward the helpless and worthless. Sometimes persons whose early experiences may be described in this way later establish relationships with others in which they receive strength from the others, and the ego strengths they already have are stabilized and supported by the relationship. The internal forces of the sense of weakness and vulnerability are held in check by the positive relationship. The loss of this particular other person in the relationship not only removes the source of daily support, but activates the earlier dormant organizers of mental life, which now are free to become dominant. Thus the early learned helplessness now shapes the person's thinking and responses to others, and there tend to be insistent demands for help that can never be enough and that, in the absence of such help, lead to defeat, giving up, and hopelessness.

In fact, the theory of Horowitz and her companions is

considerably more complex than this and describes the early roots of what is actually an intense ambivalence. However, the theory has the advantage of helping us to understand how it is that persons who seem to be functioning at fairly high levels of effectiveness in their usual life and relationships may, very shortly after the loss of a person with whom they have been closely related emotionally, sink into the mire of grief and are not be able to make any movement at all. These persons appear helpless, hopeless, and often enough, suicidal. My increasing experience is that such a reappearance of one's early low self-esteem and sense of helplessness is itself a sufficient primary dynamic in the development of unresolved grief even without the strong ambivalence that both Volkan and Horowitz and her colleagues point to.

In still other grief reactions, when there has been a sudden and violent death, particularly when the blaming of someone else for the death is involved, the intense rage that the bereaved feel toward the person or persons they hold responsible, sometimes clearly identified and sometimes not, is itself a serious barrier to the grief process. The anger sometimes has no available target toward which it can be appropriately and effectively directed, or at times is so great and in such variance with the self-image that it is repressed. Thus, in the first instance, the accumulation and even nourishing of the anger—sometimes accompanied by the thought that if one could only get even, one's needs could be satisfied—block the full expression of the sorrow and the movement of the internal process of grief. In the second instance, the denial of anger blocks the process in something of the same way as the repressed ambivalence described by Volkan.

Other variables related to the blocking of the usual grief process are the prematurity of the death, its suddenness, and the occurrence of multiple deaths in the same accident or murder. In addition to the frequency of anger in these instances, two other factors are involved. First, the deaths are unexpected and unprepared for, and the degree of dissonance is intolerable. The events do not fit what Parkes calls one's "assumptive world."[15] Second, the deaths are unprepared for in the sense that the survivors have had no opportunity to begin their anticipatory grief, deal with their own shock and anxiety prior to the death, image the death in preparation for it, and in whatever ways are necessary bring the relationship up-to-date and, in some form, say good-bye.

The fact that that sudden, violent death does in fact typically give rise to complicated and prolonged grief is supported by research in which married couples who had lost a child as a result of an automobile accident and widows and widowers who had lost a spouse in the same way were compared with one another and with a group of married couples who had lost neither child nor spouse. All of the subjects were given psychological inventories and interviewed four to seven years following the death. Results indicated that there were few differences between the two groups who had suffered losses, that the grief tended to be prolonged and intense, with large numbers of the bereaved persons and couples continuing to be pained and disturbed even many years later, and that their psychological state and their behavior were distinguishable from the group who had suffered no loss.[16]

In summary, there may be three dynamic sources of pathological grief:

1. Repressed and intense ambivalence;
2. The reactivation of latent self-images of low self-esteem and helplessness; and
3. Sudden, violent, premature death, with the strong emotional responses and the cognitive disruption that are characteristic in such instances.

These three dynamics may, of course, be overlapping in the etiology of pathological grief, and, in my own experience, often are. However, I have not always discovered repressed ambivalence as a significant factor, especially in a parent whose young child has died or has been killed.

The Pastoral Response

Most persons go through the process of grief to a relatively satisfactory resolution or readaptation without assistance from a professional person, including a minister. Therefore, I do not mean to imply that for the mental health and meaningful relationships of the bereaved they must always have special assistance beyond that of their own inner resources, relationships with family and friends, and usual activities. However, the ministry of the church goes beyond even these very important concerns to the imperative to share all of our experiences with one another within the community of faith, to go out of our way to contribute to the healing of one another and the integration of all of the profound experiences of life into our continued growth as persons, and to use all events of life as opportunities for maturing in the faith.

Assuming these are goals of our ministry, what then do we do if we begin to notice after a time that a person does *not* seem to be moving through the process of grief? This observation may be made with greater reliability and at an earlier time if the pastor is aware of the usual process of the grief reaction.

Because pathological grief is sometimes difficult to identify and is extremely complex in terms of the possible interacting forces producing it, and because a person with such a reaction needs highly specialized psychotherapy, the question is raised once again as to what a minister can possibly do. In fact, there are four periods of time and three different ways in which clergy can be especially helpful to persons who may have a pathological grief reaction. The three constructive responses of the minister are (1) early identification of clues that might point to the development of pathological grief or identification of the reaction itself; (2) the facilitation of the grief process; and (3) referral to a specialist in grief therapy. These three responses will be referred to in the context of the four periods of time.

The First Period

The first time period is, of course, at the time of the death and immediately following. The pastor will do what is done on any occasion of this sort: visit immediately and assist the person and/or family in the expression of feelings; if a family, help them to express their empathy to one another, talking openly about the death and about the person who died and the family's relationship with that person, particularly in the context of preparing for the funeral. Even at this time, it is important that the minister be alert for anyone who may have conflicting feelings about the deceased or anyone who seems to be alienated or isolated to any degree from the rest of the family. Special attention needs to be given to this person. In the light of Volkan's findings and, to some degree, my own experience that persons with unresolved grief may not have attended the funeral, or at least may have not participated in it without some serious coercion, the pastor might simply raise at some point the question of whether all members of the family are planning to attend the funeral. If someone is not, for whatever reason, a special conversation with that person is called for with a view to emphasizing the potential meaning of the service for that person.

The Second Period

The second time period overlaps the first and extends beyond it. Clergy, along with funeral directors and occasionally physicians, are the professional persons who are in a position to be engaged with persons in bereavement during those first days and weeks following the death. There are sometimes clues that might possibly be indicative of a later unresolved grief. None of these are predictive of such a reaction with certainty, but in varying degrees they should alert us to special needs a person or a family may have at this time and that call for our pastoral attention.[17]

First, notice the absence of any appearance of grief. I do not mean just not crying. Shock and denial and numbness may keep some people from crying at first, and keep many others from crying very much or in the presence of others. Even the numbness that covers up the other behaviors of grief is itself a symptom and can be distinguished from mere absence of symptoms. Numbness is like being stunned; there is noticeable lack of responsiveness about it. However, when a person appears to be truly without any of the reactions of grief within the first few days, it might well point to the strength of an underlying ambivalence or other repressed emotion that may indicate a high vulnerability to abnormal grief.

Second, look for truly excessive behavior of any kind. Granting the normality of almost any behavior and realizing that what some of us may call excessive is merely culturally conditioned for some others, we still need to pay attention to it. This behavior might be prolonged loud and uncontrollable crying, for example, or excessive handling of the dead body. Pay attention to any desire on the part of one or more family members to make excessive expenditures on the funeral. Of course, we need to realize that what is excessive for one person obviously is not for another. Even so, a large discrepancy between the actual financial capabilities of a family and what they say they want to spend for the funeral may indicate more than the usual amount of guilt, and therefore, some complication in the relationship with the dead person. Such a discrepancy would be important to note, perhaps even to discuss with the person or family.

Third, be attentive to any suicidal language, explicit or implicit. Although it may be quite normal to have such feelings in Stages Two and Three, and occasionally, though not usually, in Stage One, it is still serious enough to warrant talking with the person involved. Explicit language is just what it says: "With her dead, I might as well kill myself." There is no mistaking what is being said. Implicit language may not include the words *suicide* or *kill myself,* but the message gets across: "I just don't see how I can go on with him gone," or "Without her I'm just a burden on the kids; they'd be better off without me." In either case, it is important to talk explicitly with the person about what he or she is expressing. In the case of implicit language, about the second time a person says something like that, we should reply, "You know, sometimes when people say what you have said, they're thinking about killing themselves. I wonder if that's something that's in your mind." We need have no fear that we will put into somebody's head a thought that is not there and upon which the person may now act. If the person is not thinking about it, what we say may have the impact of calling to his or her attention the radical nature of the language being used. If, in fact, the person is thinking about suicide, he or she will be relieved to realize that someone has recognized it and is willing to talk about it.

Fourth, pay attention to family interaction. Family systems studies demonstrate that the healthiest families have among their characteristics the preparation of their members for life's inevitable losses.[18] Although they experience shock and pain as everybody else does, they also tend to be more realistic about death's being the end of life and about the reality of this particular death. In contrast, family systems that produce ambivalence and/or in which there has been unusually intense dependence on the person who died are also more likely to be death-denying, to use euphemisms for death, and to be less willing to talk about the concrete details of this particular dying and death. These families may also tend to give evidence of rigidity of thinking and feeling about a number of things. They attempt to portray themselves as a single unit, with the individuals within the family indistinguishable from one another in terms of thought and feelings. Everyone is supposed to think the same, feel the same: "We've always believed that people should control their feelings." There are invasions of the minds of other persons within the family. For example, a four-year-old child who has been pushed out of his room by the arrival of a critically ill grandmother says after her death, "I'm glad she's gone"—a very natural response for a four-year-old who had his room taken away from him. But then Mother or Father replies very sharply, "Oh, Billy, you don't really mean that." Yes, Billy does, but Billy will learn. He is to think, feel, and say only what the parents teach him to think, feel, and say. This is a family in which dependence rather than autonomy is taught, and the greater our dependence on someone the greater our anger, and the greater the ambivalence, and the greater the likelihood of an abnormal grief reaction.

Fifth, has someone in the family had a prior severe depression or a schizophrenic disorder? A person who has had a severe depression in the past is more likely to have a depressive reaction to serious loss than to go through a normal course of grief. In families where a person has or has had a schizophrenic disorder, there is a greater probability that there has already been unresolved grief that has contributed to the disorder.[19] It is, therefore, more likely that the emotional denial of death and the repressed ambivalence toward the deceased in an earlier loss will be repeated now in this one.

In the early days after a loss, ministers need to be very attentive to these sorts of behaviors. They suggest the possibility that the grief will not progress through the usual stages to resolution. It needs to be emphasized, however, that no one of these is proof in and of itself. They are merely clues, indicators, signs to be alert to as more weeks and months go by, perhaps leading to your suggestion to the family how important it is to be in some regular touch with a counseling professional to help them through their time of distress.

The Third Period

The third time period may come three, four, or six months after the death. If you notice some indication from what the person is saying about his or her experience of grief, from what you observe of the person's behavior, or from what family and mutual friends have told you, that the person does not seem to be moving through the process, then you might initiate a series of special conversations with the bereaved person in the attempt to facilitate such movement.

It should be made very clear that the grief is, in fact, unresolved, and no one should expect it to be otherwise. I am not suggesting that the person is actually in pathological grief or that the person will certainly develop such a reaction at a later time. At three or four or so months, grief can still be very intense, very painful, disturbing, disruptive. Even so, with most people, there is some noticeable movement. When there is not, the bereaved person is probably in need of special assistance.

How can the pastor provide this assistance? In a visit, you might explore the person's present experience. In the midst of the pain, the depression, the lack of energy, the inability to point to any progress, you can suggest that it might be helpful to have a couple of conversations a week for several weeks, focusing exclusively on the person's reactions to the loss. If the person agrees, how should you go about it?

We might assume, although it is not always the case, that the pastor and other persons have talked with the bereaved person for some time after the death and the funeral, that they have discussed the person who died, reviewed the circumstances of death, talked about the funeral, have done some remembering together, and that the pastor has been sufficiently empathetic to stimulate some outpouring of emotion. Such intimate and feeling-laden conversations are usually adequate to stimulate and/or support the grieving process.

When such conversations have not been effective in this regard, what is the pastor to do? A thorough knowledge of Volkan's specialized psychotherapy for persons with pathological grief, which he calls regriefing, can suggest to us a direction and some procedures.[20] While very few ministers have sufficient training in intensive psychotherapy to duplicate Volkan's entire process, some of his methods are adaptable to the conversations that any sensitive minister might have with a person in this stage of grief. His method is based on psychoanalysis, and even though he is talking about intensive therapy, there are some useful things we can learn. Volkan has three phases for this counseling process: demarcation, externalization, and reorganization.

The purpose of *demarcation* is to assist bereaved persons in making distinctions between themselves and the dead person. One way of doing this is by gathering as much information as possible about the persons in the relationship through a process of asking open-ended questions that encourage talking in concrete terms about each. This process separates the boundaries of the two individuals, emphasizing the points of contact but diminishing the sense of merging. This information gathering and discussion also provide material used to formulate a hypothesis about why the bereaved is having difficulty accepting the reality and finality of the death. Together the helper and the person in grief try to understand the dependency, which involves the fantasy that the deceased could, if still alive, gratify all the person's needs. Within this exploration is a thorough examination of the relationship in concrete detail, describing the events surrounding the death, the time immediately before and after the death, and the feelings that the bereaved person had at that time. This is essentially a procedure that facilitates the normal grief process. The person may be asked to look at a picture of the deceased and describe him or her in detail. Possible similarities and differences between the deceased and the bereaved are clarified, and there may well be some emotional catharsis. The bereaved person might also be asked to bring objects that were special to the relationship in some way (gifts, pictures, clothing, jewelry). Several of these can be brought out to look at and to hold and discuss. Photographs and mementoes stimulate the memory and feelings associated with different aspects of the relationship, bringing to light similarities and differences between the bereaved and the deceased, increasingly emphasizing the real emotional ties between them as persons. Try to discover whether any one object is more special than the others. If such a one is identified, it can become the focus of even more intensive discussion to uncover the source of its uniqueness, the particular feelings attached to it, and, therefore, the particular way it represents the dead person to the bereaved.

Externalization is not a discrete step but rather a continuation and intensification of demarcation with a much more detailed emphasis on seeking to bring into consciousness the very deepest wishes, feelings, and fantasies the bereaved might be having about the dead person. It is an attempt to bring to the outside to be heard and viewed what has been interior and unconscious. The procedures and material are sufficiently complex and difficult that they should not be attempted by someone who is not well trained in depth psychotherapy.

A major characteristic of unresolved grief is the continuing emotional denial of the death. Asking questions to elicit statements of reality concerning the actual death is very important in helping the bereaved person to accept the reality of what has taken place. Volkan has discovered, by the way, that in all of his patients with pathological grief there was some interference with full participation in the funeral; many did not attend the funeral at all, therefore allowing greater possibility for wish to overcome reality. The outcome of the process to this point (with several steps and procedures having been omitted) should be that the grief-sufferer begins to understand that one part of himself or herself has felt or known that the death has occurred, and another part has continued to feel and behave as if nothing has happened. Reviewing the relationship and the events surrounding the death assists the person in emotionally accepting the death as reality.

The final phase of Volkan's counseling process is *reorganization*. It comes after the person has been enabled to feel and verbalize repressed emotions and to discuss her or his fantasies and understand what has been taking place. The person is now free to feel sadness and to understand that the dead person represented part of herself or himself and that this is a real loss. Volkan often directs those persons who have not attended the funeral to a minister who will lead them through the ritual. Since many have not visited the grave, one or more sessions may actually be held in the cemetery, where the reality of the death is confirmed.

If there seem to be no recognizable expressions of intense repressed ambivalence, then it is pointless to continue Volkan's process. Begin to look for other core issues. Explore the life of the bereaved sufficiently to discover whether the evidences of low self-esteem, guilt, sense of worthlessness, and feelings of helplessness are reflections of the conscious self-image of the person prior to the relationship with the deceased. Whether they are or not, the conversation would then properly focus on the meaning that the relationship with the person now deceased had for the bereaved. It could be useful to focus on memories of the perceived strengths of the deceased and then to help the bereaved persons identify these strengths within themselves. Once that is done, perhaps the bereaved can begin to value these in themselves as they did in the other, and look for these same traits in others at the present time. Current relationships with their spouses, children, parents, or perhaps someone else may actually be reworked.

When a couple has lost a child, the most useful context for the procedures described above is to talk with the couple together, and if there are other children, with the whole family. Even if this is not done regularly, periodic family group sessions are an important contribution to the grief process of the couple or family because not everyone in the family has the same grieving experiences, and different individuals move at different rates of speed. It is also strengthening to the family for the pastor to assist them in their understanding of one another and their expressions of empathy to one another.

A word of caution needs to be repeated: What we have been discussing here is not just a series of gimmicky methods that anyone may use with some guarantee of success. The minister must be sensitive and perceptive, trained (it is hoped) to some degree in basic counseling procedures and relationships. He or she should use these methods as a part of an established relationship and with a reasonably long-term commitment to working on the person's grief.

As a result of conversations with the minister, the bereaved person may begin some movement toward becoming capable of living her or his own life without the physical relationship with the deceased—albeit a life with painful memories, never like it was before—but still able to accept that the person is dead, that the person is not coming back, and that relationships with others in the family and with friends are supportive and meaningful and worthwhile. However, if no such movement is noticed after a few weeks, referral to a competent mental health professional is in order.

The Fourth Period

By this time in the grief process, it will probably be six months or more after the death. This is the beginning of the fourth time period, in which a minister may play a helpful role with the bereaved. At this point, whether the minister has or has not had the sorts of pastoral care and counseling sessions just described, it is imperative that she or he take the initiative to discuss the situation realistically with the bereaved. This realism requires recognition of the fact that the person really has made no progress, is extremely unhappy, and might be helped by talking with a psychiatrist or psychologist or some other professional therapist who is informed about the procedures of grief therapy. The minister will, of course, continue on a regular basis to stay in touch with the bereaved, responding to their needs as best he or she can, including a continuing willingness to talk with them about their loss, to deal with the challenge to their faith in the midst of their grief, and to work with them on clarifying the meaning of faith to them at the present time.

Conclusion

The purpose of this chapter has been to highlight the pastor's opportunities not only to minister in the usual ways to people in their grief, but also to be alert to the first signs of unresolved grief and to be sensitive to the possibility that long-term unresolved grief may underlie the unhappiness and disturbed and disturbing behavior of people in the congregation and the larger community. If the early signs of potential pathological grief are responded to quickly and effectively, persons may be saved from years of chronic distress. If chronic pathological grief can be identified, we may be able to change the quality of our relationship with suffering persons and extend to them more effective pastoral care. In addition, they may become more receptive to our recommendations for referral to professional psychotherapists. By these means, we participate more fully in the movement toward wholeness in the lives of persons to whom Christ offers abundant life, and thereby assist in the building up of the Body of Christ.

CHAPTER TWELVE

Career Burnout Prevention Among Pastoral Counselors and Pastors

Charles L. Rassieur

If pastoral counselors are enliveners—enablers of life in all its fullness in others—our most important (and often most difficult) task is to learn how to stay as fully alive as possible! Aliveness is contagious! So is deadness![1]

The plan of this chapter is to begin with a consideration of the symptoms and the more salient causes of clergy stress and burnout, and then to lift up new areas of thought that promise to shed more light on this important topic. Finally, a framework will be discussed that will help pastors and counselors to assess their own strategies for coping with excessive stress and burnout.[2]

The Signs of Burnout

First, it must be said that the term *burnout* is not a technical term. It is a popular word that readily conveys the notion of the total exhaustion of available resources. In the diagnostic terms used by a psychologist or a psychiatrist, many cases of so-called burnout would be labeled as adjustment or affective disorders. However, many instances of mental and spiritual burnout in clergy may have very serious consequences but never fall into formal diagnostic categories.

Herbert J. Freudenberger says that the burnout syndrome may be identified by such enduring symptoms as feeling fatigued, being overcome with sadness, suffering health problems, losing one's sense of joy, being uninterested in sex, and withdrawing from social contacts.[3] Robert Wicks notes that counseling specialists may be exhibiting symptoms of burnout when they complain about their counselees: "Another group of cases today. The same old problems with new faces. I could care less."[4] Wicks correctly distinguishes between "daily burnout" and the more serious Level 2 burnout, which includes pervasive feelings of boredom, stagnation, apathy, and frustration. Level 3 burnout is very serious, and is usually indicated by chronic signs of physical and/or psychological illness.

Church professionals should be concerned when they recognize that feeling exhausted and run down is a continuing problem, perhaps accompanied by headaches or gastrointestinal disturbances. Undesired weight loss and sleeplessness or loss of appetite are often important warning signs. Approaching burnout may also be reflected by diminished resources for coping, quickness to irritation and anger, feeling helpless, or being more sensitive or suspicious of others' motives. Pastors and counselors can also be vulnerable to chemical abuse when the stress in their lives becomes unmanageable.[5]

Sources of Stress in Professional Ministry

The job description and basis of remuneration of a professional pastoral counselor, working in a counseling center, is usually quite different from that of a parish pastor. Likewise, lines of accountability and daily schedules can differ widely between pastors in the parish and those in a specialized counseling ministry. Despite these and other obvious differences in their ministries, pastoral counselors and parish clergy have much in common that predisposes them to extraordinary stress.

The Call

Most denominations emphasize the importance of their clergy's having some type of "call" from God to be ordained. The church also must recognize and affirm natural gifts for ministry in each candidate, but most ordaining bodies or judicatories look specifically for some indication from candidates that they are persuaded it is God's purpose or will for them to serve in professional ministry.

That inner sense of spiritual direction, compelling men and women to seek ordination, also motivates most clergy to be hard workers. For many pastors, whether in the parish or in a counseling center, that call is combined with much idealism about what they hope they can accomplish. Without such inspired idealism, pastoral counselors would not try to help so many very troubled people, and parish clergy would not try so hard to bring reconciliation and healing to troubled congregations. It is, however, just such idealistic enthusiasm that for many can also lead to stagnation, frustration, and apathy when they confront the disappointing realities of their work.[6] The call is essential for professional ministry and undergirds the motivation to do a job that is often discouraging and disheartening, but the call can also lead pastors to exhaustion and disillusionment when it becomes apparent they will not accomplish their dreams for their ministry.

Clergy Personality Characteristics

Of course, it is not accurate to claim that all clergy have the same type of personality. There are, however, certain personality characteristics typical of many clergy that can make counselors and pastors susceptible to stress and burnout. For example, most clergy are sensitive to their own feelings and the feelings of others. This characteristic helps pastors as they offer support in times of crisis. Sensitivity to the feelings of others also can help clergy to avoid some conflicts in the midst of tense circumstances. Yet, when this sensitivity is carried to an extreme, clergy can lose much of their own self-identity as they simply blend like chameleons into whatever others expect of them. Emotionally, such professional behavior can exact a very high price when pastors and counselors repeatedly discount and dismiss their own feelings in order to create the illusion of harmony.

Roy Oswald has noted other personality characteristics that can contribute to burnout.[7] For example, there are those who have rigid standards and high expectations for their personal performance, those who have a strong drive or need for continual achievement, and those who are hurried, impatient, easily angered, and unable to accept and live with compromise. Under a prolonged, high level of stress, clergy with such personality characteristics may show signs of burnout.

Like anyone else, clergy bring to their work a variety of unresolved conflicts from earlier developmental periods in their lives. It is not extraordinary that pastors may come from families in which there has been physical or sexual abuse, where alcohol or other chemicals have caused traumatic consequences, and where divorce has resulted in the break-up of the family. Indeed, these painful life experiences often enable pastors to understand and help others better. Those earlier years of brokenness in a pastor's life can nevertheless be the roots of behaviors or attitudes that add to stress in the present ministry. Conflicts with authority figures, compulsive work behaviors, and chronic mistrust or anxiety about people's motives can all have their beginnings in distressing experiences from a pastor's earlier years as a child and developing adolescent.

The Unstructured Work Routine

Parish pastors are basically the managers of their own time. They have to be present on Sunday mornings and at some meetings during the week; they have to appear at weddings and funerals. Most of the rest of the time they can come and go as they wish, which can be both a blessing and a curse. Lloyd Rediger has described such an open schedule as "treacherous," saying, "Sometimes it seems as though 25 hours a day, eight days a week would not be enough time to accomplish all that needs to be done."[8] The deceptive treachery of the unstructured work day can be exhausting for both the parish pastor and the counseling specialist. Effective time management is required in order to keep work demands within reasonable boundaries and the pastor's total life balanced.

The Failure to Negotiate Clear Work Objectives

Whether in a counseling center or in the parish, unclear work objectives heighten clergy anxiety and lead to unrealistic demands for performance. Many companies and firms have learned the importance of outlining clear work goals for employees, with specific objectives for measuring performance. Some clergy resist such a clearly negotiated outline of their responsibilities, saying they prefer the freedom to set their own priorities for ministry. However, failure to negotiate with one's supervisor or church council mutually agreed priorities for one's work can easily lead to role confusion and ambiguity about one's functioning. Moreover, clergy may be left open to criticism in all areas, which can easily lead to anxiety, tempting them to try to run in all directions at once.[9] On the other hand, a reasonable set of expectations and priorities understood by both pastor and lay leaders can ease the tension many clergy feel between their own self-image and the public image of what the pastor "should be."

Vocational Uncertainty

Professional ministry, whether in a parish or specialized context, has always been a risky matter. The risks for both parish pastors and counseling specialists include uncertainty regarding present and future job security. Experienced pastors know that the most promising relationship with a congregation can turn sour and end up in a conflict between pastor and parishioners within a year or two. Likewise, many talented pastors have not received the calls to the more challenging or affluent churches because of circumstances out of their control. Such seemingly unjust "breaks" can often lead one to wonder whether ministry is really worth the original excitement and idealism that accompanied the first awareness of a sense of call.

Counseling specialists often live with the uncertainties that accompany being part of a non-profit, church-related agency that frequently also competes in the secular mental health arena. Such church-related agencies may not receive the grants and gifts necessary for financial survival. Consequently, many pastoral counseling centers are continually faced with the threat of going out of business because of a lack of funding, and the counseling staff must live with the possibility of losing their jobs.

Most clergy, whether they serve in the parish or in a specialized ministry, are aware that seeking employment in the secular world, as an option in a vocational or financial crisis, can be difficult when one's primary education and experience are for professional ministry.

Social Isolation

Persons struggling with advanced stages of job-related depression or burnout consistently give the same response to the question, "How many friends do you have that you can talk to?" Their answer is predictably and sadly "None." This observation does not suggest that all persons who have only a few friends will automatically become burned out; yet, any helping professional with a limited friendship network is that much more vulnerable or susceptible to spiritual and mental fatigue and exhaustion.

Enlarging one's circle of friends is not usually an easy assignment for parish clergy or pastoral counselors. Commenting on a recent survey of over 1,200 pastors, William Hulme made this observation about clergy efforts to have collegial gatherings: "Too often they include the competitive spirit of our culture so that being guarded rather than open is the safest route with one's colleagues."[10] Hulme goes on to say that a healthy balance for ministry, which avoids social isolation, requires letting go of the inclination to try to be a perfect pastor: "The balance is restored as one gives up this drive that pressures one to be a professional 'loner,' and joins with the imperfect people of the extended family of the church."[11]

Although most clergy have a predisposition for functioning well without many close attachments to others, they still make themselves much more susceptible to emotional exhaustion when they do not cultivate and maintain vital and lively relationships that offer opportunities for nurture and support. Moreover, pastors and counseling specialists especially jeopardize their ministry when they permit their work to take the place of family or other caring relationships. The pastor who makes decisions for work that require the sacrificing of these relationships has made choices that can be devastating to both personal and professional health.

Handlers of the "Holy"

It is ironic that pastors who, in most cases, received their call to ministry through a particular worship experience or series of worship experiences should rarely have the opportunity to worship again. Instead, pastors are the priests who preside over the celebration of the rites and observances of a church. Consequently, what was at one time sacred or holy can easily become commonplace for the pastor or counselor. Then the mystery of the faith may lose its power, and pastors may miss the sense of spiritual vitality they had when they first began their theological training. Without a vibrant spiritual life, the pastor soon finds ministry to be too demanding for human resources alone. One can easily lose the necessary positive perspective for ministry when spiritual vitality has begun to wane. Hence, it is critical that pastors keep a sense of flexibility and creativity even as they search out new approaches that will keep them from becoming too familiar or even bored with the exciting mystery of God's presence in their lives.[12]

Promising New Insights for Understanding Clergy Stress

Pastors and counseling specialists may be helped by new findings and thinking that can shed fresh perspectives on the demands of professional ministry and the threats of disillusionment and burnout.

Stages of Professional Development

Thomas M. Skovholt, on the faculty of the University of Minnesota, and Michael H. Ronnestad of the University of Oslo, Norway, have interviewed one hundred practicing counselor/therapists at different stages of their professional careers. Skovholt and Ronnestad have hypothesized that counselors go through seven identifiable stages of development in their professional careers.[13] The stages begin with the untrained counselor, include the "seasoned" counselor, and end with the final stage of "integrity," which characterizes the counselor who has been practicing for at least twenty-five years. Research interviews revealed that anxiety, disillusionment, stagnation, and resignation are normal developmental concerns to be expected as counselors move through the progressive stages of their careers. For example, counselors with five or more years of experience may feel an emptiness because their work no longer challenges them as it once did. More experienced counselors must be careful of stagnation and resignation brought on by exhaustion and failure to grow intellectually.

This new research into the stages of professional development is valuable because it confirms that the potential for vocational burnout is present each step of the way along the career path. One can be overtaken at any stage of ministry with the meaninglessness or pointlessness of one's work. Recognizing the early signs of normative, developmental stresses, pastors can take timely steps toward the personal and professional growth that will effectively cope with the stress that might lead to burnout.[14]

The Differentiated Pastor in a Church Family System

Rabbi Edwin H. Friedman, in his book *Generation to Generation: Family Process in Church and Synagogue*, has brought the discipline of family therapy to the study of the several family systems that make up a congregation or synagogue.[15] He asserts that effective pastoral leadership is not a matter of charisma that forces one's views upon a resistant congregation, nor is it a consensus model in which the pastor blends with all the views of the membership. Both positions can create enormous stress for the pastor who either feels that all the work has been dumped in the pastor's lap, or who feels very frustrated because no decisions for movement or mission are emerging from the congregation. By contrast, Friedman contends for the well-differentiated pastor who defines clearly his or her personal views and perspectives *and* stays closely in touch with the church members. The result, according to Friedman, is not an avoidance of all stress as a pastor, but a reduction of the stress generated by a church that overly depends on the pastor for survival or functioning.

Friedman also challenges, from a family systems viewpoint, the conventional thinking that a burned-out pastor has brought on his or her own depression by a defect of character or a failure in pastoral leadership. Family theorists see families as organic entities with repeating histories, which systematically reproduce their problems from generation to generation. Thus Friedman asks, "What kind of congregational families are most likely to burn out their spiritual leaders? And how can clergy learn to function in such systems so that they are less likely to become the symptom-bearers for their congregations?"[16]

The Shame Response

Erik Erikson has characterized shame as an emotion associated with humiliation before others' eyes, of being completely exposed and self-conscious, like being stared at "with one's pants down."[17] Shame, and the powerful effect it has on the development of human personality, has been illuminated in two important books: *Shame: The Power of Caring* (Cambridge, Massachusetts: Shenkman Publishing Company, Inc., 1980), by Gershen Kaufman, and *Facing Shame: Families in Recovery* (New York, W. W. Norton & Company, 1986), by Merle A. Fossum and Marilyn J. Mason.

If unresolved shame and humiliation are a significant aspect of a pastor's background, the shame response will engender much troubling stress as the pastor tries to respond to normal parish and pastoral events. The shame response can make one especially sensitive to criticism or prompt one to assume excessive blame and responsibility for problems and crises that may arise in congregations. Moreover, shame-based persons easily become overly involved in others' emotional stresses. Such behavior is emotionally draining for the pastor or counseling specialist who assumes too much responsibility for the problems of the people who come for support and guidance.

The shame response can lead to excessive stress and burnout when a pastor is driven by the fear of exposure to "cover all the bases" through overwork. Perfectionism and workaholism, if examined closely, are often attempts to avoid the shame of being found to have human flaws and limitations.

A Framework for Preventing Burnout in Pastors and Counselors

A better understanding of the forces that drain enthusiasm and satisfaction can help a parish pastor or counseling specialist to avoid many of the professional pitfalls that can lead to burnout. However, there is a risk that clergy may unduly focus on the problems or negative aspects of their work instead of coping with stress by concentrating on the positive opportunities for growth and satisfaction in their ministry.

One significant correction for preoccupation with clergy problems can be found in the writings of Howard Clinebell and his emphasis on developing potential for personal and professional growth. Clinebell respects how growth can be blocked by problems or trauma occurring in the present or rooted in the past, and he has asserted that personal psychotherapy to deal with those personal obstacles to growth could be beneficial for every seminarian.[18] He persuasively calls for greater emphasis on the steps leading to the realization of the potential God has given to everyone. More specifically, Clinebell challenges pastors and counselors to focus on their own growth so they can more effectively encourage the growth of others: "As a counselor, the first and most important person for you to see through the growth-hope perspective is *yourself!* Only as you become aware of your rich potentials will you be able to see fully the potentials in others."[19]

Clinebell offers a six-point framework for achieving one's potential, an excellent approach for clergy to counter the draining stress that threatens their ministries with apathy and burnout. Basic to Clinebell's model is the necessity that each person choose to take responsibility and initiative for his or her own growth. Clinebell claims that the liberation for growth and development of potential can be found by enlivening one's mind, revitalizing one's body, renewing interpersonal relationships, finding a vital relationship to the biosphere, growing in relation to organizations and institutions, and continuing spiritual growth.[20] This hope-filled model offers the promise of an effective strategy for ending most cases of clergy and counselor burnout! Parish pastors and those in specialized ministries would do well to use Clinebell's framework for growth as a personal checklist to compare with their own strategies for coping with stress.

Enlivening One's Mind

Clinebell expands this first step to include inner growth for both intellectual and emotional development. To awaken new potential within this vital area of well-being and ministry, clergy should take such steps as:

1. *Experimenting with continuing education that draws on the five senses.* Use the action-reflection model of learning, which calls for immersion in a new life experience. Clinical Pastoral Education (C. P. E.) can provide a rich opportunity for discovering new professional potential. Likewise, educational seminars or workshops in the outdoor settings of camps or retreat centers can open vital new perspectives.

2. *Committing to opportunities for intellectual challenge.* Graduate studies have helped many pastors and counseling specialists to find renewal as they anticipate the next stage of career development for ministry. Informal study groups, whether organized around the lectionary or a specific book or topic, can also awaken a pastor from the intellectual inactivity that leads to boredom and stagnation.

3. *Seeking out other professionals for stimulating conversation.* A periodic lunch or breakfast with persons who have

experience and expertise beyond the church can open a pastor's mind to refreshing new horizons.

Revitalizing One's Body

The health and physical well-being of one's body is not an inexhaustible natural resource. One's capacity for coping with stress is linked to the vital and healthy functioning of one's body. Pastors can realize greater physical potential for coping with stress by:

1. *Monitoring and limiting the use of non-prescribed chemicals.* Some pastors have found that their decision to abstain totally from all or virtually all use of alcohol, tobacco, and caffeine has greatly increased their capacity for handling the pressures in their work.

2. *Following recognized health guidelines.* Eating sensibly and managing one's weight are directly related to effective stress management. Having sufficient, restful sleep is also essential to coping with stress.

3. *Getting sufficient exercise.* Following a minimal program for regular exercise is necessary if one wants to cope more effectively with the deadening feelings that lead to discouragement and burnout.

Renewing Interpersonal Relationships

It is in relationship with others that the potential of mind, body, and spirit finds full expression. Nurture, support, care, and love can open a wealth of potential for every human life, and especially for those who have devoted their lives to helping others. Certainly, interpersonal relationships can be filled with conflict and become painfully exhausting, but the pastor who cultivates close ties with caring and understanding persons will have a rich reservoir from which to draw for dealing with the stressful dimensions of ministry.

Pastors enhance and deepen those resources when they:

1. *Give family relationships the highest priority.* Work ordinarily requires more time in a week than family relationships do, but the married pastor who fails to turn to family members for companionship and nurture has lost a vital resource for growth and for dealing with the demands of ministry. Likewise, it is essential that single clergy have intimate and caring relationships to enrich their own lives.

2. *Seek friendships within and beyond their work setting.* Much has been said about pastors' being careful about having friends within the congregation. A pastor should never show favoritism, but such a concern does not preclude being friends with parishioners who are open and accepting of the pastor both as a professional and as a friend. Likewise, clergy in specialized ministries may count some of their colleagues among their closest friends. Friends with whom one may share some honest feelings can be an invaluable anchor for coping with life's uncertainties. Invariably, clergy who continue to find deep satisfaction in their work have trustworthy friends who invite them to be honest, open, and authentic.

Finding a Vital Relationship to the Biosphere

Human potential for coping with stress is greatly enhanced by adoption of a broader vision that includes the natural world God has created. Modern culture has taught humans that nature is to be exploited and that all other forms of life on this planet hold little intrinsic value except for food or for profit. To the contrary, awareness of the rest of the world, especially the realm of nature, builds resources for coping with stress. Individual problems and crises usually shrink in comparison with the natural world. Effective stress management might well include:

1. *Sitting in the backyard for twenty minutes.* With eyes closed, listen carefully to all the sounds of nature and feel the sun's warming rays and the breeze blowing.

2. *Taking a nature walk and observing the meaningful patterns of behavior in the flight of birds, the graceful rhythms of swimming ducks, and the scampering of a squirrel.* Bring a naturalist along who can introduce you to the deeper mysteries of God's world of plants and animals. It is virtually impossible to feel overstressed when immersed in the beauty of earth and nature.

Growing in Relation to Organization and Institutions

Every person belongs to a multitude of social systems, many of them overlapping. One's family is the most immediate social system, and beyond the family are systems of local and national government. All clergy participate in the ecclesiastical structures and systems of their denominations. Every professional national organization is a particular institutional system, as are local mental health and non-profit agency systems and the institutional structures for funding mental health and church-related counseling centers.

Stress management is enhanced as one gains confidence to participate in and even to change the important systems in one's life. Failure to take an active part in institutional structures can lead to hopelessness and a loss of empowerment. One is left very vulnerable to being overwhelmed and feeling that what one might have to offer would not matter anyway. Steps for growth, and more effective stress management, in this area could include:

1. *Taking an active instead of a reactive response to church structures.* The stress of frustration and anger in many members of the clergy often has its roots in the reactive response of their complaining about what others are doing to them in the church or its judicatories. The active response chooses to participate, to serve on committees, and to voice concerns on important issues. The active response is the best

means for countering cynicism and disillusionment with institutional failings and injustices.

2. *Making a commitment of effort or money to a national or international institutional cause.* By adopting a worldwide or national perspective on problems that affect all human beings, one is more likely to see one's own problems as manageable. Pastors need to remind themselves that they live in a worldwide community, and that through the social systems and organizations that touch them they can reach out and somehow help not only themselves but also others to deal creatively with burdening and life-threatening stresses.

Continuing Spiritual Growth

Development toward greater human potential is stifled until spiritual growth restores hope for the future and courage and imagination for living in the present. Few pastors will be overwhelmed with stress and burnout if they seek fresh approaches to recognize and cultivate the presence of God's grace in their own lives. A person wanting to take positive steps for growth in spiritual resources should consider:

1. *Experiencing new forms of worship and spirituality.* Pastors can use continuing education time to explore the worship and spiritual directions of other denominations and spiritual traditions. For example, a Protestant pastor may find it refreshing to make a prayer retreat in a Roman Catholic setting.

2. *Seeking a spiritual mentor or guide.* The Protestant tradition has not encouraged the practice of having a spiritual advisor with whom one may discuss and explore spiritual experiences. Having such a resource for spiritual direction can enrich one's potential for growth in the face of crisis or personal distress.

The Final Key

Clinebell underscores the urgency facing church professionals when he asserts that clergy, themselves, must be liberated if they are to be liberators of the human spirit for God.[21] Important liberators for clergy are judicatory leaders, and valued liberators for young pastors and seminarians are senior supervising pastors and seminary teachers. Moreover, the boards of directors and administrative directors of counseling centers influence greatly the pastoral counselors who serve in their centers. When those role models and authority figures begin sending clearer and more consistent messages to seminarians, pastors, and counselors that self-care is responsible stewardship for ministry, then the church will be served by fewer and fewer tired and disheartened clergy. All clergy can have more hope-filled ministries with greater potential for helping the people they serve. Anything less than that should not be an acceptable goal for the church and its ministry.[22]

CHAPTER THIRTEEN

Marriage and Family Counseling

Harold T. Kriesel

The evolution of the horse from Eohippus was not a one sided adjustment to life on the grassy plains. Surely the grassy plains themselves were evolved pari passu with the evolution of the teeth and hooves of the horses and other ungulates.

Turf was the evolving response of the vegetation to the evolution of the horse. It is the CONTEXT which evolves. (Gregory Bateson, *Steps to an Ecology of the Mind*)

The nature of evolution in every discipline is characterized by periods of continuous development interspersed with discontinuous quantum leaps that push knowledge to heretofore unimagined heights. Recent developments in systems approaches to marital and family therapy since Howard Clinebell's *Basic Types of Pastoral Care and Counseling* represent such a quantum leap in knowledge. Although Clinebell described the family as a social organism in his 1984 edition of *Basic Types*, he did not describe recent discoveries regarding how systems operate and the profound implications of these discoveries for the entire discipline of psychotherapy today.[1] What Howard Clinebell did do for pastoral counseling was similar to what Harry Stack Sullivan did for the discipline of psychiatry—namely, give it an

273

interpersonal and growth-oriented context rather than an intrapsychic and pathology-oriented context. The specialty of pastoral counseling and the ministry in general owe Howard Clinebell a debt of gratitude for that.

A Systems Model

Every era has its own models of reality that arise out of its own needs and technology and through which it both perceives and organizes the world around it. The ancient Hebrews lived in an environment where tribal survival was critical to individual existence. Thus their theology was heavily oriented toward the community rather than the individual. Our early Christian creeds reflect the world view of the Greek culture out of which they were born. Freud's view of reality, embodied in the sexual energies that could drive human behavior, emerged at the same time as the advent of hydraulic systems that could push pistons.

Today, on the other hand, many of our industrial centers (at least in the United States) are rusting and run-down, while high tech computer-related industries flourish. The advent of computers and information producing and retrieval systems has given us a new sensitivity to the realities of interaction and interdependence in ways we could not imagine only a few years ago. We live in a world of ROM and RAM, of monitors and modems, of parallel ports and printers that many of our elementary age children understand even better than we do. Thus it is natural for us to think of life in terms of interdependent systems rather than single causes and effects. As we progress in our ability to understand the intricacies of the environment in which we live, our models encompass more and more of reality and become ever more sophisticated.

This is especially true of systems thinking, since it has its early origins in recent developments in mathematics and physics. For instance, research in fluid dynamics has shown that systems actually reorganize themselves as they get farther and farther away from equilibrium (for example, as water approaches the boiling point, the molecules reorganize themselves into hexagons).[2] Or a systems perspective views reality in terms of active processes rather than thing-like objects.[3] Many scientists now think that only where one has a small number of subjects and tiny uncomplex systems is a Newtonian, analytical, linear (cause and effect) approach (such as that found in traditional psychotherapy) at all appropriate.[4] Persons, families, and communities are too complex for linear thinking. No longer can we envision behavior in terms of single, historical causes mediated by intrapsychic activity, resulting in individual characteristics and unchanging personalities. Rather, as Bateson says (in the quotation at the beginning of this chapter), the *context,* or the *system(s),* in which the individual is functioning is what is important. Engel has given us one of the clearest conceptual models of just what a systems model of reality encompasses, as he has illustrated it in Figure 1 below.

As one can see from this figure, reality, from a systems point of view, consists of a hierarchy of systems ranging from subatomic particles at the bottom and moving up through larger and larger systems, through persons, families, and communities. The point of this is that every level of organization is nested within a larger system of which it is a part. For those of us in the church, the model would keep going on from the biosphere to at some point include God.

This brings us to another systems concept, called *circularity,* which is critical to understanding systems. The principle of circularity can perhaps best be understood by referring to the biological systems that make up the human body. For instance, the heart, lungs, and blood vessels are interdependent parts of the cardiovascular system. Each part of this system is connected to and influences and is influenced by every other part; no part operates independently. We may

Figure 1

Hierarchy of Natural Systems*
(Levels of Organization)

BIOSPHERE

↕

SOCIETY NATION

↕

CULTURE-SUBCULTURE

↕

COMMUNITY

↕

FAMILY

↕

TWO-PERSON

↕

PERSON
(experience & behavior)

↕

NERVOUS SYSTEM

↕

ORGANS/ORGANS SYSTEMS

↕

TISSUES

↕

CELLS

↕

ORGANELLES

↕

MOLECULES

↕

ATOMS

↕

SUBATOMIC PARTICLES

*From "The Clinical Application of the Biopsychosocial Model," by G. L. Engel. Copyright © 1980 *The American Journal of Psychiatry*. Used by permission.

think of our hearts beating as an isolated event. In reality, however, each part of our bodies influences our heartbeat, and vice versa. A diseased lung will cause changes in heart function, which will cause changes in lung function, which will cause changes in another part of the cardiovascular system, and so on. The reality of how systems function is circular in nature rather than linear. Disease in one part of the system affects and is affected by every other part of the system. Likewise, treatment that heals one part of the system may also affect another part of the system (sometimes negatively), as with chemotherapy in the case of cancer. Circularity means that, especially as systems become more complex, we can no longer think in terms of a beginning and an end. There is no place where disease or health begins, but only processes that go back and forth and affect each other simultaneously and constantly.

As simple as these two basic systems concepts of context and circularity seem, we are not accustomed to applying them to social groups, such as families and communities. We still tend to think of human problems as belonging to the individual and that there are single root causes for particular behaviors.

Family Systems Approaches

Family therapists, however, beginning in the early 1950s, began to examine social systems to determine whether they exhibited characteristics similar to the natural world. Could human behavior be understood in terms of context and circularity instead of the reductionistic and linear models that dominated psychology and psychiatry up until that time?

Structural Family Therapy

Because of this background in biological and natural sciences, many of the early family systems pioneers came from a medical background. One of the most influential early family therapists, Salvador Minuchin, was trained as a psychiatrist before he became director of the Philadelphia Child Guidance Clinic and developed what has become known today as the Structural Family Therapy approach. Minuchin worked with urban slum families, and later with psychosomatic families, trying to discover how they operated as systems and what maintained and changed their behaviors. Minuchin came to believe that the structure and corresponding set of rules that governs each family system and reflects the relative power of each family member determines how well a family functions within its environment.[5] For instance, if the mother's efforts to discipline a misbehaving child are rendered ineffectual by the father's constant public criticizing and covert undermining of the mother's efforts, the probability that the child will become a behavior problem is increased. In this case, the child's ability to exert power inappropriately in the family is strengthened by a weakened parental hierarchy. At the same time, the child may be reinforcing the father's criticism of the mother. The circular nature of family interaction, along with the importance of appropriate power in the family, can thus be seen.

Minuchin also looked at families in terms of how close or distant they were (enmeshed or disengaged) and in terms of how flexible or rigid the boundaries were between sub-groups within the family and between the family and its environment. For instance, a family that was overly enmeshed might have difficulty in letting go of children in late adolescence/early adulthood. Signs of this kind of family dysfunction might appear in the form of psychosomatic illness in children or parents, or in various kinds of behavioral or emotional problems in the children.[6] On the other hand, a disengaged family might not be able to provide the emotional nourishment necessary for children to become capable of being close to others their own age. Minuchin also believes that certain types of family organization predispose persons in that family toward psychosomatic illness, delinquency, and other problems. Therefore, the goal of therapy with families is, many times, to change the power structure, the family system, which will in turn change individual behaviors.

Family Communication

Other early contributors to family systems therapy included an interdisciplinary group, based in Palo Alto, California, called the Mental Research Institute (MRI). The MRI included Don Jackson, Gregory Bateson, Virginia Satir, and others. Beginning with research into the interactional aspects of schizophrenia, this group gradually began to focus on how family communication affected such varied things as ulcerative colitis, asthma, and school performance in children. Out of this work, they developed and enlarged the concepts of family homeostasis, the "double bind" hypothesis, and circular causality.

Family homeostasis refers to that tendency in the family to maintain its balance at a current level so that it is not destroyed (similar to maintaining a balance of sugar and insulin in the bloodstream). Problems arise, however, when the system needs to change (for example, when it is time for children to leave home), but the family system tries to maintain homeostasis at a previous level.

The *"double bind" hypothesis* refers to a situation in which someone is in an ongoing relationship and the other person in that relationship says, in effect, "Do not do so and so, or I will punish you," and at the same time says, "If you do not do that thing, I will punish you." In addition, the person is forbidden to leave or to comment on his or her predicament. For example, a father slaps his child for crying while telling the child that he is doing it because he loves him or her. The Palo Alto group thought that repetitive double bind situations created the environment for dysfunctional behavior.

Circular causality refers, as was previously described, to the fact that family systems tend to act in recursive rather than linear ways. In other words, rather than A causing B causing C, A influences B, which influences A, which influences C, which influences B, and so on. Behaviors in the family are related to other behaviors so that the focus for therapy becomes the system itself.[7]

The Family Life Cycle

Jay Haley, another pioneer in the family systems field, developed what he called a "strategic" approach to family therapy. Haley based his approach on "the normal family life cycle," as shown below.

At each stage of this family life cycle, family members enter and exit the family systems in various ways, upsetting the family homeostasis and precipitating an emotional crisis. At each stage of the cycle, families are required to make major developmental changes. If they do not, they become "stuck," or even regress to earlier stages.

Using this normal or typical life cycle as a criterion for what ought to be occurring at different stages of family life, Haley began to view human problems and human dysfunctions of all types as occasions where people were "stuck" at a particular stage in the cycle after they should have moved on to the next. Therapy, then, consists of helping families to get "unstuck" and to move on to the next appropriate stage for them.[8]

An example of this was this writer's work with a thirty-year-old woman whose father had died when she was seven years old. The death was sudden and she, her father's favorite, did not get to talk with him, say goodbye, or grieve at the funeral since she was not allowed to attend. Her presenting problem in counseling centered around her inability to commit to an adult relationship with a man. As therapy progressed she began to realize that she had never said goodbye to her father and was thus not ready to say

THE STAGES OF THE FAMILY LIFE CYCLE*

Family Life Cycle Stage	Emotional Process of Transition: Key Principles	Second Order Changes in Family Status Required to Proceed Developmentally
1. Between Families: The Unattached Young Adult	Accepting parent offspring separation	a. Differentiation of self in relation to family of origin b. Development of intimate peer relationships c. Establishment of self in work
2. The Joining of Families Through Marriage: The Newly Married Couple	Commitment to new system	a. Formation of marital system b. Realignment of relationships with extended families and friends to include spouse
3. The Family With Young Children	Accepting new members into the system	a. Adjusting marital system to make space for child(ren) b. Taking on parenting roles c. Realignment of relationships with extended family to include parenting and grandparenting roles
4. The Family With Adolescents	Increasing flexibility of family boundaries to include children's independence	a. Shifting of parent child relationships to permit adolescent to move in and out of system b. Refocus on mid life marital and career issues c. Beginning shift toward concerns for older generation
5. Launching Children and Moving On	Accepting a multitude of exits from and entries into the family system	a. Renegotiation of marital system as a dyad b. Development of adult to adult relationships between grown children and their parents c. Realignment of relationships to include in laws and grandchildren d. Dealing with disabilities and death of parents (grandparents)
6. The Family in Later Life	Accepting the shifting of generational roles	a. Maintaining own and/or couple functioning and interests in face of physiological decline, exploration of new familial and social options b. Support for a more central role for middle generation c. Making room in the system for the wisdom and experience of the elderly, supporting the older generation without overfunctioning for them d. Dealing with loss of spouse, siblings and other peers and preparation for own death. Life review and integration.

*From Betty Carter and Monica McGoldrick, *The Family Life Cycle: A Framework for Family Therapy.* Copyright © 1980 by Allyn and Bacon. Reprinted by permission.

"hello" to any man now. In therapy she progressed from the small girl, who hadn't said goodbye, to a grown woman ready to move into the appropriate stage in her life cycle.

Another important concept in Strategic Family Therapy that is also found in Structural and other systems approaches is that of triangling (one instance of how circularity works in families). Haley, along with Bowen and many other family therapists, noted that many, if not most, child and adolescent problems consist of a family structure that contains an overly involved parent-child dyad (a cross-generational coalition) and another parent who seems peripheral. From this basic structure, Haley went on to discover that when a child displays behavioral problems of any kind, most of the time it can be assumed that at least two adults are triangled into the problem. Furthermore, it is also usually the case that the child is both a participant and a vehicle for dysfunctional communication between the adults in the family. Therefore, as noted above, problems cannot be understood apart from the *context* in which they occur. A child's behavioral problem cannot be understood apart from the function that it serves within the family and/or larger system.

Although there are many other schools of family therapy, such as Bowen's family-of-origin approach and the Milan group, the approaches described here will provide a substantive beginning in the study of family systems counseling. Minuchin provides an excellent introduction in thinking about the structure of the family system. The MRI group focuses on the effects of communication styles within the family. Haley et al. stress the importance of understanding the normal family life cycle, along with various strategies for getting families "unstuck."

Implicit in each of these three approaches are two basic assumptions about systems. First, to understand any system, we must first understand the context(s) within which it functions. For the family, that means that we must understand its structure, its place in the life cycle, and its communication patterns. Second, we must understand how structure, life cycle, and communication interact in a recursive, or reciprocal, way within the family we are counseling. Consider the following example.

A thirty-five-year-old woman was referred to me by her physician because she had declared that God had told her to stop taking insulin for her diabetes, so she had stopped two days before. Upon inquiring, I learned that she had had to end her career as a practical nurse several years before and since that time had devoted herself to raising her son and daughter. Her husband had left the family a year before, and since that time, her daughter had become her confidante. The daughter did not seem to mind having to take days off from high school to care for her mother, since she had never done well in school. The mother came from a very religious home where the Lord's guidance was sought for every aspect of daily life. At the same time, it was common in the mother's family of origin to ascribe one's own wishes to God and to communicate them indirectly to others in this way. The son had left home six months previously to enter the armed services. The daughter had gone out with a boy for the first time a week ago, and, on returning home, had gotten into an intense argument with the mother over where she had been and what she had done.

It is clear here that the appropriate parent-child boundary between mother and daughter was weakened by both the mother's illness and the father's departure. The mother was overenmeshed with the daughter, who for her own reasons did not mind staying home from school to care for the mother. Communication within the family was indirect and relied on a spurious religious framework for validation of personal feelings. Life cycle stage also affected the situation in that the daughter had reached an age where she had begun dating, with all of the parental separation anxieties that accompany that process. In addition, the mother's physical illness provided a context for the entire situation by changing her identity from successful professional to disabled patient.

Treatment for the mother consisted of intensive crisis therapy, involving herself and both children. Religious issues were put into a family context, life cycle issues were explained to the children, and new roles were envisioned for the mother that would replace the declining parental responsibilities from which she gained much self-esteem. Insulin injections resumed! This case illustrates how a family systems approach that takes into account family structure, life cycle issues, and communication patterns can quickly solve what appear to be intractable human problems.

At the same time, this example also shows that a family systems approach to psychotherapy is not primarily a modality that is appropriate for some situations but not others; rather, it is at its core an ontology (or *Weltanschauung*), a way of talking about how the world *is*. From this world view, every level of system can only be known in terms of its context, and every living system can only function in a circular manner if it is to remain a living system. The point of all of this is that only by focusing on the system from a non-deterministic (a contextual and circular) perspective can we hope to effect any change.[9]

Finally, a family systems approach also calls for the recognition that we are a part of every system with which we interact. As Gertrude Stein is reputed to have said, "There is no there, over there." When we are counseling with a family, what we are counseling is not a family system "over there" but a family system of which we have become a part.

Implications for Pastoral Care and Counseling

Although the implications of a family systems approach for pastoral care and counseling are many, I want to focus on what I believe to be the primary lesson that such an approach can teach us. It seems to me that the core truth of a systems approach is that we are all one with each other. We are all connected with the systems of which we are a part and are a part of us. It is our nature to effect and be affected by these systems in a non-deterministic way. James Lovelock has recently written a fascinating book describing what he calls "The gay hypothesis."[10] In this book, he presents a picture of the earth as literally being a living organism. He buttresses this point of view with a number of observations that suggest that the earth is actively engaged in regulating its own functioning. Indeed, it appears to be doing this in a way that attempts to counteract many of the ecological disasters that humankind is currently afflicting on it. Whether the earth can continue to do this in a way that is compatible with life as we know it is open to question. I believe that the point Lovelock makes—namely, that we are all one with and depend on each other as a living system—speaks to the heart of pastoral care and counseling as a function of the church's ministry.

Although in pastoral care and counseling our focus is primarily (although certainly not exclusively) on human interaction, a systems approach can give us a renewed sensitivity to and deeper understanding of our essential interconnectedness. Scott Peck, *The Different Drum: Community Making and Peace*, comments on our separateness and gives us a model for interconnectedness.

> In our culture of rugged individualism—in which we generally feel that we dare not be honest about ourselves, even with the person in the pew next to us—we bandy around the word "community." . . . If we are going to use the word meaningfully we must restrict it to a group of individuals who have learned how to communicate honestly with each other, whose relationships go deeper than their masks of composure, and who have developed some significant commitment to "rejoice together, mourn together," and to "delight in each other, make other's conditions our own."[11]

Peck's description of community gives us as pastoral counselors the "heart" for which a systems model is the form. The purpose of dealing with context and circularity in structural, communication, and strategic formats is so that we may build communities that respect both individuation and interdependence in a healthy balance. Systems approaches provide us with a vehicle that we can use to move toward true community. Systems approaches can also be used as guidelines for healthy community, whether that takes its form within the family or within other social groupings.

For most of us who do pastoral care and counseling, people come to us in the midst of a crisis of one kind or another. That crisis almost always makes them open to forming a quick community (system) of sorts with us. Because we are part of a larger worshiping community, we, of all caregivers, want to make sure that people recognize their community (system) with us as being temporary. As responsible caregivers, we want to orient people back into the more permanent systems of family and church and other communities of which they are a part. Because of our commitment to and participation in our worshiping communities (systems), pastoral counselors are natural systems therapists.

Systems approaches to family therapy lead us back to one of the basic tenets of our faith: the importance of connectedness. Although systems approaches may represent a quantum leap in terms of the discipline of psychotherapy, they only recall the living prayer that we are as lovers and friends of this world. Sallie McFague has said it most eloquently in her book *Models of God: Theology for a Nuclear Age*:

> If the world, the cosmos, is our point of contact with God, THE place where we join God to work on a project of mutual importance—the well-being of the body for which we have been given special responsibility—then it is here that we find God, become aware of God. This means that we look at the world, all parts and aspects of it, differently: it is the body of

God, and hence we revere it, find it special and precious, not as God but as the way God has chosen to be visible, available, to us. . . . It is not then mere earth or dead matter; it is "consecrated," formally dedicated to a divine purpose. We do not know in all ways or even in many ways what this purpose is, but the world is not OURS to manipulate for OUR purposes. If we see it as God's body, the way God is present to us, we will indeed know we tread on sacred ground.[12]

As systems pastoral therapists, we are part of God's consecrated world, working within all of its levels of systems and in all of its blessedly redundant circularity.

CHAPTER FOURTEEN

Marriage in the Second Half of Life

Robert W. Wohlfort

At the time of our crossing over into the second half of life, we have a story to tell, and we have a story to create. The story is not a collection of anecdotes about life, but a creative tale of what being alive this long has meant. When there are two to reminisce and to create, recollection and anticipation are compounded in their diversity, complexity, excitement, grief, foreboding, and hope.

This chapter concerns the telling of the marital story of the past and the creating of the marital story of the future. All of us have a past, and we have an anticipated future. It is crucial to pause to remember and to create. If we do not, we will die—perhaps not a physical death (although some may wish for it) but our souls and our spirits will simply be echoes of an unreflected past, captured by the resignation of moving ahead into stagnant sameness. An empty resignation will emerge, and the present marriage will be jettisoned with no understanding of what occurred or what could have been created.

Telling a story is an art that can be learned, honed, practiced, and lived. It is an art that comes more easily to us who are older because we are becoming more keenly aware that we are closer to death than to birth; we have a different perspective on creating, making, building, and on the unchangeable. History, art, poetry, literature, and music are increasingly our intimates. We are the older generation, and our calling becomes one of caring for what we have helped to build and strengthening our wisdom to continue to be effective citizens of our part of creation.

The Second Half of Life

Only in part is the second half of life measured by the clock and by the years. More important, the second half is a time of opportunity and a time of threat that is not marked by age and calendar but by circumstance, development, decision, and "where" the persons are. A married couple, both of whom are age forty-five, with two adolescent children at home is quite similar to a wife and husband, age fifty-three and fifty-five, with two adolescent children at home. For my purposes, I wish to de-focus chronology and highlight development. I will play down *chronos*, or calendar time, and highlight *kairos*, or opportunity time, proper time, right time, spiritual time, mythological time, and, in eschatological terms, the endtime. *Chronos* is not to be ignored, but it will not be central.

Marriage in *kairos* is my focus. Within this focus I have made choices. My paradigm is the marriage that has included children, knowing that there are marriages that do not. My paradigm is the marriage that has existed in a first half and is now moving into a second, knowing that many marriages have not existed before the transition (although many of those men and women did have a prior union with another in the first half of their lives). My paradigm is the marriage of a woman and a man, knowing that there are long-term and successful homosexual unions that are entering the second half of life. Whatever the paradigm, the couple is faced with the same basic invitation to the future: to tell individual stories; to tell joint stories; and together, having shared more and more of their histories, to engage in creating the future.

Learning to Tell the Story

Telling the story is as old as civilization and is an essential dynamic in the sustenance of life. Before there was the written word of the Pentateuch, persons were chosen to be keepers of The Story, men and women who handed down The Story verbally from one generation to another. The Story of Yahweh was distinctive from the stories of other gods of the Middle East: how Yahweh brought creation into being; how he selected Sarah and Abraham; how the special relationship between Yahweh and Israel developed. The Story goes on and is preserved so that the generations that follow will be grounded in who they are and whose they are.

On Reformation Day, Lutherans tell the story of Martin Luther (as most Protestants do) to remind themselves of their tradition, their emphasis, and their focus as part of the Christian family. From time to time, Roman Catholics recollect the papacy of John XXIII and tell the story of his reform, of his person, of his convening the Second Vatican Council—thus reminding themselves of their tradition, their emphasis, and their focus.

Families who gather for reunions, holidays, and anniversaries tell family stories. For at least some family members, renewal of pride in the family occurs, and the family's values, beliefs, and styles are affirmed.

To *not* tell the story is to act as if an individual, a family, or a marriage has no history, is sufficient unto itself, and is responsible for creating all aspects of itself. No person, family, or couple is without context, roots, and memories, and no person, family, or couple can escape the impact of these roots, no matter how fervently they wish for that escape.

Storytelling is an art that we who are or will be part of a marriage in the second half of life will do well to learn. One of the best teachers in this skill is Erik Erikson, who has given to the world a rich and full life (at this writing he is in his ninth decade). Analyst, teacher, and clinician to youth and adults, his major contribution is his schema of eight stages of psychosocial development that span the life cycle.[1] For each period of a person's development, Erikson has posited a dynamic of the syntonic and the dystonic—vital "tasks" for infants, children, adolescents, young adults, and older persons to achieve. In each stage of life the person is "working" in the lively tension of competing dispositions that, when kept in a creative balance, help the person to develop an outlook on life that will serve as a building block for healthy living. For example, newborns are vitally involved in the area "of trust and a sense of mistrust: their balance, we claim, helps create the basis for the most essential overall outlook on life, namely, hope, which must be awakened by our primal, or maternal, caretaker(s)."[2]

For the purposes of this chapter, we move to the seventh and eighth stages of psychosocial development:

> We come to the adult reality in the world in which generativity within the cross generational setting of the technologies and cultures must "take care" of what is being procreated, produced, and created. This vital strength of *care* (as we have formulated it) is the widening concern for what has been generated by love, necessity, or accident; it overcomes the ambivalence arising with irreversible obligation. Thus care attends to the needs of all that has been generated.
>
> And then, indeed, we really come to the last stage, with which we are trying to deal, above all, in our attempts to reflect on and to learn from our present study. Will we be able to use and to confirm what in regard to the last stage we have formulated so far, although our formulations contain such high terms as *integrity* and *wisdom?* Integrity, we suggested, now is and must be the dominant syntonic disposition, in search of balance with an equally pervasive sense of despair. As for the final strength, wisdom, we have formulated it thus: *Wisdom* is detached concern with life itself, in the face of death itself. It

maintains and learns to convey the integrity of experience, in spite of the decline of bodily and mental functions.[3]

Generativity in tension with *stagnation* and its predominant strength of *care*; *integrity* in tension with *despair* and its predominant strength of *wisdom*—these are essential tools of telling and creating the story of marriage in the second half of life. The other essential tools are two traditional functions of pastoral care: reconciling and healing. The *reconciling* function seeks to reestablish broken relationships between persons and between persons and God. The *healing* function seeks to restore a debilitated person to a condition of wholeness on the assumption that his or her restoration achieves a new level of spiritual insight and welfare.[4] With these concepts of generativity-stagnation (care), integrity-despair (wisdom), reconciling, and healing as our tools, we seek to reflect on telling and creating the story of marriage in the second half of life.

Reconciliation and Marriage in the Second Half of Life

I believe that it is in the interaction of the dynamics of reconciliation and generativity-stagnation (care) that the most crucial step is taken in creating the story line for marriage in the second half of life. These ingredients, carefully and conscientiously blended together, create a critical mass that is both exciting and frightening and helps the couple to glimpse the future of their individual and future lives. What is seen may cause them to wince, but not to look portends a drift into stagnation, poor caring, and irreconciliation that could last for decades and/or cause separation and divorce, the reasons for which cannot be articulated. It must be acknowledged that to gaze through the lenses of reconciliation, generativity, and care can result in the dissolution of a long union. So be it! The unexamined, and thereby the stagnant, life is not vital life. Reconciliation is not limited to a marital union's remaining intact; a person can become more reconciled to his or her own self (and even to the other!) through the dissolution of a dysfunctional union.

Reconciliation: A Time to Remember

The first movement in reconciliation—the very first movement—is to remember. To remember is to begin to tell the story, which is the beginning of creating the story of an anticipated individual and marital future, or (perhaps) to begin to put the pieces in place so that, self-consciously, the marriage will not continue. In this treatment of remembering, I will consider the memories that wound and the memories that sustain.

I am indebted to Henri J. M. Nouwen, Dutch-born Roman Catholic priest, for the clarity of thought regarding our need to remember. In his book *The Living Reminder*, Nouwen writes of and quotes from Elie Wiesel, the holocaust survivor who has made us sensitive to the absolute necessity of remembering that "what is forgotten cannot be healed." Nouwen continues:

> In his many books about the holocaust, Elie Wiesel does not remind us of Auschwitz, Buchenwald, and Treblinka to torture our consciences with heightened guilt feelings, but to allow our memories to be healed and so to prevent an even worse disaster. . . . By cutting off our past we paralyze our future; forgetting the evil behind us we evoke the evil in front of us.[5]

Elie Wiesel is from the Hungarian town of Sighet. In 1944, all the Jews of this town were deported to the concentration camps, Wiesel and his family among them. After twenty years, Wiesel returned to Sighet and with anguish wrote: "I was not angry with the people of Sighet . . . for having driven out their neighbors of yesterday, nor for having denied them. If I was angry at all it was for having forgotten them. So quickly, so completely . . . Jews have been driven not only out of town but out of time as well."[6]

Wiesel cites a response that I encounter with some frequency in my work as a therapist, especially in my work with couples: the desire to forget or downplay unpleasant memories. There appears to be an intense need to obliterate the pains of the past and to live as if they had not occurred. Again, Nouwen is on target concerning this issue:

> But by not remembering them we allow the forgotten memories to become independent forces that can exert crippling effect on our functioning as human beings. When this happens, we become strangers to ourselves because we cut down our own history to a pleasant, comfortable size and try to make it conform to our own daydreams. Forgetting the past is like turning our most intimate teacher against us. By refusing to face our painful memories we miss the opportunity to change our hearts and grow mature in repentance.[7]

There can be no reconciliation without remembering—*not* for the purpose of fashioning and collecting ammunition but for realizing how we wound as well as how we have been wounded, which opens up the possibility (not the certainty) for healing. The longer we live the more there is to remember. The role of memories increases in our individual and marital existence. With time and with interaction, these memories become less and less factual and more dependent and interdependent on *how* they are recollected. "The events of our lives are probably less important than the form they take in the totality of our story."[8] Henri Nouwen's statement is crucial for the understanding and creation of the marital story. He continues: "Different people remember a similar illness, accident, success, or surprise in very different ways, and much of *their sense of self* [my italics] derives less from what happened than from how they remember what happened, how they have placed the past events into their own personal history.[9]

The work of healing the memories of wounds received and wounds inflicted is critical work. At best, when they reminisce about their individual and marital lives, the husband and the wife begin to gain a perspective of how much more alike they are than different, if—and this is a big if—they are able to listen to and respect their own and the other's recollection of the past. To be most reconciling, these recollections will not focus on their absolute historical accuracy but on how they are conveyers to one another of who each person is.

To be sure, there are times when the facts are of primary importance. Agreements and contracts are significant ingredients in marital life, but if too much emphasis is placed on what and who is correct, the marriage and the telling of its story fall into stagnation and degenerate into the dusty world of fact-finding at the sacrifice of vital living.

Sustaining Memories

Memories can be used as weapons and can thereby be employed for the purpose of wounding. Memories can help persons to endure and can thereby sustain them through a time that might otherwise appear hopeless. As a marital therapist, frequently I am struck by how difficult it is for a couple to bring to memory what could be sustaining remembrances. Often, it seems, the difficulty is the result of wounding memories, and to recall sustaining ("good") memories, emphasizes the pain even more. The whole of the marital story, both wounding and sustaining, must emerge. Critical as it is not to forget the pain, so it is also critical not to neglect those times that were satisfying. Granted, to recall those memories could increase the pain because of the stark contrast of the then and the now, but not to do so is to do violence to the whole of the story.

Not to recall the memories of sustenance is to create the illusion that this marital union never had its good times. Rarely is this perspective even close to being accurate. Instead, persons deny sustaining memories and attempt to avoid the grief of what has been lost over time. The task at hand is to be able to tell *all* of the story, including the parts that have been sustaining (life-giving) to each person and to the couple, despite the pain that might emerge.

Often, the couple can be assisted in the recollection of sustaining memories by directed storytelling; for example, by a deliberate and leisurely look at the family photo albums, including the wedding album. Family movies and videotapes can rekindle hope and excitement in the couple, hope being future expectation based on *realistic* present reality. The risk of directed storytelling is that grief and the anger over what has been lost may be so great as to impede the possibility of reconciliation.

When a marriage becomes troubled, it is difficult to recollect the times when marital dynamics and life were different. In being able to live back into those times, not for the purpose of trying to return to them but for the purpose of lifting out of them what was good for each person and for the couple, possibilities for future life emerge. What usually emerges are the dynamics of each life in lively and creative tension with the marital life.

Separate and Together

An essential art in being married is knowing how to be an individual in the union without being so individualized that the union is characterized by two persons living parallel and non-intersecting existences—and conversely, knowing how to be a vital couple without being so fused and enmeshed that the essential individuality of each person is lost.

Some couples are too close and need absence and distance

from each other so that there can be space for the nurturing aspects of sustaining memories to take hold and for individual life to flourish. If the two are always together, there is little opportunity for each to appreciate the uniqueness of the other and of himself or herself because there is no sustaining and separate other, only an "us." The adage "Absence makes the heart grow fonder" does have significance. Absence allows each person to have the opportunity to reflect on the other free of the everyday dealings that can obscure depth. In the quietness of absence, sustaining memories can emerge.

Some couples are too distant, so that what is developing is a rather solid set of individual lives that provides no joint arena for the infusion of sustaining memories. The distance may be a defense against the belief, or the reality, that there are too few memories of sustenance in this marriage. The closing of the distance could announce that there is shaky ground indeed for the creation of a vital union for the second half of life.

Memories and the Need for Professional Help

I have alluded to and even made implicit remarks about the fact that some couples may need a marital therapist to assist them into and through the transition of marriage in the second half of life. I wish to make this resource more explicit.

I have heard it said that in the course of a long-term marriage, the couple will have experienced six or seven "marriages." This is to say that a marital union is a dynamic enterprise that is called upon to be quite different at the various developmental times of life. The marriage of the couple without children is quite different from the same couple's parenting two middle-school aged children and one close to high school graduation, while being primary caregivers for one or more elderly parents.

More often than not, the couple that is the possessor of reasonable personal resources traverses the transitions from one "marriage" into another with relative ease. The resources of the extended family, of friends, and of the family community often are of great value in times of transition. Frequently, as a life boundary is crossed, the rituals of the communities of faith (confirmation, bar mitzvah, and the like) are occasions of sustenance and support for the family and for the marriage. But it is not always so. Assistance may be needed at any of the points of transition, and the preparation of the marriage for the second half of life is no exception. The issues of being generative and caring for what has been created present special challenges to the heart and soul of the man and the woman. Regrets over the past, missed opportunities that cannot be recovered, ambivalent feelings that the children are emerging into their own lives, and ache over what may be occurring in the lives of the offspring may require the aid of a counselor. Also, as the wife and the husband look into their personal and professional futures and anticipate life as a couple again (or perhaps for the first time for the couple that was pregnant when married), they may discover enough good reasons to call on the resources of a marital therapist to assist at this transition.

The time of transition into the second half of life can unmask individual dynamics, stresses, stressors, and emotional turmoil or illness. With so much occupying each mate in the first half of life, it is possible for individual dynamics to be ignored or overlooked. Fast-paced social and professional lives can be used as covers for alcoholism. The myriad of tasks and demands related to child care can mask chronic depression. A biologically based bi-polar illness, with its wild mood swings, may have received accommodation because there was so much to do. With the onset of life's second half and its call to review and to create, these and scores of other illnesses, stressors, and struggles may work their way to the surface. The help of a professional therapist could be life-giving.

Reconciliation and the Uniqueness of Each Marriage

Earlier, I described reconciliation as the pastoral care function that seeks to reestablish broken relationships between persons and between persons and God. Implicit in this function is the fact that any relationship between two persons, and the relationship between a person and his or her God, is special and is unique.

For a couple to reminisce and to join in creating their future, one important fact emerges: Each and every marriage is unique—despite all the general principles that exist; despite all the texts and marriage guides that have been published; despite all the moral, ethical, societal, and theological statements that have emerged regarding the nature of relationships. "Our everyday experience tells us that although there are many ways in which these [marital] relationships are like all others, there are significant ways in which they are special and different."[10] This statement by John Patton—a pastoral psychotherapist, writer, and teacher—alerts us to the specialness of each marital story. As each marriage and/or individual life extends in time, experience, and knowlege, that specialness increases. In a union that has endured for twenty-five years, it is easy to lose sight of this vital and generative truth. The wife may say: "I know what he is going to say before he opens his mouth." And the husband may say: "I can finish her sentence before she is half-way through it." Sometimes this kind of interaction is regarded as "cute," but I regard it as dangerous because it carries with it the notion that the partners know everything they need to or will ever know about each other (stagnation!).

To enter the second half of life is to enter that time of life when dreaming and planning about a very different kind of life and living are possible. For most couples, obligations recede. Each person is in the position to contribute dreams for the future. For these dreams to have the chance to be a vital component of that future, they need to be received in a hospitable manner by the partner. Henri Nouwen puts this thought well when he states:

> Someone who is filled with ideas, concepts, opinions and convictions cannot be a good host. There is no inner space to listen, no openess to discover the gift of the other. It is not difficult to see how those "who know it all" can kill a conversation and prevent an interchange of ideas. Poverty of mind as a spiritual attitude is a growing willingness to recognize the incomprehensibility of the mystery of life. The more mature we become the more we will be able to give up our inclination to grasp, catch and comprehend the fullness of life and the more we will be ready to let life enter into us.[11]

To be stagnant with the other is to be in broken-relatedness. Reconciliation is needed if vitality (generativity) is to return or be born. An important movement in the reconciling process is the claim that while millions of marriages and millions of marital stories may be told and written, "*Our* memories, *our* history, *our* future, *you* and *I* are unique. We have lived many years and have created much. . . . but I do *not* know all about you and you do *not* know all about me!"

This affirmation must be a personal marital credo in order for the couple to create a generative and vital future union. This affirmation recognizes the mysteries of the self and the other and gives recognition to the separateness of the husband and the wife in the midst of their togetherness.

Healing and Marriage in the Second Half of Life

Clebsch and Jaekle tell us that "the healing function seeks to help a debilitated person be restored to a condition of wholeness on the assumption that the restoration achieves a new level of spiritual insight and welfare."[12] I believe it is eminently fair to speak of healing in a marriage as the restoration of the union, which restoration is at a new level of spiritual, emotional, and relational welfare.

The concepts of generativity, integrity, and healing are dynamically complementary. But

> the intimacy which is the essential quality of marriage can only be described irrationally. . . . [Marriage] also precipitates creativity, and not just biologically, but in a general sense, and it does this by disturbing the homeostasis, by disrupting the individual's organization, his solidity, his quieting down. It is more difficult to burn out at 25 if you suddenly find yourself a mate, and you settle into a permanent battle as to who's going to do what to who with whose gun.[13]

Frieda and Charles

These reflections on healing and irrationality bring to my mind a vignette from the life of my aunt and uncle: Frieda and Charles. The absolute facts of this event are lost, but the essence of this irrational interaction are preserved for the family. Frieda and Charles died many years ago. The vitality and irrationality of their living confirms why, despite the passing of the decades, they have grown in importance to me.

One evening, well into the second half of their individual and marital lives, they began to argue. Words escalated, and when words were not enough, Frieda smashed her dinner plate on the edge of the table. (She did not throw it at her husband!) Charles's reponse was to break his plate in a similar fashion. She broke her coffee cup; he broke his. She made shards of her saucer, and he followed suit. The irrationality escalated until all the china on the table and in the cupboard was scattered about the dining room floor, not a piece unbroken. Exhausted and with nothing more to say or destroy, they began to laugh—deep laughter from the depths of their individual and marital souls (I can hear them now)—and their union grew in strength, spirit, depth, integrity, and wisdom.

I do not recommend destruction of property; yet, there is a vitality, a generativity, a caring, an integrity, and a wisdom encased in the whole of this story that is worthy of our consideration. It is fascinating to me that this vignette from their marital life has made its way into the ethos of our family culture. This fact is not surprising if we allow ourselves to expand our vision of a marriage beyond that of a legal, public, private, and social arrangement. If we allow ourselves to embrace the spiritual and mythical dimensions of the marital union, then we will be incorporating into ourselves a dimension of marriage that, by definition, is a healing definition: marriage at new levels of spiritual, emotional, and relational welfare.

Marriage as a Spiritual and Mythological Journey

The perspective of marriage as a spiritual and mythological journey is especially applicable to the creation of the marital story for the second half of life. Joseph Campbell—scholar, writer, and professor—describes marriage thus:

> There are two completely different stages of marriage. First is the youthful marriage following the wonderful impulse that nature has given us in the interplay of the sexes biologically in order to produce children. But there comes a time when the child graduates from the family and the couple is left. I've been amazed at the number of my friends who in their forties or fifties go apart. They have had a perfectly decent life together with the child, but they interpreted their union in terms of their relationship through the child. They did not interpret it in terms of their own personal relationship to each other.
> Marriage is a relationship. When you make the sacrifice in marriage, you're sacrificing not to each other but to the unity in a relationship. . . . You're no longer this one alone; your identity is in the relationship. Marriage is not a simple love affair, it's an ordeal, and the ordeal is the sacrifice of ego to a relationship in which two have become one.[14]

Joseph Campbell invites us to go beyond the rational enterprises of workshops and technique, beyond the private and social arrangement, and into the heart and soul and spirit of the union. Any venture into the heart and soul and spirit of the matter must be, in large measure, spoken of in images, in poetry, in metaphors, so that while we affirm the uniqueness and specialness of each marital history and creation, we are attuned to and comforted by our bond with the very fabric of all creation. For all its practicalities, our marital life is part of the great and dramatic mystery of all of Life. Joseph Campbell speaks:

> [Marriage is] not simply one's own thing, you see. It is, in a sense, doing one's own thing, but the one isn't just you, it's the two together as one. And that's a purely mythical image signifying the sacrifice of the visible for a transcendent good. This is something that becomes beautifully realized in the second stage of marriage . . . of the two experiencing that they are one. If they are still living as they were in the primary stage of marriage, they will go apart when their children leave.[15]

Alchemy

Alchemy is the medieval chemical "art" that sought to transmute the baser metals into gold and to discover the universal solvent and the elixir of life. This mythical concept is, not surprisingly, a part of Carl Jung's theoretical and therapeutic work. It is the stuff of love songs, ancient and modern; of poetry; of opera; and of literature. *Crossing to Safety,* by Wallace Stegner, is a novel about the long and beautiful friendship of Larry and Sally Morgan and Sid and Charity Lang. We follow their separate and intertwined life courses from their young adult lives at the University of Wisconsin into their older age in Vermont. The novel's dust cover reads, in part:

In a world where, as Stegner has said, the accident of a germ or the skewing of a gene can unmake lives, each of these very different people learns to live as a baby learns to walk: by collapse and recovery, injury, failure, despair, persistence, and most of all by the affectionate support of others. Each achieves a different safety by a different route. All of them owe their precarious, threatened foothold to the love of friends. Through the *alchemy* of friendship, what could have been a story of broken dreams and broken lives becomes a story of acceptance and affirmation.[16]

The alchemical image is not a reference to magic or illusion. Alchemy is healing, a process to move the relationship to new levels of spiritual, emotional, and relational welfare. It is the mythological chemical art of generativity and integration (to use our Eriksonian paradigm) that seeks ever-expanding dimensions of caring and wisdom. And when we know that generativity is in tension with stagnation, that integrity is in tension with despair, then we not only tolerate "collapse . . . recovery, injury," but we also understand them to be essential parts of the human condition and essential components of our individual and marital stories.

The Context of the Marital Journey

I hope that what I have written so far has brought some clarity to the nature of marriage, particularly to the marital union in the second half of life. Perhaps it is becoming self-evident why some marriages reconcile and undergo healing and some do not. As I come to the conclusion of this chapter, I want to explore, briefly, one more area of marital life: the context in which present-day American marriages exist. I have written of marriage as a spiritual and mythological journey against the backgrounds of remembering, reconciling, healing, and the telling and creating of the story. Each marital journey is taken at a particular point in time, and it is my contention that the particular historical context of each marriage profoundly influences the process and the outcome of each union.

This chapter was written toward the end of the 1980s, a time when there was much emphasis on individual fulfillment and a time when America was badly suffering from damage to its idealism and identity in the wake of twenty-five years of national trauma: the assassinations of President John F. Kennedy, Malcom X, Martin Luther King, Jr., Robert Kennedy; the long, costly, bitter, and divisive war in Vietnam; the scandal of Watergate and the resignation of President Richard Nixon; the Iran-Contra scandal; a large and mounting national debt; an alarming increase in drug abuse; an escalation in the number of homeless persons in one of the world's most affluent nations; and the spectre of nuclear annihilation. Responding to the atmosphere of America at this time in our history, Clebsch and Jaekle wrote in the preface of their revised edition of *Pastoral Care in Historical Perspective*:

> Today clients in swelling numbers seek therapy not because they feel bad but because *they do not feel good*. The helper, to be sure, may uncover hurt beneath or besides aimlessness, or pain hidden in ennui, but the contemporary client is ready for more than cure, more than recovery of a status quo ante. We today suffer from lack of spiritual "weight" and purpose for our lives, and we would gladly embrace hurting if to do so brought meaning and significance. We quest not for restoration but uplift—literally, "relevance"; we thirst not for knowledge but for wisdom; we hunger not for adjustment but for fulfillment.[17]

A vital marriage, by definition, is a union hungering for fulfillment (generativity, integrity, care, and wisdom). Our present national context does not enhance this fulfillment. Our national marital, and individual, purposes tend to be narcissistic and violent in nature, and this narcissism and violence mitigate against successful relationships, against seeing others as persons in their own right. Our voracious appetite for instant gratification is at war with the complexities of the time needed to create viable relationships. Fulfillment has a chance to flower when the relationship has a "heart"—the hearts of the wife and of the husband. (Again we are in the domain of the mythological.) Joseph Campbell said: "The heart is the organ of opening up to somebody else. That's the human quality as opposed to the animal qualities which have to do with self-interest."[18] It is difficult to open up in an atmosphere of self-absorption, instant gratification, and violence. It is no accident that the Tin Man of *The Wizard of Oz* is an enduring character as he seeks to receive a heart. He is functional and likeable, but his sleek, cold, stiff, hollow body is a striking metaphor of what is missing in all the lands of Oz.

In the 1960s, many Americans had the heart to give themselves "to America" and to the civil rights movement, only to have their hearts deeply wounded, even broken, by the deaths of their leaders and the trauma of having their devotion betrayed by war and scandal. To repeat myself, I am calling attention to the American scene because the context in which we take our marital journeys affects individual and relational lives. I have attended conferences on family life that alert therapists to the underlying anxieties families have about the nuclear holocaust. This anxiety state is especially apparent in our children. Our lives, our spirits, and our hearts are not at rest and available when our context is so disturbed. Howard Clinebell, in whose honor this book is written, has done much to sensitize the pastoral care movement to this contextual issue. His passion for personal and interpersonal wholeness and his vision brought into being Pastoral Counselors for Social Responsibility, a network of pastoral care specialists seeking to bring an end to the nuclear weapons build-up that threatens the future of our planet and the atmosphere in which persons can have and give their hearts.

It takes courage to have and to give the heart because when the heart is given, say in a marriage, there is under the best of circumstances (mythologically speaking) the realization that:

> The true marriage is the marriage that springs from the recognition of identity in the other, and the physical union is simply the sacrament in which that is confirmed. It doesn't start the other way around, with the physical interest that then becomes spiritualized. It starts from the spiritual impact of love-Amor.[19]

Our present American scene is not a supportive context for Joseph Campbell's profound sense of marital love and commitment. Under ideal circumstances, by the time a marriage enters into the second stage, the second half, its heart and the hearts of the individuals involved are subject to extreme exposure and vulnerability. Some will realize, perhaps beyond any doubt, that their marriage never was a deep spiritual union. Some marriages will be able to recover or create the spiritual dimension through hard work, which might include therapy. Other partners will have kept the mythological, irrational, and spiritual components at the forefront of their living. We live in less than ideal and supportive times, and this stress must be taken into account as we tell our stories and create our futures.

The task of reminiscing will strengthen or weaken the hearts of the couple and, ideally, bring them to reconciliation that will bring them closer. Remembering will shed light on a less than vital union but could assist the partners in agreeing to continue because they prefer such living to being alone and, perhaps, assist them in creating a measure of the mythological core. Reconciliation, as I have discussed it here, can enable a husband and a wife to divorce because they now know why their individual and marital vitality is so low. Healing and generativity and integrity and caring and wisdom come in many forms.

I Need You

Frequently, when it is apparent that a marriage is good, vital, dynamic, and generative, there is the recognition of the complementariness of the partners. Given what has been written in this chapter, this complementariness may well be expressed through the vulnerable witness of "I need you!" This is not the need of a person as one half of a circle seeking the other half in a mate, but the need discovered through an enduring union in which each partner has a keener sense not only of his or her weak points, blind spots, and underdeveloped areas, but more important, of how the one has led the other into depths, heights, awarenesses, and mysteries that would have remained undiscovered. There is an increased sense of being alive in a marriage of generativity and integrity. Such an aliveness is neither automatic, easy-to-come-by, or even possible for every couple joined in marriage. Conversely, this vitality is not an impossible dream available only to the select few who are privy to the secret code to the mysteries of the universe.

By telling its story, the couple seeks:

to incorporate what has been generated in life (as well as what has become stagnant) and to care for what has been created by love, necessity, or accident;

to integrate their individual and the marital life experiences without slipping into despair about their time together;

to take the recollection of their individual and marital lives and move toward reestablishing their bond with each other (reconciliation); and to move their relationship to new levels of spiritual, emotional, and relational well being (healing).

Each of us has stories to tell, and each couple has stories to tell. These stories exist whether they are expressed or not. To paraphrase an earlier quotation from Henri Nouwen: In refusing to engage in telling our stories in their fullness, we turn our most intimate teachers against us. If we participate in this betrayal, we drastically reduce our opportunities for reconciliation, healing, and vitality.

CHAPTER FIFTEEN

Sexuality and Pastoral Care

Carolyn J. Stahl Bohler

To become whole persons, we need to accept and celebrate our sexuality. Our striving to be whole provides a positive model for parishioners, even as their attempts at expressing wholeness encourage us. Ministers and priests have in the past often been seen as persons who sacrificed or denied their own sexuality, but ministers today see that we are called to be aware that we are sexual beings who pastor sexual persons. This chapter deals in a practical way with the person and task of the minister. We will reflect on sexuality as a dimension of our lives and inevitably as an element in our pastoral care.

A father who is a parishioner comes to the minister and asks, somewhat casually, but very seriously, "Pastor, how should I teach sex to my children?" If the pastor is squeamish about sex, he or she may not hear the question, may even slough it off with a joke, "You're asking me?" There may be quite a concern in that family, but the pastor has closed the door to care.

At a college youth meeting, a young woman asks her minister, "How do I say no to my boyfriend, if I am not ready yet to have sex?" The minister is being asked a real question, one that the woman has probably rehearsed ten times in anticipation of the meeting, to say it just right. If the minister gets flustered, becomes embarrassed, or changes the subject to how different men and women are, she or he is avoiding not only the topic of sexuality, but the young woman who is trying to be responsible.

If we have faced, explored, expressed, and questioned our own sexuality, then we will certainly feel the concern that this father and this young woman have and be able to respond out of knowledgeable empathy. Moreover, if we reflect on and accept our own sexuality, we will be more integrated persons ourselves. We may enjoy life more—or face the difficulties of life more. Certainly, our spouses and close friends will benefit from the healthy integration of sexuality into our lives. Vulnerability is a strength, not a weakness, for both men and women.[1] We do not need, nor can we expect, to have these matters resolved completely, but we do need to face sexuality in ourselves and in others. I recognize my questioning and vulnerability, even as I expect the reader to question and to wrestle.

One of the very human qualities of the people we find in the Bible is their sexuality. They wrestled, as we do, with all the ambiguities entailed in sexual relations. When we preach, we do not need to skip over passages that involve sexual expressions in the Bible; we can see the people as people—human, like us. Yet, we also need to remember that the Bible *describes*; it does not always *prescribe*. We encounter Sarah, asking her husband to have a child by Hagar. This describes Sarah's actions and Abraham's response. We do not need to say that their decisions in their day prescribe our behavior today. We can see that they wrestled with hard issues, and we do, too. Five relevant themes emerge from our biblical tradition.

Creation

The first theme is a doctrine of the Judeo-Christian tradition that needs to be grasped not only intellectually but also, and especially, at a feeling level: *Creation is good; the Word became and becomes flesh—that is, incarnation continues.*

"And the Word was made flesh, and dwelt among us" (John 1:14*a* KJV). People throughout Christian history have had a hard time believing this radical claim that *their* bodies are important and very good.[2] God not only *was* present in Jesus the Christ, but God *is* present in each of us. Incarnation continues.

Our bodies are blessed and touched and breathed into by God. We are said to be made in the image of God, as male and female. Our relationship with the deity is even described at times using bodily, relational metaphors, as when God speaks as a woman carrying Israel in her womb and nursing her (Isa. 46:3-4; 49:15).

The Bible includes a "symphony of love" in which a woman says about her lover, "O that you would kiss me with the kisses of your mouth!" (Song of Sol. 1:2 RSV). Her yearnings are realized, "O that his left hand were under my head, and his right hand embraced me!" (2:6 RSV). She implores the daughters of Jerusalem to let love happen according to its own rhythm:

> I adjure you, O daughters of
>   Jerusalem,
>   by the gazelles or the hinds of the
>   field,
> that you stir not up nor awaken
>   love
>   until it please.
> (Song of Sol. 2:7 RSV)

Our bodies are the temple of the Holy Spirit, as Paul said to the people at Corinth (I Cor. 6:19-20). Clearly, sexuality is a part of God's pleasure as well as our joy in being God's creatures, but so many Christians, including pastors, fear that pleasure, particularly bodily pleasure, is wrong.

The primary reason in Christianity for an attitude opposed to pleasure is what James Nelson describes as a misinterpretation of the centrality of the cross. We see the cross and think of it as exalting pain, suffering, or crucifixion. Nelson, however, prefers the theology of Matthew Fox, who suggests that the purpose of the cross is to show that there can be an end to all crucifixions and the ushering in of a new age of shalom.[3]

Parallel to this exaltation of suffering is a focus on serving others at the expense of ourselves. When we pose relationships in either-or frameworks, we arrive at the bizarre conclusion that *either* we care for others, *or* we care for ourselves. We think we must choose between the two alternatives, but in reality they are bound together. When we consider the pleasure of lovemaking or the bodily joys of hugging our children and friends, or the physical closeness of breast-feeding, we see that most of the genuine enjoyment of our bodies is in relation to another. Our satisfaction is simultaneously a deep caring and a giving to the other. Our stinginess regarding pleasure robs those around us as much as ourselves.

Still another reason for our ambivalence regarding sexual pleasure is the fact that in its heterosexual expression, men and women are required to be intimate and vulnerable with each other. For some couples, radical honesty in an intimate relation with the other sex is overwhelming. They need religious taboos to help them to avoid their own existential fears.

Each of us experiences the created goodness to some degree and wrestles in some way to accept the legitimacy of pleasure and the joy of being physical bodies. No one avoids this wrestling, and no one is able to completely dismiss this joy.

I well remember the positive understanding of our bodies and sex that our teacher inadvertently shared with a few of the girls in my junior high Sunday school class. We were walking through the church parking lot when she mentioned that she was enjoying menopause, that she was free from worrying about becoming pregnant and able to enjoy sex much more.

What a crucial set of affirmations she made in that comment: People over fifty enjoy sex; people can enjoy sex in a long-term marriage relationship; menopause is natural and fine, even potentially enjoyable; and our bodily experience of aging has some good qualities. She told us girls these things just as we were beginning to have our menstrual periods. The entire childbearing years separated us in age, but a huge bond of sisterhood united us in the quest for an affirmation of our bodies and our sexuality.

I have counseled various people who had difficulty accepting the goodness of their bodies. One man who was very eager to marry typified persons whose religion and sexuality interfere with each other. He was in his thirties, quite responsible and faithful, given to much reflection on his relationship with God. After several sessions, I asked him whether he masturbated. He told me that he did not, that he perceived masturbation to be too self-oriented, just for his own pleasure. I asked this question because he seemed extremely frustrated sexually. This frustration was getting in the way of his being natural and comfortable with women. He had told me that he had not had intercourse with a woman, that he wanted to, but only if he were married. It dawned on me that he might not be allowing himself any sexual pleasure until he married. If I had denied the aspect of sexuality in the counseling discussion, I would have helped him to perpetuate his very problem. Pastoral counselors should look for what Gestalt therapists call "holes" in a personality—aspects that are denied or not experienced. Whatever is missing needs to be named.

We were made as sexual beings, and God called that good. Many of us want to be very responsible in sexual relationships. It is not always easy to find the right person with whom to express our sexuality. In the meantime, to give ourselves pleasure may be one way that we can affirm our gift of sexuality while giving us time to gain perspective in our relationships.

Single people *can* be whole. We must grasp the fact if we are going to counsel single people effectively. Intimacy with others and a healthy integration of sexuality into our lives can be achieved by those who choose to be single and celibate. Celibacy does not mean a denial of sexuality; yet, celibacy will not be the norm for all responsible single adults.[4]

Think of ways you experience your body as good. Think of ways you enjoy pleasure and sexual expression now. Think of ways you wrestle to experience the goodness of your body, its sexuality, and its potential for pleasure. Think of people to whom you minister who may be wrestling experientially with this doctrine.

Fall

The second sexually relevant theme evident in our faith tradition is *There was and is a "fall" into existence. That existence, in contrast to pure essence, is inevitably messy and imperfect.*

Consider a cake recipe on a three-by-five card. Imagine the cake. Do you see a perfect image? Unfortunately, however, it does not exist. Now, if you gather the ingredients, follow the directions exactly, and make the cake, you will have something good to eat, but it is not perfect. It cannot be perfect—it sags a bit here, is a little too dry, or a little too sweet.

If you are not accustomed to baking cakes, you might think about buying a toy, then following the directions while looking at the perfectly built one on the box. Those stickers we put on the bicycle Christmas Eve are never spaced quite as perfectly as the one on the box, but our children cannot play with the picture on the box—they need a bicycle that exists.

Paul Tillich described the Fall as a "fall" into existence. As pure essence, pure possibility, things can be perfect. When we bring something into existence, we lose perfection. That, for me, is a very humble and encouraging view of the Fall. We are not bad, inherently evil in some way, but we *do* exist; therefore, we are not perfect. This is not the end of things, however, for we can grow. Paul Tillich spoke of our growing until we take on what he called New Being, which is taking on Jesus the Christ.

In order to grow, we must have more knowledge—of facts, of feelings, of God, of others. In the myth, Eve and Adam began without knowledge and with no self-reflection. Then began their search for discernment, freedom, understanding, consciousness; they sought knowledge, especially the knowledge of what separated good from evil. Mythically, we can exist with abstract perfection, but when consciousness dawns, we humans become self-conscious and, therefore, imperfect. Their quest for knowledge brought Eve and Adam into existence as persons, and their existence required of them a continued quest for knowledge and growth.

We suggest in many areas of life that it is better to know more—more about foods so that we can eat more healthfully; more about our neighbors in order to interact better; more about politics in order to participate wisely. Granted, we cannot learn all there is to know, but we realize that it is good, not harmful, to gather knowledge.

Yet, in sexual matters there is often a peculiar shift of opinion. People sometimes think that it is better *not* to know, or better for younger people not to know about sex. For example, Gary Bauer, Undersecretary of Education and Chairperson of a White House task force on the American family during the Reagan administration, was quoted as saying that his group's goal was "to tell children [that premarital sex] is wrong and explain why it's bad for them—not to teach them so much about sex that they can engage in it in early adolescence."[5]

Why do people hold this anti-knowledge position? Perhaps because they think that if a person does not know about sex, she or he will not have sexual intercourse or explore sexually.

But statistics concerning attitudes of teenagers prove otherwise. The less knowledge they have, the more trouble people get into with sex. Here our first guideline is connected with the second. A positive attitude toward sex leads people to get facts and, therefore, to reduce irresponsible sexual behavior and its consequences. Studies have shown that young women who have negative attitudes toward sex are much less inclined to get adequate knowledge regarding effective birth control, yet do engage in sexual intercourse at times and are then at greatest risk of pregnancy, disease, and abuse. The higher the denial of one's sexuality the more likely one is to get into trouble in sexual matters.[6]

It is clear that the safest, most responsible behavior results when men and women are able to affirm that they are sexual beings and are able to decide whether, when, and how to express their sexuality out of knowledge and equality between the partners in the relationship. Rather than fearing that anyone could have too much knowledge or knowledge too soon, we need to fear naïveté and inequality among teenagers or among pastoral counselors and clients. Knowledge and equality are the greatest insurance for thoughtful, responsible behavior.

The need for knowledge regarding sexuality is crucial whether that sexuality be expressed heterosexually or homosexually. The more one knows about homosexuality, the more responsible one can be in one's own sexual expression. Up to now people seem to have considered sex education optional. The consequences have been venereal disease, which is often remedied by antibiotics. Now, more of us grasp the fact that we cannot choose not to educate. Life is possibly at stake. Unfortunately, the heterosexual community is quite capable of denying the possibility of acquiring AIDS. We pastors must have knowledge ourselves; we must share that knowledge with both youth and adults.

Connected with the imperative to know, to learn, and to teach as soon as possible—not when we finally feel comfortable with it—is the need to have realistic moral standards for sexual conduct. It is fine to have idealistic norms, but these norms are useless if they are portrayed as laws to be obeyed by all. We need to trust others, and ourselves, to develop realistic guidelines for conduct that are actually followed. Our idealistic norms differ, even in the same denomination, but our realistic guidelines reveal even greater divergence. We need to stay in dialogue, to hear and to accept one another, even as we challenge one another.

The norm of fidelity in marriage is not merely idealistic, but it is a realistic guideline. Honesty and commitment are given and expected as a couple enters into marriage as a covenant. Fidelity becomes more realistic the more each person in the marriage experiences herself or himself as a whole person, with vulnerabilities, longings, needs, and uncertainties, and the more each shares that struggle toward wholeness thoughtfully and courageously. This is derived from a variety of sources. Clearly the Bible has ample guidance for covenants in loving relationships. Also, practitioners of psychotherapy have shown me that people who can trust each other with honesty and commitment will be able to mature in their relationship. I admit that I intuitively want this value in my own marriage. I know it is important to my husband myself, so my own needs and values help to make this relevant and realistic for me.

I can share this guideline with a couple I am counseling, but I need to grasp that it may not be realistic for them at this moment. Part of my therapeutic strategy may be to work to empathize with their frames of reference. Because my value is so strong, I may seek ways to introduce the relevancy of the guideline of fidelity. If, however, I am more intent on getting them to accept the "guideline" than on working with their resistance to doing that, I may fail both to evangelize the couple and to join therapeutically with them enough to make a difference in their pattern of relationship.

We ministers need to provide guidance, but it cannot be merely in the form of idealistic norms. If we say, "Do not have sexual intercourse before you marry," to a couple we are counseling in premarital sessions, we are for the most part opting ourselves out of providing any guidance at all. Granted, there will be some people for whom this is a realistic, cherished guideline. Others may "obey." Others will marry sooner than they really should (given their psychological and spiritual maturity) in order to "obey." Most will simply be left to find their own guidance. They will look to their peers, who may well pressure them to become sexually active before they are prepared, educationally or psychologically.

We need to lift up for the couple who plan to marry the right to say no and yes in informed ways, not intimidated by others. We need to lift up facts about how they can share with each other sexually, without having intercourse. We need to discuss birth control and AIDS prevention. If we present only the idealistic guideline of no sex, we may persuade ourselves that we can ignore these crucial topics.

Male ministers have a special responsibility to discuss sexuality because fathers avoid sex education more than mothers do. Yet, males "have a great deal of influence on couples' contraceptive behavior."[7] Males need to communicate their values and their moral struggles.

Ignorance of facts about sexuality is widespread, even among middle-aged adults. A couple in their early forties, one of whom was a member of the clergy, thought that they should have sexual intercourse every night, that this was expected of married couples. When they discovered (while they were preparing to teach a program for college students) that couples vary immensely in their frequency of intercourse, they were set free to have realistic expectations for their own marriage.

Knowledge of the counseling process and the dynamics

possible between the client and the counselor is crucial in pastoral care. In my helping ministry as a pastor, chaplain, and professor, I have been asked on more than one occasion by both women and men to become involved with them sexually. Several times I was surprised, angry, and disappointed. I was embarrassed that I had not seen any clues to the other's desires and that the other could so misuse my desire to help. When I anticipated the other's desires and was able to deal with that in a healthy way as a part of the counseling process, even then a part of me wanted to deny what was happening.

Many pastors, male and female, have had similar experiences.[8] How we handle these situations will affect our own lives and those of the others involved, as well as the reputation of our entire profession. We need both knowledge and internal freedom to handle these situations responsibly. We need to grasp the enormous authority invested in us as *the minister*. We need to know how important it is to be genuinely human with another, to be clear in our values, and to know that people survive our "no." We also need to know how to refer people to other counselors when that is wise. Finally, we need to have such a clear experience of equality between women and men that we do not consider the "other sex" either more fragile than our own or more powerful than our own.

Colleagues with whom I shared these ideas at a pastor's school reminded me that a typical reaction to such occurrences with parishioners—or colleagues—is for us to feel guilty. We tend to hide what occurred, sometimes from ourselves and almost always from other colleagues or denominational supervisors. We fear that we will be condemned immediately (and we may be, by unthinking colleagues). However much we learn from psychotherapists about listening skills or imagery or dialogue techniques, we are reluctant to hear from the psychotherapists that many forms of transference and projection do occur in therapeutic relationships.

We ministers need to challenge ourselves to see whether we

evoke sexual emotions from our clients, just as we need to check to see whether we evoke anger. People do become angry with us and are at times envious of us; they express gratitude to us; they hate us and are jealous of our power and authority; they care about and appreciate us. It is not surprising that at times they also fall in love with us. Yet, just as we can handle anger creatively without needing to absorb the anger as our responsibility, so also we can handle the sexual feelings without putting down the other, without taking responsibility for the other's feelings, and without experiencing those feelings as demands placed upon us.

We as ministers might become attracted to a person whom we are counseling. It is imperative that we recognize our moral responsibility not to confuse the professional relationship with our private emotional longings, for it is impossible to put aside the enormous authority invested in us by the other. We can never have "equal" power when we are functioning in our role as counselor. It is not wrong to have the feelings, but it is wrong to act upon them, and virtually always inappropriate to name them.

Think of knowledge that brought you some freedom at the same time it incurred in you a greater sense of responsibility. Think of how you have made realistic guidelines for yourself that you can and do follow. Think of how your pastoral care has helped others to find realistic guidelines.

Social Context

Biblical criticism shows us that stories and texts have to be understood within their setting. Likewise, *sexual expressions have meanings and consequences that can only be understood in their social contexts. These meanings and consequences vary over time, across cultures, and between genders.* We are wise to appreciate these meanings and their changes as we face our own sexuality and care for one another.

In the comic strip "Cathy," Cathy Guisewite shows the changes that can take place in the social meaning of sexual expression. As Cathy is getting dressed to go out on a date, she reflects: "I'm wearing the 'heirloom lace' of my grandmother's generation . . . with the conscience of my mother's generation . . . coping with the morals of my generation. . . . No matter what I do tonight, I'm going to offend myself."[9]

People like Cathy, her mother, and her grandmother are our parishioners. The assumptions we begin with cannot be the same for each generation. We fit into a generation; the cultural setting at the time we entered puberty and young adulthood greatly affects our outlook on sexual matters. What our experiences have been as a man or a woman can alter our capacity to empathize with certain situations. For example, a member of the clergy who married twenty years ago and longed to have a child, but could not, may need to work to transcend his experience to grasp the panic of a pregnant twenty-two-year-old woman who insists she must finish her schooling before having a child.

A young clergyperson may assume that rape victims see themselves as victims if this minister has a friend who was raped, has been in rape recovery groups, and speaks consistently of the event as an act of violence. Yet, there are many people who still blame the victim, and many women who were raped do wrestle, sometimes for years, with internalizing that blame. In order to care for a rape victim, the minister must listen to that person's experience. Keeping in mind that the Bible describes the lives of people in a very different time and culture, the minister could share the story of Tamar, a strong woman who did not assume a victimized identity, but was raped anyway and suffered the cultural consequences of her day (II Sam. 13).[10] Whatever the stories, the pastor should offer insights with compassion and empathy, not with the notion that this particular woman should behave or feel a certain way.

In 1963, there was serious concern for population growth; the pill was not yet available, abortion was illegal, and pregnant teenagers were generally not admitted into the regular high school programs. A pastor who counseled a pregnant teenager then would have had a different set of influences than she or he would today. Now, an array of birth control methods is legally available, but there are still various social and economic hindrances to obtaining them; AIDS can be acquired in one sexual encounter; abortion is legal but not always available; and parents are still unwilling to share information openly.

Pastoral care for teenagers depends on the context. We cannot pastor today the same as we did twenty-five years ago. The relativity of context is seen dramatically when we realize that a girl of fourteen in biblical times, or in some contemporary cultures other than our own, would probably already be betrothed or married. While stories across contexts may build bridges of empathy and bring a sense of relativity to solutions, actual answers must emerge from the fresh moment. One matter that is not relative is the need for speaking in a prophetic voice to the systems that perpetuate the abuse of teenaged girls.

The sizeable increase in the number of women pastoring churches has altered the counseling possibilities for both men and women. A parishioner can in many cases choose whether to go to male or female clergy to discuss an issue. Female and male colleagues on the same staff or in neighboring churches can work together to offer team counseling as well as feedback and peer supervision of their counseling.

In the past few decades, vasectomies have been much more common and have offered men a responsible way to take part in the prevention of pregnancy. Males are able to state clearly, by their own actions, when they do not want (more) children. If a man chooses not to have a vasectomy, he may be communicating either that he is not certain that he does not want to have more children or that he does not want his body affected by the decision.

Because pastoral care includes concern for the health of parishioners, medical factors—such as prevalent diseases and their treatment—alter the emphasis of counseling over time and in different geographic settings. Syphilis was a terrible disease until penicillin was discovered. There was a window of history during which sexually active people did not fear much disease, for venereal diseases were apparently curable. Now AIDS is here. The reasons for sexual behavior have altered, as disease is either dreaded or denied. Seldom did pastors deal with fear of disease a decade ago, but today people come to us, terrified of becoming involved sexually with anyone, no matter what precautions they take. We need to hear the fear, or the denial of fear, as we help people find realistic guidelines for themselves.

Denominations have the power to change meanings and consequences in the lives of clergy. It was not long ago that pastors were not allowed to continue their ministries if they divorced. Now, divorce is often the turning point that leads people to seminary. Today, a mere vote of a denomination's governing body can mean acceptability or rejection of gay and lesbian clergy's gifts and graces.

Within a decade, or even less, sexual meanings and consequences change. We cannot easily impose our meanings on others or expect that the consequences that exist for us will be the same for the next generation. We need to keep thinking and caring in context, whether that care is to understand and guide our own generation, our parent's generation, or our children's generation.

Think of important choices you have made in relation to your sexuality that were affected by the time and cultural circumstances in which you made the choices. Think of the meaning and consequences of your choices—and how they would be different in different decades or different economic classes, or if you were the opposite gender. Think about how your pastoral care was different a decade ago and imagine some differences ten years hence.

Forgiveness

The fourth theme echoing from our tradition is that *both forgiveness and transformation are possible at any age. This growth process is as available for matters regarding sexuality as it is for any other dimension of our lives.*

The recorded comments of Jesus about sexual matters are not many, but they are striking precisely because of their contrast with the prevailing spirit and practice of the time. Jesus insisted on the fundamental equality of the sexes and on the supreme importance of love and forgiveness in sexual matters as well as in every other area of life. To the people who asked Jesus what he thought they should do with the woman who was caught in adultery, he said, "Let him who is without sin among you be the first to throw a stone at her." When the crowd had dissipated, Jesus looked up and said to her, " 'Woman, where are they? Has no one condemned you?' She said, 'No one, Lord.' And Jesus said, 'Neither do I condemn you; go, and do not sin again' " (John 8:7-11 RSV). Jesus combined forgiveness with his expectation of transformation.

I heard a young person say that she thought she had to hurry up and have sex because adults don't like it and, after all, when one gets to be an adult, one is not desired for sex much anymore. Her expectations can be transformed if adults demonstrate that they are responsible, joyous sexual beings and that they find same-aged adults attractive. Unfortunately, this teenager's notions are reinforced in premarital and marriage counseling if the minister holds assumptions about the lack of meaningful sex over time for adults and the need to treasure sex when young.

Sometimes we become so focused on sexual expressions

outside of marriage that we forget that some married couples have difficulties sharing sexually with each other. When couples have challenges in their communication, it is often difficult for them to ask for help, but when the difficulties involve sexuality, the resistance to asking for help increases even more. Yet, forgiveness and transformation are possible for married couples at any age. Clergy can offer guidance, often by recommending a book (such as *The Gift of Sex: A Christian Guide to Sexual Fulfillment* by Clifford and Joyce Penner[11]), but we need also to be ready to make referrals to other professionals. It is as important to find responsible sex therapists, when that is needed, as it is to locate responsible lawyers.

We can be transformed even in how we go about talking about sexuality. When I went to an obstetrician during my first pregnancy, I was struck by the natural and calm way he spoke of sexual intercourse and all the anatomical parts of the body. I soon thereafter had to teach, for the first time, the sexuality segment of a course on marriage and family counseling. I recall standing before a mirror, saying, "Sexual intercourse," "vagina," "penis," practicing speaking of sexual matters. Students say I still blush at times when I mention sexual matters. I am a sexual person, with inhibitions and awkwardness as well as a desire to speak honestly and openly. I am still in a transformation process. Each of us is being transformed.

Even denominations can be transformed. Protestant denominations have subtly encouraged their clergy to marry, because single clergy are sometimes perceived to be threatening to individuals in churches. These denominations need to reconsider the impact that this pressure has on single clergy, so that clergy do not marry more to fit in to the system than to follow God's guidance to marry a particular person at a particular time. The United Methodist Church's General Conference statement (1984, 1988) for "celibacy in singleness" is a dramatic example of a church body's encouraging denial or distortion of sexuality and decisions regarding marriage. The more we hear individuals speak genuinely of their own struggles the more we as pastors will care for our institutions as well as for individuals, since systems affect the individuals within them.

Think of times when you experienced forgiveness or transformation in relation to being sexual. Consider whether there is anything for which you now want forgiveness or transformation. Reflect on how you might have been an agency of forgiveness and transformation for others, or how you could be now.

The Church

The final theme from our tradition is that *the church has a crucial role to play in teaching.* Others may need to "borrow" our authority for a while, to temporarily use our norms until they can find their own. They may need to see us facing our sexuality honestly in order to have permission to do that themselves.

Many denominations have excellent sex education materials. For example, The United Methodist Church has a training program for sex educators (who can be laypersons or clergy), but annual conferences vary in their use of this program. Abingdon Press provides books for graduated levels of reading to teach sex education in responsible ways.[12]

Many students in seminaries and colleagues in ministry tell me that they avoid visiting people in their homes because of their fear of sexual overtones in the visit. The publicity given to the sexual involvements of some TV preachers has fostered in some of these ministers a fear of actual or perceived involvement. It certainly is wise not to be naïve, but we can be creative—we can visit people at their work settings, for example. We can ask other laypersons to go with us on visits.

When I served a church, I asked my husband (who is a layperson) to go with me to visit a few male parishioners I had never met. I did consider how to maintain safety and carefulness, but it did not seem appropriate to avoid the visits altogether.

I recall preaching on the Eve and Adam passage one time during the four years I served that church. A young man who attended only that one day said he was not returning because "all that minister talks about is sex." Just as we can be misunderstood on any topic we discuss, so also we will be misunderstood by some when we discuss sexuality. That small number of misunderstandings should not deter us from seeking to integrate sexuality into our lives and our ministry.

Think of what your local church and denomination have done throughout your lifetime to teach responsible sexuality. Think of what you could do now.

Conclusion

Matters of sexuality touch on aspects of our theology—such as incarnation, revelation, grace, salvation, forgiveness, and confession. We are embodied people, so we have children, we touch, we have disease, we caress, we have intercourse, and we even abuse each other. Our embodiedness is a mixed blessing. Today we experience dire consequences when we use our bodies unwisely. Still, we cannot say that because the consequences are so dire we must deny our sexuality—we cannot deny any aspect of ourselves successfully. It is the imperative of ministers to do all we can to affirm our bodies and sexuality; yet to do that in a climate in which we and others will find viable norms that can really be followed. Our goal is to teach people to be self-knowing, to consider their partners equals with whom they can reflect and to seek to grasp God's guidance in their relationships. This discernment process holds the greatest hope for wise choices.

CHAPTER SIXTEEN

Pastoral Care in Recovery from Addiction

Robert H. Albers

Introductory Considerations

The Issues

Historically, the relationship between the religious community and the community of those recovering from addiction to mood-altering substances might be accurately described as ambivalent. On the one hand, as Conley and Sorensen have pointed out, the religious community has been at the forefront of providing compassionate concern to those afflicted with and affected by addiction.[1] On the other hand, there is ample evidence to substantiate the fact that the religious community has assumed and demonstrated a posture of moralistic condemnation and pious judgmentalism, devoid of understanding love.

Howard Clinebell, in his seminal work on alcoholism, delineated seven attitudinal perspectives assumed by the religious community with respect to the relationships between sin and those who suffer from addiction.[2] The spectrum ranges from regarding addiction as moral terpitude and evidence of the depth of human sin to compassionate concern toward those afflicted with a life-threatening illness.

The ambivalence in the religious community is exacerbated by the fact that the research done by the scientific community has failed to isolate a singular etiology. A variety of theories has been postulated, including the learning theory, the physio-pharmacological theory, the social-cultural theory, the personality profile theory, the psychoanalytic theory, and the moral-religious theory.[3] Each theorist has marshalled convincing evidence for the veracity of a given postulation, and approaches to addressing the issues have been developed that are concomitant with the particular presuppositions and assumptions of a given theory.

The multiplicity of theories and perspectives has prompted me to affirm that addiction to mood-altering substances is a multi-faceted life-style disorder that threatens the totality of a person's existence in body, mind, and spirit. It not only affects the individual's personal life but creates havoc in the person's social existence as well. Like the ripple effect of a stone thrown into a placid pond, addiction, with its concomitant effects, moves from the person afflicted to affect all of her or his significant relationships. Recovery implies not only freedom from the substance and its multiple implications for the addict, but also freedom for those significant others whose lives have been grasped and squeezed by the tentacles of this unrelenting and enslaving phenomenon. Addiction has been termed "the family disease" in the common parlance of professionals who seek to work in a creatively healing way with the family, significant others, and the individual. But understanding and healing must pervade the wider and larger social systems of human existence as well as the individual's circle of significant relationships. Among those larger systems that need to experience a metamorphosis in attitude, awareness, and action is the religious community.

An Interdisciplinary Approach for Growth Through Community

If addiction is viewed as affecting the totality of a person's physical, emotional, social, and spiritual life, then a holistic approach to recovery is critical. The scientific community and the religious community each have significant contributions to make, and it is imperative that they work in tandem for the sake of the individuals and their families who are in the recovery process. The component strands that comprise an individual and her or his social system become unraveled in the course of the addictive process and must be rewoven in a healthy and holistic manner. If such a possibility is to be realized, an interdisciplinary approach to dealing with addiction becomes the sine qua non.

Continued attention needs to be given to issues involving intervention and treatment as well as to preventive measures, but more is needed. Once the recovery process has been initiated through treatment or significant involvement in a recovery group, the individual and her or his family and significant others need a healthy milieu, or matrix, in which to develop and grow. In the addictive process growth and development are arrested for the individual afflicted as well as for significant others who are affected. Evidence to substantiate that reality has been cited by Howard Clinebell in his research delineating ten personality traits found in those addicted to alcohol.[4] Each of the traits indicates that growth has been truncated for the addict. Those near and dear to the addict experience similar deleterious effects when it comes to their personal development. In order to experience a healthy and meaningful life in recovery, those afflicted and affected by addiction require a nourishing and nurturing environment in which to grow.

A significant experience of community is the key that unlocks the door of isolation and estrangement and unleashes the potential for new and creative social and spiritual relationships. Twelve-step recovery groups—such as Alcoholics Anonymous, Alanon, Alateen, Adult Children of Alcoholics, Narcotics Anonymous, and forty or more other groups dealing with addictive and compulsive behavior—have provided the kind of environment wherein caring plus confrontation has resulted in significant growth.[5] It is important that the religious community support and supplement rather than attempt to supplant the efforts of such groups. These groups are friends, not foes, and intend to be complementary, not competitive, when it comes to healing and health. It behooves members of the religious community to understand the intention and purpose of recovery groups, just as it is important for members of recovery groups to accept and to understand the function of the religious community. Recovery groups enable people to deal with the dis-ease occasioned by addiction; the religious community has been established to deal with the dis-ease of alienation from God, other people, nature, and oneself. Both recovery groups and the religious community have as a principle concern the healing and health of people, and both appeal to the salutary nature of a holistic spirituality.

If the thesis is correct that the spiritual key to recovery from addiction is a significant experience of community, then the pastoral care provided for people in this process must be communal in nature. For the religious community, this means taking into account the theological foundations that anchor the faith community in its ministry.

Theological Foundations for Recovery Ministry

The Mandate to Minister to the Broken and Oppressed

Even a cursory overview of the Scriptures depicts God as one who reaches out to the troubled, the oppressed, the sick, and the enslaved in order to grant freedom and deliverance from their plight. The Exodus is seen as the significant salvific activity of God in the Old Testament, who in mercy delivered Israel from the physical, political, social, economic, and religious oppression of Pharaoh. The Christ event, in similar fashion, constitutes the heart and center of the New Testament proclamation. In Christ, God has decisively acted to redeem humankind from death, darkness, disease, and destruction.

Jesus viewed himself as inaugurating and implementing the kingdom, or reign, of God in a new way through his ministry. The evangelist Luke characterizes the essence and nature of this ministry by portraying Jesus as the fulfillment of the prophetic words of Isaiah. On the sabbath, Jesus read these words in the synagogue gathering:

> The Spirit of the Lord is upon me,
> because he has anointed me to
>   preach good news to the poor.
> He has sent me to proclaim release
>   to the captives
> and recovering of sight to the blind,
> to set at liberty those who are
>   oppressed,
> to proclaim the acceptable year of
>   the Lord.
> (Luke 4:18-19 RSV)

He closes the book and indicates that in his own person and ministry this prophecy is being fulfilled. He not only proclaims these words, but enacts them in his ministry of healing love to those crippled in body, mind, and spirit by debilitating diseases. He enjoins the disciples, and therefore the religious community, to demonstrate the reality of the kingdom of God in the world by engaging in outreach to the disenfranchised, the diseased, and the downtrodden, thereby emulating his own ministry.

People who are afflicted by addiction, and those around them who are affected by the same, understand fully the meaning of Jesus' words. Many lose possessions, property, and personal integrity when a mood-altering substance becomes their all-consuming passion. No price is too high to pay for the drug of choice, and no life sinks so low as a result of that insatiable need. Families, friendships, and fortunes dissolve as a consequence. Addicted persons experience and significant others observe the reality of bondage to a chemical substance. Release for those imprisoned in this life-style is imperative; yet, they are often blind to the reality of the situation and, because of their sense of shame, will vehemently deny that anything is wrong. An opening of the eyes of the blind to see with clarity what is transpiring is urgently needed. Individuals and families become stigmatized because of addiction and often experience oppression through ostracism, isolation, or intentional neglect.

There is ample biblical evidence to substantiate the fact that the religious community has a mandate to minister to the chemically dependent and their families. The dominical example and injunction is to reach out, touch, care for, and heal those who are sick and to facilitate their deliverance from the bondage that enslaves them. Because those persons and families caught in the throes of addiction are often incapable of reaching out for help, the task of the religious community is to reach out to them, to go to the highways and by-ways of life and if necessary compel them to come in so that they too may participate in the life God has intended for them. The religious community is motivated by the ethic of love, which is inclusive and does not have the luxury of choosing and selecting whom it will love.

The Centrality of Grace

Theologically, grace constitutes the foundation of the religious community's existence. Grace is acknowledging the fact that God has done for humankind what humans could not do for themselves. Grace informs the shape of proclamation and forms the basic matrix for ministry. Incorporated in a grace-oriented community are confession, absolution, forgiveness, reconciliation, and newness of life. These are critical issues for people and families who are in recovery. A word of grace is a clarion call to freedom.

Paul Tillich has defined and described the message of the faith community as "accepting the fact that you are accepted."[6] Perhaps more than any other word, *acceptance* is most critical in the vocabulary of those in recovery. Initially, there is the necessary acceptance and acknowledgment of one's condition as a person in need of recovery. It is imperative that the family likewise accept that reality and accept its own complicity in the process. There is need for the acceptance of assistance when it is offered. Often those offers of assistance and acceptance are spurned because the persons enmeshed in the addictive system are fearful that they will not be accepted if the truth is known about the situation. While they desire acceptance, they often derail attempts at being accepted because they are convinced of their own unacceptability.

A grace-informed pastoral care is one that is patient and persistent. It acknowledges the reality of the human condition. It recognizes that the hunger and thirst that cannot be assuaged by perishable materials require what is imperishable, what comes from God alone. As the afflicted and those affected by their addiction come to experience the reality of acceptance by others, they experience the powerfully liberating nature of God's grace for them. When grace as acceptance is proclaimed and implemented, the floodgates open, allowing the resentment, hostility, bitterness, suspicion, and rage to pour out. The love and mercy of God is then poured into life, and renewal occurs. Pastoral care in recovery recognizes that grace is neither quantified nor qualified by human determination, but is freely poured out upon all. The old life is surrendered, and the new life can be accepted as a gift.

The Message of Hope

Despair is the constant companion of those who are mired in the vicious cycle of addiction. Addicts have often imaged their experience as the dark night of the soul, as entering into an endless tunnel with no hope for light at the end. Many engage in valiant efforts to free themselves from their addictive cycle but find it impossible to do so. It is like being trapped in quicksand—the more they struggle to extricate themselves the more rapidly they sink into discouragement, depression, and despair. Family members or significant others have the same experience. Repeated efforts to be of help have been rejected, concern has been spurned, and periodic short-term abstinence creates only mirages of hope that quickly vanish into thin air as the one addicted reaches for the bottle, the pill, or the needle once again.

A message of hope is desperately needed for all who are involved in this experience. It is critically important in the provision of pastoral care that this not be a false hope that piously promises that all will be well. Rather, it must be a hope that is born out of struggle and out of the conviction that there is a power greater than ourselves, who can create order out of chaos and engender hope where there was only despair. Frequently, those who are in recovery recount the depth of despair experienced while in the bonds of their addiction. Self-destruction becomes an attractive option, for often the darkness of death appears paradoxically to be the only ray of light and hope, the only escape from the interminable darkness of addiction. Jürgen Moltmann's insistence that hope provides the basic foundation for human existence, meaning, and purpose finds an eager and expectant ear among those struggling to recover.[7]

Hope, like love, needs to be incarnated in the lives of those who are in recovery. Contact and sharing with others who have had similar experiences of struggle is of immense value. Hope springs eternal for those who do not have to walk alone, for those who realize that they are not unique, for those who know that another choice does exist. One recovering person stated that he had been a drunkie and junkie since his juvenile years and fully expected to die in that condition, never once giving thought to the fact that there was ever any hope for an existence apart from alcohol and drugs.

The Primacy of the Faith Community at Work

These fundamental theological affirmations must be more than pious platitudes uttered in a vacuum; they need to become incarnationally enfleshed in the faith community. As has already been suggested, the faith community reacts with ambivalence in the face of the phenomenon of addiction. If the faith community exists to express and experience love for God and for humankind, then certain steps need to be taken in order to enable the community to be a help rather than a hindrance. The following steps are suggested as a way of mobilizing the community.

ATTEMPTS AT EDUCATION

Education has often been asked to assume principle responsibility and bear the brunt of the load in dealing with most issues. It is successful only to the degree that there is receptivity on the part of people who are willing to learn and understand. Chemical dependency affects such a large portion of the population either overtly or covertly; yet, so educational efforts often fail to reach those who may benefit most. The subject matter in and of itself is taboo because there is a conspiracy of silence among the afflicted and the affected. Participation in educational efforts in and of itself would constitute a threat. The fear of being identified as one who is struggling with addiction in oneself or in a significant other precludes participation.

Nonetheless, attempts at educational efforts in the faith community need to continue. Accurate data needs to be presented. Appreciation for those who have come to learn must be expressed. The issues must be directly addressed early in the educational process among young children. The use and abuse of mood-altering substances is no longer only an adult or adolescent affair; it involves children who are in grade school. New educational materials for children are now being produced that attempt to address the issues involved.

ADJUSTMENT OF ATTITUDES

Perhaps the most difficult task is adjustment of the attitudes often held by people in the faith community. Attitudes are spawned as the result of the influence of parents, peers, teachers, clergy, public opinion, and personal experience. Once in place, attitudes seem riveted deep within a person's psyche and are not easily changed.

A person who has grown up in a chemically dependent family system is likely to have internalized a strong negative attitude as a consequence of the pain, suffering, and nightmarish existence she or he has experienced. Anger, rage, and hatred may be so strong that the person is not open to shifting perspectives on the issue. Other family members may be so involved in protectionism, enabling, and other codependent behavior that any shift in perspective constitutes a betrayal of family loyalty. The readjustment of attitudes in this community toward a more objective, healthy, and growth-producing posture meets with incredible resistance.

People often feel that their situation is unique or different and that no one else can fully understand why they have adopted the attitude that holds sway in their lives. For those few who indeed may not be directly or even indirectly touched by the addictive cycle, an attitude of indifference, superiority, or judgmentalism may prevail. The point is that healing and health may be precluded because of entrenched attitudes. Addressing these problems in attitude is a primary concern for pastoral care by the faith community.

AWARENESS OF IMPLICATIONS

The manifold implications of chemical dependency in the lives of people is incalculable. Persons in the faith community need to be alerted to the fact that the issue involves more than the individual who is addicted to mood-altering substances and her or his family or significant others. When the implications of chemical dependency are investigated, a complex and intricate mosaic of interlocking and interconnected concerns appears.

Chemical dependency has intergenerational implications. Patterns of use and behavior can often be traced within the family system. Children who have a parent or parents who are chemically dependent have a 25 percent greater chance of becoming chemically dependent themselves. Family relationships and ways of communicating with one another and society as a whole are influenced strongly by the presence of addiction in the family system. The adult-children-of-alcoholics syndrome and the adult-grandchildren-of-alcoholics phenomenon point to the importance of viewing chemical dependency from an intergenerational perspective.

Domestic violence and sexual abuse are often companion phenomena where drug and alcohol addiction are an issue. This is not to suggest that there is always a corollary, but the incidence of alcohol/drug-induced violence can be substantiated by engaging in conversation with those who are closest to the chemically dependent person. The number of persons, particularly females, who have experienced incest in the family or rape within marriage is staggering as their stories are unfolded in recovery groups. The physical, emotional, social, and spiritual scars occasioned by domestic and sexual violence complicate the recovery situation immensely. Raising the level of awareness and consciousness in the religious community with respect to these phenomena is critically important.

ACTIVATING THE RESOURCES

Ministry to the chemically dependent and their families or significant others involves identifying and activating all of the available resources in the community. Addiction, as has been suggested, is a multi-faceted phenomenon, requiring a multi-dimensional strategy. One primary resource for the faith community that is often overlooked or ignored is the people who are currently in recovery.

Experience may not be the only teacher, but it is a good instructor when it comes to this kind of ministry. As a pastor involved in this kind of ministry, I discovered that the most important resources available are people who have a substantial amount of quality sobriety (at least two years) and recovering family members who can commiserate with others who are experiencing the effects of chemical dependency. The expertise is experiential, and when people who are wrestling with the effects of addiction and codependency can actually speak to others who have survived and now are experiencing sobriety with serenity, the impact is great. Many people who are in recovery belong to a support group—such as AA or Alanon—an outpatient group, or a growth group and are usually more than eager to be of assistance to others who are in search of help.

Some communities have trained professionals to work with chemical addiction. In keeping with the holistic approach to recovery, their expertise is needed if intervention and treatment are going to be sought. Whether inside or outside the faith community, many professionals in the field of addiction have acknowledged the importance of spirituality as a key component in recovery. These trained professionals are often available to conduct conferences and seminars for the religious community.

The religious community might serve as the repository for available resources in a given area. The location of twelve-step groups and treatment centers as well as the names, addresses, and phone numbers of interventionists, social welfare workers, and key people in recovery are but a few of the resources one might gather in an attempt to minister to the whole person and the whole community. People and agencies who are involved in political, economic, medical, and legal work as it pertains to chemical dependency should also be identified.

The "people resources" within the religious community also play a vital role if their disposition toward those who struggle with chemical dependency is one of concern rather than condemnation, of inclusion rather than exclusion, and of compassionate caring rather than moralistic judgmentalism. Since chemical dependency estranges, isolates, and alienates people from their primary social units of support, including the religious community, persistent and patient love is fundamental to reaching them.

The Pastoral Role in the Recovery Process

General Considerations

The minister, priest, or rabbi is the called, elected, or designated leader of the religious community. As such, the concerns of the individual, family, community, and wider systems that are related to issues of addiction, recovery, prevention, intervention, and life-style renewal fall within her or his area of professional responsibility. The minister is only one member of the interdisciplinary team who may work with issues of addiction. The minister is a member not only of the religious community but also of the wider community in which she or he serves, and thus ought to realize that singular responsibility for holistic ministry to the chemically dependent and their families or significant others does not reside with her or him as a clergyperson. Ministers have developed notorious reputations for being independent, "Lone Rangers" as it were. Effective ministry with the chemically dependent and others affected by addiction requires that the minister participate as the spiritual shepherd on the interdisciplinary team, but not assume responsibility for the whole process.

The minister must also become aware of her or his own attitudes with regard to chemical dependency. A number of people who are involved in ordained ministry are adult children of alcoholics/addicts. One must come to terms with one's own feelings, experiences, and disposition before it will be possible to minister to others more objectively. This consciousness-raising process can be excruciatingly painful for the minister, but it is a necessary prerequisite so that one's own prejudices and biases do not unduly stand in the way of effective ministry.

The minister is in a position to play a number of key roles in the total scope of chemical dependency concerns. As a professional, the minister is a generalist who is often privy to people's private lives and situations through the life cycle. The minister is often consulted for counseling when crises occur, since compassion, concern, and confidentiality are assumed as givens. The minister has access to, and in some cases is expected to be in, the homes of parishioners. This provides the opportunity to observe people in their own settings and circumstances and to assess the relationships they have with significant others. Often, clues are dropped that all is not well within the family system. The minister, in the privacy of the parishoner's home, has an occasion to pursue concerns that may involve chemical dependency issues. The minister also has occasion to observe and to participate in the interaction that occurs with other members of the community in gatherings, meetings, worship, study, and significant occasions in life passages.

Historically, clergy are often approached by members of the wider community who have no affiliation with a church. The position is one of public as well as private trust. If the minister has established a reputation for being understanding, compassionate, and concerned, people who are desperately looking for an empathetic listener may seek out this minister as a general resource for dealing with chemical dependency as well as other critical life issues.

Specific Roles and Functions

In addition to these general roles, there are specific roles the minister assumes by virtue of the office that are significant in ministry to chemically dependent persons and their families or significant others.

In dealing with chemical dependency, the minister can function as a coordinator in both the religious community and the wider community setting. If the minister is aware of local, regional, and state resources, he or she will be able to appropriately direct people who have specific chemical dependency needs to them (whether for intervention, treatment, referral to a Twelve-Step group, or some other need).

The minister can often function as a catalyst to facilitate movement in a relational system that is paralyzed and immobilized. If the minister recognizes the symptoms and signs of the addictive syndrome, she or he may need to describe objectively what is happening to the person or persons. The pastor must be willing to risk and to expect resistance, rebuff, and rejection. While it is important to avoid the role of rescuer and to avoid assuming responsibility for someone's recovery, the minister is in a strategic position to be a catalyst for action.

The historic role of confessor assumes a position of priority in ministering to chemically dependent persons and their families or significant others. Anger, hostility, depression, despair, violence, guilt, shame, and a host of other negative emotions, experiences, and encounters need to be aired. The minister needs to be prepared to hear the painful details of the story. Assisting people in assuming responsibility for their own attitudes, actions, and behavior is a critically important function. As confessions are made, a word of absolution and forgiveness is pronounced for those who seek relief. Clergy are often called upon to hear fifth steps in the twelve-step recovery process. The fifth step is not to be construed as a confession in the ecclesiastical sense of the word, but it is an opportunity for the person involved to admit before God and another human being the exact nature of her or his wrongs.

Chemical dependency invariably results in fractured relationships with God, with others, and with self. The minister often functions as the facilitator of reconciliation. At the heart of a healthy spirituality is a sense of serenity. The effects of the dis-ease must be dealt with in a forthright manner. Brokenness, estrangement, and alienation are overcome through the act of reconciliation so that the persons involved may experience a new peace that passes all human understanding.

One of the more important functions of the minister is to assist in effecting reentry into the community following treatment for the chemically dependent person and her or his family or significant others. As has already been indicated, the power of shame results in isolation from the wider community. Many people have expressed to me as they were about to leave treatment that they will find it difficult to go out in public and, specifically, to return to public worship services. The minister needs to exercise patience and not coerce the recovering person or the family to return for worship against his or her will. Time is a great healer, and constant support, concern, and love for all involved is critical. The minister also needs to interpret the situation for the religious community and assist the community in facilitating reentry.[8]

Reentry to the community for the alcoholic/addict and her or his significant others is analogous to the reentry of a spaceship into the earth's atmosphere. Prior to recovery, the community has seen the person as a "space cadet," one who is "out in orbit" or "high" on mood-altering substances. Addicts themselves speak of being "zoned out" and "high," oblivious to the world around them. As the recovery process is initiated and the person is no longer "spaced out," he or she is once again confronted with life in the "real world." It is a frightening process to face reality. As with the spaceship's reentry into the earth's atmosphere, reentry into the community must be done with precision, proper timing, and purposeful planning. Reentry at the wrong angle or the wrong time may result in great damage or destruction. The minister is in a strategic position to interpret this reality to the religious community as well as to the chemically dependent person and her or his significant others.

Remember that community is the key to recovery. The alcoholic/addict will need an abstinent peer group in order to sustain sobriety and to grow as a recovering person. A twelve-step support group seems still to be the best vehicle for facilitating that process, but those who are afflicted and affected also need the community of faith to nourish and nurture them as resurrected and renewed persons who are beginning a new journey in sobriety. The abstinent community and the religious community can work in tandem to assist in this critical growth process. The minister, as the leader of the religious community, is in a strategic position to assist in the critical reentry procedure. A supportive minister is of invaluable service to all who are involved.[9]

Pastoral care provided in the recovery process from addiction is but one of many responsibilities assumed by the minister. However, because of the pervasive nature of addiction and the multiplicity of people who are afflicted and affected, it is a pastoral ministry that deserves the attention of all members of the clergy who have as their objective in ministry the holistic health and well-being of their parishioners.

Major Publications by Howard Clinebell

Basic Types of Pastoral Counseling. Nashville: Abingdon Press, 1966. (German, Finnish, Korean, Japanese, and Chinese editions.)

Basic Types of Pastoral Care and Counseling: Resources for the Ministry of Healing and Growth. Nashville: Abingdon Press, 1984. (Revised edition of *Basic Types of Pastoral Counseling.*)

(Editor) *Community Mental Health: The Role of Church and Temple.* Nashville: Abingdon Press, 1970.

Contemporary Growth Therapies: Resources for Actualizing Human Wholeness. Nashville: Abingdon Press, 1981. (German edition.)

(With Charlotte H. Clinebell) *Crisis and Growth: Helping Your Troubled Child.* Philadelphia: Fortress Press, 1971. (German and Finnish editions.)

(Editor) *Global Peacemaking and Wholeness: Justice-based Theological, Psychological and Spiritual Resources.* Proceedings of an Institute for Religion and Wholeness Conference, May 17–19, 1984.

(With Martha Hickman) *Growing Through Grief: Personal Healing.* Nashville: United Methodist Communications Productions, 1984. A series of six video teaching tapes with a *User's Guide.*

Growing Through Loss: A Howard Clinebell Resource. Nashville: United Methodist Communications Productions, 1983. A series of six, ninety-minute video teaching tapes showing a grief group from beginning to end, led by Clinebell; with a *Leader's Guide.*

Growth Counseling for Marriage Enrichment: Pre-Marriage and the Early Years. Philadelphia: Fortress Press, 1975. (German, Dutch, Japanese, and Chinese editions.)

Growth Counseling for Mid-Years Couples. Philadelphia: Fortress Press, 1977. (Japanese and German editions.)

Growth Counseling: Hope-Centered Methods of Actualizing Human Wholeness. Nashville: Abingdon Press, 1979. (German, Korean, and Finnish editions.)

Growth Groups: Marriage and Family Enrichment, Creative Singlehood, Human Liberation, Youth Work, Social Change. Nashville: Abingdon Press, 1977. (Paperback edition of *The People Dynamic.*)

Growth Counseling: New Tools for Clergy and Laity. Nashville: Abingdon Press, 1973. (Fifteen do-it-yourself cassette courses with *User's Guide*—part I: "Enriching Marriage and Family Life"; part II: "Coping Constructively with Crises."

(With Charlotte H. Clinebell) *The Intimate Marriage.* New York: Harper & Row, 1970. (German and Spanish editions.)

The Mental Health Ministry of the Local Church. Nashville: Abingdon Press, 1972. Paperback edition of *Mental Health Through Christian Community.*

The People Dynamic: Changing Self and Society Through Growth Groups. New York: Harper & Row, 1972. (Australian edition.)

(With Harvey Seifert) *Personal Growth and Social Change.* Philadelphia: Westminster, 1974.

(Coeditor) *Spirit-Centered Wholeness, Beyond the Psychology of Self.* Lewiston, N.Y.: Edwin Mellen Press, 1988.

Understanding and Counseling the Alcoholic Through Religion and Psychology. Nashville: Abingdon Press, 1956. Revised edition, 1968.

(Editor with Howard W. Stone) *Creative Pastoral Care and Counseling Series.* Philadelphia: Fortress Press. 18 vols.

Introduction

1. All case material presented in the book has been disguised to protect the privacy of the individuals concerned. Many of the cases are compilations of individuals. In others, the sex, occupation, location, or other identifying details have been changed.

2. Encountering Sin in Pastoral Counseling

1. Margaret S. Livingstone, "Art, Illusion, and the Visual System," *Scientific American,* 258 (1988).
2. J. Teicholz, "A Selective Review of the Psychoanalytic Literature on Theoretical Conceptualizations of Narcissism," *Journal of the American Psychoanalytical Association,* 26 (1978): 831-62.
3. This summarizes work of the ego-psychologists, the object relations school, and self-psychology (Kohut). For a good overview, see Stephen Johnson, *Characterological Transformation: The Hard Work Miracle* (New York: W. W. Norton, 1985).
4. H. Kohut, *The Restoration of the Self* (New York: International Universities Press, 1977).
5. The phrase *the fragile self* is the contribution of Philip Mollon and Glenys Parry in their excellent article "The Fragile Self: Narcissistic Disturbance and the Protective Function of Depression," *British Journal of Medical Psychology,* 57 (1984): 137-45. In a gestalt therapy context, the self is a dynamic process, indicating the act of integration, giving rise to the personality, the gestalting of a person. The somewhat awkward phrase *fragile self-process* seeks to capture this process sense.
6. The term *shame* has been used in a number of ways (see Hunter Beaumont, *Shame: Phenomenology, Theory, Treatment* [Perth, Australia: Gestalt Therapy Institute of Perth, 1985]). It describes the feeling of being ashamed, or it may describe the entire process of inner collapse, or it may describe the clinical syndrome of fragile self-processes. The literature suggests several alternative clinical terms for this inner collapse. Kohut suggested the term *narcissistic injury,* which captures the subjective feeling of hurt and anger that often accompanies this state (see note 4 and also Heinz Kohut, *The Analysis of the Self* [New York: International Universities Press, 1971]). Masterson has suggested abandonment depression, suggesting a deep

organismic response to abandonment (James Masterson, *The Real Self* [New York: Brunner/Mazel, 1985]). *Shame* has the advantage of being a simple word that does not encourage placing the blame for the experience outside of the client's responsibility.

7. See Beaumont, *Shame.*
8. The instrumental relationship is contrasted to the "I-Thou" relationship in the work of Martin Buber. See Martin Buber, *I and Thou* (New York: Charles Scribner's Sons, 1958).
9. Ali Beg, "A Note on the Concept of Self and the Theory and Practice of Psychological Help in the Sufi Tradition," *Journal of Interpersonal Development,* 1 (1970): 58-64.

3. Ethics in Pastoral Care and Counseling

1. James N. Poling, "Ethical Reflection in Pastoral Care, Part I," *Pastoral Psychology,* 32, 2 (Spring 1984): 106-14; "Ethical Reflection in Pastoral Care, Part II," *Pastoral Psychology,* 32, 3 (Spring 1984); "An Ethical Framework for Pastoral Care," *Journal of Pastoral Care* 42, 4 (Winter 1988): 299-308.
2. Howard Clinebell, *Basic Types of Pastoral Care and Counseling* (Nashville: Abingdon Press, 1984), p. 139.
3. See William Frankena, *Ethics* (Englewood Cliffs, N.J.: Prentice-Hall, 1973).
4. Stanley Hauerwas, *Community of Character: Toward a Constructive Social Ethic* (Notre Dame: University of Notre Dame Press, 1981).
5. James Fowler, *Stages of Faith* (New York: Harper & Row, 1981).
6. See Archie Smith, Jr., *The Relational Self: Ethics and Therapy from a Black Church Perspective* (Nashville: Abingdon Press, 1982).
7. See Barbara Andolsen et al., *Women's Consciousness, Women's Conscience* (New York: Harper & Row, 1985); Marie Fortune, *Sexual Violence: The Unmentionable Sin, Ethical and Pastoral Perspectives* (Philadelphia: Pilgrim Press, 1983).
8. "The Unique Death of Eli Creekmore." Videotape produced by KCTS, Seattle, WA, 1987.
9. For comparison, see the method for practical theological reflection in James Poling and Donald E. Miller, *Foundations for a Practical Theology of Ministry* (Nashville: Abingdon Press, 1985), pp. 69ff.

4. Social Systems in Pastoral Care

1. Juan Luis Segundo, *The Community Called Church,* vol. 1 (Maryknoll, N.Y.: Orbis Books, 1973), p. 27.
2. Leonardo Boff, *Liberating Grace* (Maryknoll, N.Y.: Orbis Books, 1981), p. 65.
3. Ibid.
4. Dermot A. Lane, *Foundations for a Social Theology, Praxis, Process, and Salvation* (Dublin: Gill and Macmillan, 1984), p. 23.
5. Walter M. Abbott, J. J., ed., Vatican II, *Gaudium et Spes* (New York: Guild Press, 1966).
6. Lane, *Foundations for a Social Theology, Praxis, Process, and Salvation,* p. 110.

7. Ibid., p. 112.
8. Boff, *Liberating Grace*, p. 84.
9. National Conference of Catholic Bishops (NCCB), *The Challenge of Peace and Our Response* (Washington, D.C.: U. S. Catholic Conference Incorporated, 1983); *Economic Justice for All* (Washington, D.C.: U. S. Catholic Conference Incorporated, 1986).
10. NCCB, *The Challenge of Peace and Our Response*, p. 102.
11. Robert Bellah et al., *Habits of the Heart: Individualism and Commitment in American Life* (Los Angeles: University of California Press, 1985), p. 15.
12. NCCB, *The Challenge of Peace and Our Response*, p. 102.
13. NCCB, *Economic Justice for All*, pp. ix, x.
14. Ibid., p. 83.
15. Ibid., p. 88.
16. Ibid., p. 89.
17. John Paul II, *On Social Concern: Encyclical Letter of John Paul II* (Boston: St. Paul Books, 1988), p. 71.
18. UNO, United Neighborhood Organization; EVO, East Valleys Organization; SCOC, South Central Organizing Committee; VOICE, Valley Organized in Community Effort. All are Hispanic community organizations in the Los Angeles area.
19. Boff, *Liberating Grace*, p. 85.
20. See John Paul II, *On Social Concern*, pp. 70-71.
21. Ibid., pp. 69-70.

5. Pastoral Care Across Cultures

1. Kurt Anderson, "The New Ellis Island," *Time* (June 13, 1983): 1-5.
2. G. Stanley Hall, *Adolescence* (New York: Appleton, 1904); see also Hall's *Life and Confessions of a Psychologist* (New York: Appleton, 1923). Hall's works are cited by Thomas Alexander and Samuel Sillen, *Racism and Psychiatry* (Secaucus, N.J.: Citadel Press, 1974), pp. 7-8.
3. See C. J. Jung's discussion of American behavior in his *Contributions to Analytical Psychology* (New York: Harcourt Brace, 1928); and his "Your Negroid and Indian Behavior," *Forum* 83 (1930): 193-99.
4. C. J. Jung, as quoted by Brill in *The Basic Writings of Sigmund Freud*, A. A. Brill, trans. (New York: Modern Library, 1938). These thoughts of Jung are cited by Alexander and Sillen, *Racism and Psychiatry*, pp. 13-14.
5. W. I. Thomas, "The Psychology of Race Prejudice," *American Journal of Sociology* 9 (1904): 593-611.
6. Must reading for everyone working to increase his or her cultural sensitivity is Alexander and Sillen, *Racism and Psychiatry*.
7. See Edwin H. Richardson, "The Problems of the Indian in the Affluent Society," papers presented at Region 8 Indian Health Meeting, Rapid City, S.D., May 1973; at the South Dakota Senate Educational Committee hearing, August 1976; and at the South Dakota Indian Commission for Alcohol and Drug Abuse, 1975. Richardson refers to these papers in "Cultural and Historical Perspectives in Counseling American Indians," in *Counseling the Culturally Different: Theory and Practice*, Derald W. Sue, ed. (New York: John Wiley, 1981), pp. 9-10.

8. See Rene A. Ruiz, "Cultural and Historical Perspectives in Counseling Hispanics," in Sue, *Counseling the Culturally Different*, p. 190.
9. See G. Kagiwada and I. Fujimoto, "Asian American Studies: Implications for Education," *Personnel and Guidance Journal*, 51 (1973): 400-405.
10. See H. H. L. Kitano, *The Evolution of a Subculture* (Englewood Cliffs, N.J.: Prentice-Hall, 1969).
11. See Derald W. Sue, "Cultural and Historical Perspectives in Counseling Asian Americans," in Sue, *Counseling the Culturally Different*, pp. 113-40.
12. M. Korman, *Levels and Patterns of Professional Training in Psychology* (Washington, D.C.: American Psychological Association, 1973), p. 105.
13. Monica McGoldrick, John K. Pearce, and Joseph Giordano, eds., *Ethnicity and Family Therapy* (New York: Guilford Press, 1982), p. 3.
14. See A. M. Greeley, *Why Can't They Be Like Us?* (New York: Institute of Human Relations Press, 1969); *The American Catholic* (New York: Basic Books, 1978); and *The Irish Americans* (New York: Harper & Row, 1981).
15. David W. Augsburger, *Pastoral Counseling Across Cultures* (Philadelphia: Westminster, 1986), p. 18.
16. See Monica McGoldrick and Randy Gerson, *Genograms in Family Assessment* (New York: W. W. Norton, 1985).
17. Archie Smith, Jr., *The Relational Self: Ethics and Therapy from a Black Church Perspective* (Nashville: Abingdon Press, 1982), p. 38.
18. Augsburger, *Pastoral Counseling Across Cultures*, p. 23.
19. Paulo Freire, *Pedagogy of the Oppressed* (New York: Herder & Herder, 1970), p. 19.
20. See S. Sue, D. Allen, and L. Conaway, "The Responsiveness and Equality of Mental Health Care to Chicanos and Native Americans," *American Journal of Community Psychology* (1975). See also S. Sue, H. McKinney, D. Allen, and J. Hall, "Delivery of Community Mental Health Services to Black and White Clients," *Journal of Consulting and Clinical Psychology* 42 (1974): 594-601.

6. Cultural Collisions: A Perspective from Africa

1. This chapter is adapted from my essay "Polygamy in Pastoral Perspectives," in *Families in Transition: The Case for Counselling in Context*, Masamba ma Mpolo and Cécile De Sweemer, eds. (Geneva: World Council of Churches, 1987), pp. 97-126. It illustrates two major concerns of Howard Clinebell: that pastoral counseling is integral to pastoral care (and vice versa) and that cultural dimensions *must* be taken seriously while doing counseling.
2. The 1964 Ivory Coast law forbidding polygamy says that no one can contract a new marriage without abolishing the first one (Law no. 64-375, art. 2). The polygamous husband cannot contract another marriage without dissolving other marriages he has been involved in (Law no. 64-381, art. 13). See R. Daniel, "Image de la famille en Côte d'Ivoire," *Jeune Afrique*, 745 (April 18, 1975): 62. The 1970 Tanzanian law on marriage recognizes these forms of marital union: monogamy, polygamy, and potential polygamous marriage. The engaged couple must choose one of these forms before officially taking marriage vows. Generally, young women choose monogamy, and any subsequent change has to be decided before the court with the participation

of state and church officials. See "La famille en Tanzanie," *Fêtes et raisons* (Paris) 29 (1975): 7.

3. The first two examples are provided by Adrian Hastings, *Christian Marriage in Africa*, abridged ed. (Nairobi: Uzima Press, 1981), pp. 20-21.

4. See Masamaba ma Mpolo, "Polygamy in Pastoral Perspectives," for an extensive discussion of more specific cultural practices relating to polygamy and polyandry.

5. Ferdinand Ngoma, *L'initiation Ba-Kongo et sa signification*, doctoral thesis, Sorbonne, 1963, p. 25.

6. See Joseph van Wing, *Études Bakongo*, 2nd ed. (Brussels: Desclée, 1959), p. 127.

7. See Laurent Mpongo in *Revue du clergé africain* (Mayidi, Zaire), 27, 1 (January 1972): 39.

8. See Bokembo, "Autorité parentale et délinquance juvénile en Afrique," *Psychopathologie africaine* (Dakar) 5, 1 (1969): 114.

9. Ibid., 38.

10. See David Mace and Vera Mace, *Marriage, East and West* (New York: Doubleday, 1960).

11. See E. G. Parrinder, *The Bible and Polygamy* (London: SPCK, 1958), p. 6.

12. Ibid., p. 7.

13. The following explanation is suggested by C. R. Smith: "The phrase 'husband of one wife,' found in the Epistle of Timothy, about both bishops and deacons, cannot mean that these officers were to be monogamists while other Christians might be polygamists, for there were no polygamists even among the heathen. The phrase probably means that a man who in his heathen days had been divorced and had married again—and who therefore had more than one wife living—must not be appointed to Church office." In Parrinder, *The Bible and Polygamy*, p. 51.

14. E. Hillman, *Polygamy Reconsidered: African Marriage and the Christian Church* (Maryknoll: Orbis Books, 1975), p. 167. Also refer to Manas Buthelezi, "Polygamy in the Light of the New Testament," *African Theological Journal*, 2 (1969): 58-70.

15. Hillman, *Polygamy Reconsidered*, p. 8.

16. See Hastings, *Christian Marriage in Africa*, pp. 21-22.

17. See the following works of African women: Awa Thiam, *La parole aux négresses* (Paris: Denoël, 1978); Alo Rotimi, *Our Husband Has Gone Mad Again* (Ibadan University Press, 1977); Miriama Bâ, *Une si longue lettre* (Dakar: Les Nouvelles Editions Africaines, 1980); Rose Zoé-Obianga, "L'engagement de la femme dans l'Afrique actuelle," in Kofi Appiah-Kubi et al., *Libération ou adaptation? La théologie africaine s'intérroge* (Paris: L'Hamarthan, 1979); Mercy Amba-Oduyoye, "Feminism: a Pre-Condition for a Christian Anthropology," *African Theological Journal* 11, 3 (1983); Mazaza Mukoko, "La polygamie est-ce une bonne chose?" in *Report on the Pan-African and Ecumenical Consultation on Christian Family and Family Life Education, Yaoundé, 17-23 April 1983* (Geneva: World Council of Churches [Office of Family Education], 1983); and Louise Tappa, "Un regard systématique sur le phénomène polygamie-polyandrie aujourd'hui," in *La polygamie et l'Église* (Yaoundé: Faculté de théologie protestante, 1982).

7. Prayer and Meditation in Pastoral Care and Counseling

1. Ana-Maria Rizzuto, *The Birth of the Living God* (Chicago: University of Chicago Press, 1979), p. 210.
2. See Merle Jordan, *Taking on the Gods* (Nashville: Abingdon Press, 1986), p. 36.
3. See Wilfried Daim, *Depth Psychology and Salvation*, trans. K. F. Reinhardt (New York: Ungar, 1963), p. 119.
4. Gerald G. May, *Addiction and Grace* (San Francisco: Harper & Row, 1988), pp. 13-14, 16.
5. Howard Clinebell, *Basic Types of Pastoral Care and Counseling*, rev. ed. (Nashville: Abingdon Press, 1984), p. 128.
6. See Hans Kohut, *The Analysis of the Self* (New York: International Universities Press, 1971).
7. David C. Jacobsen, *Clarity in Prayer: Telling the Small Truth* (Corte Madera, Calif.: Omega Books, 1976), p. 93.
8. See Peter Taylor Forsyth, *The Soul of Prayer* (London: Independent Press, Ltd., 1949).

8. Imagination in Pastoral Care and Counseling

1. Belden C. Lane, "Language, Metaphor, and Pastoral Theology," *Theology Today* 43, (January 1987): 488.
2. See Julian of Norwich, *Showings*, trans. Edmund Colledge and James Walsh (New York: Paulist Press, 1978); St. John of the Cross, *Dark Night of the Soul*, trans. E. A. Peers (New York: Doubleday, 1959); St. Ignatius, *The Spiritual Exercises of St. Ignatius*, trans. Louis J. Puhl (Chicago: Loyola University Press, 1951).
3. Sallie McFague, *Metaphorical Theology: Models of God in Religious Language* (Philadelphia: Fortress Press, 1982), p. 13.
4. Lane, "Language, Metaphor, and Pastoral Theology," p. 489.
5. See Gordon Kaufman, *The Theological Imagination: Constructing the Concept of God* (Philadelphia: Westminster Press, 1981) and David Tracy, *The Analogical Imagination: Christian Theology and the Culture of Pluralism* (New York: Crossroad Press, 1981).
6. See Avery Brooke, *How to Meditate Without Leaving the World* (New York: Seabury, 1979).
7. See G. Michael Cordner, "The Spiritual Vision Within," *The Journal of Pastoral Care*, 35, 1 (March 1981): 42.
8. See Ina Progoff, *The Practice of Process Meditation* (New York: Dialogue House, 1980).
9. Jerome L. Singer, "Towards the Scientific Study of Imagination," in Singer, *Imagery: Theoretical and Clinical Applications*, vol. 3 (New York: Plenum Press, 1983), p. 9.
10. See Joseph Schorr, Psychotherapy Through Imagery, 2nd ed. (New York: Thieme-Stratton, 1983).
11. See Jerome L. Singer, *Imagery and Daydream Methods in Psychotherapy and Behavior Modification* (New York: Academic Press, 1974).
12. See Hanscarl Leuner, *Guided Affective Imagery: Mental Imagery in Short*

Term Psychotherapy, trans, Elizabeth Lachman (New York: Thieme-Stratton, 1984).

13. See K. David Schultz, "Imagery and the Control of Depression," in *The Power of Human Imagination: New Methods in Psychotherapy,* eds. Jerome L. Singer and Kenneth S. Pope (New York: Plenum Press, 1978), p. 306.

14. Thomas A. Droege, *Guided Grief Imagery: A Resource for Grief Ministry and Death Education* (New York: Paulist Press, 1987), p. 6.

15. Cordner, "The Spiritual Vision Within," p. 42.

16. There is considerable literature on the use of imagination in the health fields—imaging for coronary problems, for cancer, and so on.

9. Depression

1. See A. T. Beck et al., *Cognitive Therapy of Depression* (New York: Guilford Press, 1979), p. 1.

2. The terms *melancholy* and *depression* are used interchangeably in this chapter.

3. Morton Bloomfield, *Seven Deadly Sins* (East Lansing: Michigan State College Press, 1952), p. 96.

4. Quoted in Hubertus Tellenbach, *Melancholy,* trans. Erling Eng (Pittsburgh: Duquesne University Press, 1980), p. 5.

5. See Beck, *Cognitive Therapy of Depression,* p. 2.

6. A. T. Beck, *Depression* (New York: Harper and Bros., Hoeber Medical Division, 1967), pp. 255-61.

7. Ibid., p. 17.

8. See Howard Stone, *Suicide and Grief* (Philadelphia: Fortress, 1972), pp. 31-34.

9. One of the most helpful and easy to use inventories is the Beck Depression Inventory by A. T. Beck, *Depression,* pp. 186-207 and 333-37. Other scales are the Zung Self-Rating Depression Scale by W. W. Zung, "A Self-rating Depression Scale," *Archives of General Psychiatry* 12 (1965): 63-70; the Raskin Depression Scale by A. Raskin et al., "Differential Response to Chlorpromazine, Imipramine, and Placebo: A Study of Sub-groups of Hospitalized Depressed Patients," *Archives of General Psychiatry* 23 (1970): 163-73; the Hamilton Rating Scale for Depression by M. Hamilton, "A Rating Scale for Depression," *Journal of Neurology, Neurosurgery, and Psychiatry* 196, 23: 56-62.

10. Beck, *Depression,* p. 57.

11. See Roy W. Fairchild, *Finding Hope Again: A Pastor's Guide to Counseling Depressed Persons* (New York: Harper & Row, 1980), p. 33.

12. You may also wish to review *Suicide and Grief* or *Crisis Counseling,* both by Howard Stone, and *The Prediction of Suicide* by A. T. Beck, H. L. P. Resnik, and D. Lettieri, eds. (Bowie, MD: Charles Press, 1974) for further information on assessing and managing suicidal persons.

13. Robert P. Lieberman, "A Model for Individualizing Treatment," in *Behavioral Therapy for Depression,* ed. Lynn Rehm (New York: Academic Press, 1981), p. 244.

14. A. T. Beck, *Cognitive Therapy and the Emotional Disorders* (New York: International Universities Press, 1976), p. 296.

15. Ibid., p. 263.

16. Roberto Assagioli, *Psychosynthesis* (New York: Hobbs, Dorman & Company, Inc., 1965), p. 22.
17. See Peter M. Lewinsohn et al., *Control Your Depression* (Englewood Cliffs, N.J.: Prentice-Hall, 1978), p. 125.
18. See Victor Frankl, *Man's Search for Meaning*, trans. Ilse Lasch (New York: Washington Square Press, 1963), pp. 151-214.
19. See Lewinsohn, *Control Your Depression*, pp. 154-56.
20. See Beck et al., *Cognitive Therapy of Depression*, p. 2.
21. See ibid., p. 204.
22. Ibid., p. 9.
23. See Howard Stone, *Using Behavioral Methods in Pastoral Counseling* (Philadelphia: Fortress Press, 1980), pp. 31-44.
24. See P. Hauck, *Overcoming Depression* (Philadelphia: Westminster Press, 1976); A. T. Beck and R. L. Greenburg, *Coping with Depression* (New York: Institute for Rational Living, 1974); A. Ellis and R. Harper, *A New Guide to Rational Living* (Englewood Cliffs, N.J.: Prentice-Hall, 1975).
25. Fairchild, *Finding Hope Again*, p. 33.
26. See especially the helpful book by William A. Barry and William J. Connolly, *The Practice of Spiritual Direction* (New York: Seabury Press, 1982); or Kevin J. Culligan, "The Counseling Ministry and Spiritual Direction," *Pastoral Counseling*, ed. Barry Estade (Englewood Cliffs, N.J.: Prentice-Hall, Inc., 1983); or my book *The Word of God and Pastoral Care* (Nashville: Abingdon Press, 1988), pp. 92-123.

10. Loss and Grief

1. Elisabeth Kübler-Ross, *On Death and Dying* (New York: Macmillan, 1959).
2. See Bernard Schoenberg et al., "Loss of External Organs: Limb Amputations, Mastectomy, and Disfiguration," in *Loss and Grief* (New York: Columbia University Press, 1970).
3. See Thomas H. Holmes and Richard H. Rahe, "The Social Readjustment Rating Scale," *Journal of Psychosomatic Research II* (1967): 213-18.
4. Colin Murray Parkes, *Bereavement* (New York: International Universities Press, 1972).
5. John Bowlby's version of this theoretical understanding of grief is spelled out in his *Attachment and Loss*, vol. 2 (New York: Basic Books, 1973), and in *The Making and Breaking of Affectional Bonds* (London: Tavistock Publications, 1979).
6. Parkes, *Bereavement*, p. 22.
7. For example, see Kenneth R. Mitchell and Herbert Anderson, *All Our Losses, All Our Griefs: Resources for Pastoral Care* (Philadelphia: Westminster Press, 1983).
8. See Norman Paul, "Psychiatry: Its Role in the Resolution of Grief," in Austin H. Kutscher, ed., *Death and Bereavement* (Springfield, Ill.: Thomas, 1969).
9. See Norman L. Paul and George H. Grosser, "Operational Mourning and Its Role in Conjoint Family Therapy," *Community Mental Health Journal*, 1, 4 (Winter 1965): 339-45.
10. There have been a couple of good volumes on this in the field of pastoral care. For example, see William M. Clements, *Care and Counseling of the Aging* (Philadelphia: Fortress Press, 1979), and William E. Hulme, *Vintage*

Years: Growing Older with Meaning and Hope (Philadelphia: Westminster Press, 1986).

11. In my book *Losses in Later Life* (Mahwah, N.J.: Paulist Press, 1989), I outline seven major losses of the second half of life and discuss in detail some of their unique dangers and potentials for spiritual growth.

12. For a further discussion of this point, see chapter 4, "Grief and Growth," in my *Grief and Growth* (Mahwah, N.J.: Paulist Press, 1985).

13. For example, see Donald Capps, *Life Cycle Theory and Pastoral Care* (Philadelphia: Fortress Press, 1983).

14. This statement and those that follow would also apply to synagogues, and maybe even more so to synagogues than to churches.

15. See Granger E. Westberg, *Good Grief* (Philadelphia: Fortress Press, 1973).

16. The loss of a pastor is sometimes made more complicated by the "transferences" that some parishioners place on this perceived authority figure. Such transferences contaminate the parishioners' grieving.

17. Some denominations have responded by creating a new specialized ministry by using an interim minister or supply pastor, who makes a career of filling in at congregations who are in between permanent pastors. Such interims are often skilled pastoral care specialists and are very knowledgeable about grief dynamics.

18. One of the more important books in this regard is Edwin H. Friedman, *Generation to Generation: Family Process in Church and Synagogue* (New York: The Guilford Press, 1985).

19. The classic study of ritual as a rite of passage is Arnold van Gennep, *The Rites of Passage* (Chicago: University of Chicago Press, 1960).

20. For a discussion of the decline of ritual in Western civilization, see Geoffrey Gorer, *Death, Grief, Mourning in Contemporary Britain* (London: Cresset, 1965).

21. I first heard this suggestion from Thomas B. Robb at the Office of Aging, The Presbyterian Church (USA). See his book, *The Bonus Years: Foundations for Ministry with Older Persons* (Valley Forge: Judson Press, 1968).

11. Unresolved Grief

1. Some of the material in this chapter has appeared previously. Several paragraphs were first published in an article entitled "Awareness of Unresolved Grief: An Opportunity for Ministry" (*The Christian Ministry*, July 1980, 19-23), with rights being retained by the author. Another few paragraphs are paraphrased from another article by the author, "Recognizing abnormal grief symptoms in the families you serve," (*The Knight Letter*, June 1982, 7-9 and July 1982, 10-13). Another section from this article is reprinted with only minor changes and is properly footnoted in context. This material is used with the written permission of The International Order of the Golden Rule, an association of funeral directors (P.O. Box 3586, Springfield, IL, 62708).

2. R. Scott Sullender, *Grief and Growth* (Mahweh, N.J.: New York: Paulist Press, 1985).

3. See William V. Arnold, *Introduction to Pastoral Care* (Philadelphia: Westminster Press, 1982); Howard J. Clinebell, *Basic Types of Pastoral Care and Counseling,* rev. and enlarged (Nashville: Abingdon Press, 1984);

Charles Gerkin, *Crisis Experience in Modern Life* (Nashville: Abingdon Press, 1979); David K. Switzer, *The Minister as Crisis Counselor*, rev. and enlarged (Nashville: Abingdon Press, 1986) and *Pastoral Care Emergencies* (Mahwah, N.J.: Paulist Press, 1986).

4. See Edgar N. Jackon, *Understanding Grief* (Nashville: Abingdon Press, 1957); Kenneth R. Mitchell and Herbert Anderson, *All Our Losses, All Our Griefs* (Philadelphia: Westminster Press, 1983); Wayne E. Oates, *Pastoral Care and Counseling in Grief and Separation* (Philadelphia: Fortress Press, 1976); Yorick Spiegel, *The Grief Process: Analysis and Counseling* (Nashville: Abingdon Press, 1977); Sullender, *Grief and Growth*; and David K. Switzer, *The Dynamics of Grief* (Nashville: Abingdon Press, 1970).

5. Clinebell, *Basic Types of Pastoral Care and Counseling*, pp. 226-27.

6. Jackson, *Understanding Grief*, chapter 11; C. Murray Parkes, *Bereavement: Studies in Adult Grief*, rev. (New York: International Universities Press, 1984), chapter 8; Therese A. Rando, *Grief, Dying and Death* (Champaign, Ill.: Research Press, 1984), chapter 4; Switzer, *Pastoral Care Emergencies*, chapter 7.

7. Parkes, *Bereavement*, p. 27.

8. See Elisabeth Kübler-Ross, *On Death and Dying* (New York: Macmillan, 1969).

9. See Rando, *Grief, Dying and Death*, p. 27.

10. Mitchell and Anderson, *All Our Losses, All Our Griefs*, p. 84.

11. For varying proposals of stages of grief, all reflecting important insights and providing useful guidelines, see Arnold, *Introduction to Pastoral Care*, pp. 164-66; Wayne E. Oates, *Anxiety in Christian Experience* (Philadelphia: Westminster Press, 1955) pp. 52-55; C. Murray Parkes, "Seeking and 'Finding' a Lost Object," *Social Science and Medicine* 4 (1970): 187-201; "The First Year of Bereavement," *Psychiatry* 33 (November 1970): 444-67, also summarized in Switzer, *Pastoral Care Emergencies*, pp. 152-54; Spiegel, *The Grief Process*, pp. 59-83; see also Mitchell and Anderson, *All Our Losses, All Our Griefs*, pp. 61-82.

12. Vamik D. Volkan, "The Recognition and Prevention of Pathological Grief," *The Virginia Medical Monthly* 99 (May 1972), 537.

13. Ibid.

14. Mardi J. Horowitz, Nancy Wildner, Charles Marmar, and Janice Krupnick, "Pathological Grief and the Activation of Latent Self-Images," *American Journal of Psychiatry* 137, 10 (October 1980): 1157-1162.

15. C. Murray Parkes, "Psycho-social Transitions: A Field for Study," *Social Science and Medicine* 5 (1971): 103-5.

16. See Darrin R. Lehman and Camille Wortman, "Long-term Effects of Losing a Spouse or Child in a Motor Vehicle Crash," *Journal of Personality and Social Psychology* 52, 1 (1987): 218-30.

17. See David K. Switzer, "Recognizing Abnormal Grief Symptoms in the Families You Serve," *The Knight Letter* (July, 1982): 11-12.

18. See W. Robert Beavers, *Psychotherapy and Growth: A Family Systems Perspective* (New York: Brunner/Mazel, 1977), pp. 152-55.

19. See Norman L. Paul and George H. Grosser, "Operational Mourning and Its Role in Conjoint Family Therapy," *Community Mental Health Journal* (1965): 340.

20. See Vamik K. Volkan and C. R. Showalter, "Known Object Loss, Disturbance in Reality Testing, and 'Re-grief' Work as a Method of Brief Psychotherapy," *Psychiatric Quarterly* 42 (1968): 358-74.

12. Career Burnout Prevention Among Pastoral Counselors and Pastors

1. Howard Clinebell, *Basic Types of Pastoral Care and Counseling: Resources for the Ministry of Healing and Growth,* rev. (Nashville: Abingdon Press, 1984), p. 419.
2. The term *stress* will be used interchangeably in this chapter to refer to both *stressors,* which are external demands for accommodation, and *stress,* which is technically the physiological and emotional responses made by our bodies and minds to the stressors in our environment.
3. Herbert J. Freudenberger with Geraldine Richelson, *Burn-out: The High Cost of High Achievement* (New York: Bantam Books, 1981), pp. 17-19.
4. Robert J. Wicks, "Countertransference and Burnout in Pastoral Counseling," in *Clinical Handbook of Pastoral Counseling,* eds. Robert J. Wicks, Richard D. Parsons, and Donald E. Capps (New York: Paulist Press, 1985), pp. 90-95.
5. See Richard C. W. Hall, Earl R. Gardner, Mark Perl, Sondra K. Stickney, and Betty Pfefferbaum, "The Professional Burnout Syndrome," *Psychiatric Opinion* 1, 4 (April 1979): 12-17.
6. See Jerry Edelwich with Archie Brodsky, *Burn-out: Stages of Disillusionment in the Helping Professions* (New York: Human Sciences Press, 1980), pp. 42-190.
7. See Roy M. Oswald, *Clergy Burnout: A Survival Kit for Professionals* (Minneapolis: Ministers Life Resources, Inc., 1982), p. 15.
8. G. Lloyd Rediger, *Coping with Clergy Burnout* (Valley Forge, Penn.: Judson Press, 1982), p. 63.
9. See Charles L. Rassieur, *Stress Management for Ministers* (Philadelphia: Westminster Press, 1982), pp. 104-12.
10. William E. Hulme, Milo L. Brekke, and William C. Behrens, *Pastors in Ministry: Guidelines for Seven Critical Issues* (Minneapolis: Augsburg Publishing House, 1985), p. 138.
11. Ibid., pp. 153-54.
12. See William E. Hulme, *Managing Stress in Ministry* (San Francisco: Harper & Row, 1985). Hulme shows persuasively that the pastor's faith can in fact be a primary resource for the effective management of stress in ministry.
13. See Thomas M. Skovholt, University of Minnesota, and Michael Helge Ronnestad, University of Oslo, *Optimal—and Alternative—Stages of Counselor/Therapist Development* (Unpublished research paper: December 1987).
14. For effective intervention in career developmental stress, clergy are encouraged to consider going to a church-related career development center. The address of a nearby center may be obtained by writing to the Church Career Development Council, Room 774, 475 Riverside Dr., New York, NY, 10115.
15. Edwin H. Friedman, *Generation to Generation: Family Process in Church and Synagogue* (New York: The Guilford Press, 1985).
16. Ibid., pp. 197, 216-219.

17. Erik H. Erikson, *Identity: Youth and Crisis* (New York: W. W. Norton & Company, Inc., 1968), p. 110.
18. See Howard Clinebell, *Basic Types of Pastoral Care and Counseling: Resources for the Ministry of Healing and Growth* (Nashville: Abingdon Press, 1984), p. 420.
19. Howard Clinebell, *Growth Counseling: Hope-Centered Methods of Actualizing Human Wholeness* (Nashville: Abingdon Press, 1979), p. 71.
20. Ibid., pp. 19-41.
21. Ibid., p. 70.
22. For further reading, see Brooks R. Faulkner, *Burnout in Ministry: How to Recognize It—How to Avoid It* (Nashville: Broadman Press, 1981); Gary L. Harbaugh, *Pastor as Person: Maintaining Personal Integrity in the Choices and Challenges of Ministry* (Minneapolis: Augsburg, 1984); Wayne E. Oates, *Managing Your Stress* (Philadelphia: Fortress Press, 1985); William Willimon, *Clergy and Laity Burnout* (Nashville: Abingdon Press, 1989).

13. Marriage and Family Counseling

1. See Howard Clinebell, *Basic Types of Pastoral Care and Counseling* (Nashville: Abingdon Press, 1984), p. 284.
2. See B. J. Engebretsen, "Beaver, Bluestem, and Bluegrass: Human Health and the Changing Ecology of the Des Moines River Watershed," *Family Medicine* XVII, 5 (Oct. 1985): 196.
3. See H. T. Kriesel and D. M. Rosenthal, "The Family Therapist and the Family Physician: A Cooperative Model," *Family Medicine* XVIII, 4 (July 1986): 198.
4. See G. M. Weinberg, *An Introduction to General Systems Thinking* (New York: John Wiley and Sons, Inc., 1975).
5. See H. J. Aponte and J. M. VanDeusen, "Structural Family Therapy," in A. Gurman and D. Kniskern, eds., *Handbook of Family Therapy* (New York: Brunner/Mazel, 1981), p. 313. Also see S. Minuchin, *Families and Family Therapy* (Cambridge: Harvard University Press, 1974); M. Ritterman, *Using Hypnosis in Family Therapy* (San Francisco: Josey-Bass, 1983), pp. 66ff.
6. See F. Pittman, "The One That Got Away," in R. Simon, ed., *The Family Therapy Networker* 8, 8 (Nov.–Dec. 1984): 42-46. See also H. T. Kriesel, "The Psychosocial Aspects of Malignancy," in C. E. Driscoll, ed., *Primary Care: Management of the Cancer Patient* (Philadelphia: Harcourt, Brace, Jovanovich, 1987), p. 277.
7. See K. Tom, "Circularity: A Preferred Orientation for Family Assessment," in A. Gurman, ed., *Questions and Answers in the Practice of Family Therapy* (New York: Brunner/Mazel, 1981), pp. 84-87.
8. See Cloe Madanes, *Strategic Family Therapy* (San Francisco: Josey-Bass, Inc., 1981), p. 20. See also J. Haley, *Uncommon Therapy: the Psychiatric Techniques of Milton H. Erickson* (New York: Norton, 1973); J. Haley, Jr., *Leaving Home* (New York: McGraw-Hill, 1980).
9. An excellent discussion of the interaction of structure and causality can be found in P. F. Dell, "Understanding Bateson and Maturana: Toward a Biological Foundation for the Social Sciences," in A. Gurman, ed., *Journal of Marital and Family Therapy* 11, 1 (January 1985): 1-20.

10. J. E. Lovelock, *Gaia: A New Look at Life on Earth* (London: Oxford University Press, 1979).
11. M. Scott Peck, *The Different Drum: Community Making and Peace* (New York: Simon and Schuster, 1987).
12. Sallie McFague, *Models of God: Theology for an Ecological Nuclear Age* (Philadelphia: Fortress Press, 1987), p. 185.

14. Marriage in the Second Half of Life

1. See Erik H. Erikson, "Identity and the Life Cycle," *Psychological Issues* 1 (1959): 1-171.
2. Erik H. Erikson, Joan M. Erikson, and Helen Q. Kivnick, *Vital Involvement in Old Age* (New York: W. W. Norton and Company, 1986), p. 33.
3. Ibid., pp. 37-38.
4. See William A. Clebsch and Charles R. Jaekle, *Pastoral Care in Historical Perspective* (New York: Jason Aronson, Inc., 1983), pp. 8-10. *Sustaining* and *guiding* are the other two of the four traditional pastoral functions. The work of Clebsch and Jaekle traces the historical roots and uses of these four functions. It is, however, the work of Henri J. M. Nouwen that lifts them up as vital components of contemporary spiritual and interpersonal life (see below).
5. Henri J. M. Nouwen, *The Living Reminder: Service and Prayer in Memory of Jesus Christ* (New York: Seabury Press, 1977), pp. 17-18.
6. Elie Wiesel, *Legends of Our Time* (New York: Hart, Rinehart and Winston, 1968), pp. 123, 128.
7. Nouwen, *The Living Reminder*, pp. 21-22.
8. Ibid., p. 19.
9. Ibid.
10. John Patton, *Is Human Forgiveness Possible?* (Nashville: Abingdon Press, 1985), p. 26.
11. Henri J. M. Nouwen, *Reaching Out* (New York: Doubleday, 1975), p. 74.
12. Clebsch and Jaekle, *Pastoral Care in Historical Perspective*, p. 8.
13. Carl Whitaker, *From Psyche to System: The Evolving Therapy of Carl Whitaker*, eds. John R. Neill and David P. Kniskern (New York: The Guilford Press, 1982), p. 187.
14. Joseph Campbell with Bill Moyers, ed. Betty Sue Flowers, *The Power of Myth*, (New York: Doubleday, 1988), p. 7.
15. Ibid.
16. Wallace Stegner, *Crossing to Safety* (New York: Random House, 1987), dust cover; italics added.
17. Clebsch and Jaekle, *Pastoral Care in Historical Perspective*, pp. viii-ix.
18. Campbell, *The Power of Myth*, p. 189.
19. Ibid., p. 190. Amor is the love of a person-to-person relationship.

15. Sexuality and Pastoral Care

1. See Jean Baker Miller, *Toward a New Psychology of Women*, 2nd ed. (Boston: Beacon Press, 1986), pp. 29-48.
2. See James B. Nelson, *Between Two Gardens: Reflections on Sexuality and Religious Experience* (New York: The Pilgrim Press, 1983), p. 16.

3. See ibid., p. 37, citing Matthew Fox, *A Spirituality Named Compassion* (Minn: Winston Press, 1979), chap. 4; and *Whee! Wee, Wee All the Way Home* (Wilmington, N.C.: Consortium Books, 1976).
4. Ethicist Karen Lebacqz suggests that "appropriate vulnerability" can be a responsible realistic sexual ethic for single people. She translates Genesis 2:25 as most adequately rendered, "And the man and his wife experienced appropriate vulnerability." Karen Lebacqz, "Appropriate Vulnerability: A Sexual Ethic for Singles" *The Christian Century* (May 6, 1987): 436.
5. Allen J. Moore, "Teen-age Sexuality and Public Morality," *The Christian Century* (September 9-16, 1987): 749.
6. See Meg Gerrard, "Emotional and Cognitive Barriers to Effective Contraception: Are Males and Females Really Different?" in Kathryn Kelley, ed., *Females, Males, and Sexuality: Theories and Research* (Albany: State University of New York Press, 1987), p. 219.
7. Ibid., p. 237
8. In its "Events and People" section, *The Christian Century* reported: "A study conducted by the Professional Ethics Group of the Center for Ethics and Social Policy at the Graduate Theological Union-Berkeley and funded by the Lilly Endowment indicates that one in four clergy has had some kind of sexual contact with a parishioner and one in ten has had an affair with a parishioner" (*The Christian Century* [March 7, 1990]: 240).
9. Lebacqz, loc. cit.
10. See Phyllis Trible, *Texts of Terror* (Philadelphia: Fortress Press, 1984), pp. 37-57.
11. See Clifford Penner and Joyce Penner, *The Gift of Sex: A Christian Guide to Sexual Fulfillment* (Waco, Texas: Word, 1981).
12. Donald and Rhonda Preston, *Before They Ask: Talking About Sex from a Christian Perspective* (Nashville: Graded Press, 1989); Dorlis Brown Glass, *Created by God: About Human Sexuality for Older Boys and Girls* (Nashville: Graded Press, 1989); Joan Miles, *Our Sexuality: God's Good Gift* (Nashville: Graded Press, 1989); and Joan Miles, *Male and Female: Blessed by God* (Nashville: Graded Press. 1989).

16. Pastoral Care in Recovery from Addiction

1. See Paul C. Conley and Andrew A. Sorensen, *The Staggering Steeple* (Philadelphia: Pilgrim Press, 1972).
2. Howard J. Clinebell, *Understanding and Counseling the Alcoholic*, rev. ed. (Nashville: Abingdon Press, 1968), pp. 167-78.
3. For learning theory, see Vernon Johnson, *I'll Quit Tomorrow* (New York: Harper & Row, 1973); for the physio-pharmacological theory, see Frank A. Seixas, ed., *Currents in Alcoholism* (New York: Grune and Stratton, 1978); for the social-cultural theory, see William M. Filstead et al., eds., *Alcohol and Alcohol Problems* (Cambridge: Ballinger, 1976); for the personality profile theory, see Howard J. Clinebell, *Understanding and Counseling the Alcoholic*; for the psychoanalytic theory, see Eva Marie Blum, "Psychoanalytic Views on Alcoholism," *Quarterly Journal of Studies on Alcoholism*, 27:2

(1966); and for the moral-religious theory, see *Alcoholics Anonymous*, 2nd ed. (New York: Alcoholics Anonymous World Services, 1955). See Howard J. Clinebell, "Philosophical-Religious Factors in the Etiology and Treatment of Alcoholism," *Quarterly Journal of Studies on Alcoholism*, 24 (1963) 473-88.

4. See Clinebell, *Understanding and Counseling the Alcoholic*, p. 53.

5. See Howard J. Clinebell, *Growth Counseling* (Nashville: Abingdon Press,), p. 55.

6. Paul Tillich, *Systematic Theology*, vol. 2 (Chicago: University of Chicago Press, 1957), p. 179.

7. Jürgen Moltmann, *Theology of Hope* (New York: Harper & Row, 1967).

8. For further information with regard to the congregations, see Thomas Hamilton Cairns, *Preparing Your Church for Ministry to Alcoholics and Their Families* (Springfield, Ill.: Charles C. Thomas, 1986). See also Stephen P. Apthorp, *Alcohol and Substance Abuse: A Clergy Handbook* (Wilton, Conn.: Morehouse-Barlow Co. Inc., 1985).

9. For a more detailed exposition of the pastoral role, see Robert H. Albers, *The Theological and Psychological Dynamics of Transformation in the Recovery from the Disease of Alcoholism* (Ann Arbor: University Microfilms, Inc., 1982), note particularly chaps. 11–12.

LIST OF CONTRIBUTORS

Robert H. Albers (M.Div. Wartburg Seminary; Ph.D. Claremont) is Associate Professor of Pastoral Theology and Ministry at Luther Northwestern Seminary in St. Paul, Minnesota.

Hunter Beaumont (Ph.D. Claremont) is a past President and Training Faculty Member of the Gestalt Therapy Institute of Los Angeles. From 1980–1983 he served as Guest Professor of Clinical Psychology at Universitat Ludwig Maximillian, Munich, Germany, where he is now engaged in the international training and supervision of psychotherapists and pastoral counselors.

Carolyn J. Stahl Bohler (Ph.D. Claremont) is Emma Sanborn Tousant Associate Professor of Pastoral Theology and Counseling, United Theological Seminary, Dayton, Ohio. She has authored numerous works, including *When You Need to Take a Stand* (1990), *Prayer on Wings: A Search for Authentic Prayer* (1990).

John B. Cobb, Jr., is a long-time colleague of Howard Clinebell on the Faculty of the School of Theology at Claremont. Founder and Director of the Center for Process Studies and publisher of the journal *Process Studies*, he has also served as Avery Professor of Religion at the Claremont Graduate School.

Merle Jordan (Th.D. Claremont) is Associate Professor of Pastoral Psychology at Boston University School of Theology and the Coordinator of Training for Pastoral Psychology at the Danielson Institute of Boston University. He is also the author of *Taking on the Gods: The Task of the Pastoral Counselor.*

Harold T. Kriesel (Ph.D. Claremont) is the Director of Behavioral Science in the Family Practice Residency Program at St. Joseph's Hospital in Phoenix, Arizona and also in private practice as a pastoral counselor and psychologist.

Bridget Clare McKeever, SSL, (M.A. Duquesne; Ph.D. Claremont) is Associate Professor of Pastoral Care and Counseling at St. Meinrad School of Theology, St. Meinrad, Indiana.

Masamba ma Mpolo (Ph.D. Claremont) is a minister of the Baptist Church of Western Zaire and teaches Pastoral Care and Counseling at the Protestant Faculty of Theology in Kinshasa. From 1978–1986, he served as Executive Director of the Office of Family Education for the World Council of Churches.

Christie Cozad Neuger (Ph.D. Claremont), a United Methodist minister, is currently an Assistant Professor of Pastoral Theology at Princeton Theological Seminary. She has served as a parish pastor, hospital chaplain and pastoral psychotherapist.

James N. Poling (Ph.D. Claremont) is Associate Professor of Pastoral Theology and Counseling at Colgate Rochester Divinity School/Bexley Hall/Crozer Theological Seminary in Rochester, New York. His research interests are theology and ethics in relation to violence in families and communities.

Charles L. Rassieur, (Ph.D. Claremont) a Presbyterian minister, is a licensed consulting psychologist in New Brighton, Minnesota. He has written three books for clergy and the practice of ministry, including *Stress Management for Ministers* (1982).

Paul G. Schurman is professor of Pastoral Counseling at the School of Theology at Claremont, where he is also the Director of Training at the Clinebell Institute. Prior to this position, he served as Area Director of Pastoral Care and Counseling for the Ohio East Area of the United Methodist Church.

R. Scott Sullender, (M.Div., Th.M. Princeton; Ph.D. Claremont), a Presbyterian minister, is the Director and a pastoral counselor at the Walnut Valley Counseling Center in Walnut Valley, California. He has authored several books on the subject of grief, including *Grief and Growth* and *Losses in Later Life.*

David K. Switzer (Th.D. Claremont) is Professor of Pastoral Theology at Perkins School of Theology, Southern Methodist University, Dallas, Texas, and a part-time psychiatric hospital chaplain. He is the author of: *The Dynamics of Grief; The Minister as Crisis Counselor; Parents of the Homosexual; Pastor, Preacher, Person,* and *Pastoral Care Emergencies.*

Robert W. Wohlfort (Th.D. Claremont), pastor in the Evangelical Lutheran Church in America. He has been Executive Director and is now a pastoral psychotherapist with The Pastoral Counseling and Consultation Centers of Greater Washington (D.C.). He is also interested in gerontology as it related to religion and therapy.

Howard W. Stone (Ph.D. Claremont), a pastor in the Evangelical Lutheran Church of America, is Professor of Pastoral Care at Brite Divinity School, Texas Christian University, Ft. Worth, Texas. Along with Howard Clinebell, Jr., he edited the successful Creative Pastor Care and Counseling Series and has written several books used by pastors and students including: *The Caring Church; Crisis Counseling; The Word of God and Pastoral Care; The Caring Christian; Schliermacher's Practical Theology* (edited with James Duke).

William M. Clements (Ph.D. Claremont), a United Methodist minister, is Professor of Pastoral Care and Counseling at the School of Theology at Claremont. From 1975–1990, he served as an Assistant and then associate Professor in Family Practice at the University of Iowa and at Emory University. He has authored and edited articles, chapters, and books including *Ministry with the Aging* and *Religion, Aging and Health: A Global Perspective.* He is editor of the *Journal of Religious Gerontology* and the new interdisciplinary *Journal of Religion in Psychotherapy.*